CULTURE AND HISTORY

CULTURE AND HISTORY

*Prolegomena to the Comparative
Study of Civilizations*

BY

PHILIP BAGBY

UNIVERSITY OF CALIFORNIA PRESS

BERKELEY AND LOS ANGELES

1963

University of California Press
Berkeley and Los Angeles
California

English Edition
Longmans, Green & Co. Limited
London, England, 1958

Second printing, 1963
(First Paper-bound Edition)

To

A. L. KROEBER

il miglior fabbro

ACKNOWLEDGMENTS

I AM especially indebted to Professor A. L. Kroeber, not only for his massive labours in laying the foundations of the science of culture, but for the personal encouragement which he has given me, and the inspiration of his example. Professor C. F. C. Hawkes and Mr. W. H. Walsh have very kindly read my first drafts and made many helpful comments and suggestions, from not all of which perhaps I have been wise enough to profit. I have also greatly benefited by conversation, discussion and even argument with numerous friends and acquaintances, among whom I can only mention Sir Isaiah Berlin. Last but not least, I must thank Mrs. Joan Weber for her patience and care in seeing the manuscript through its various stages.

CONTENTS

1

INTRODUCTION

THE 'philosophy of history' is the term customarily used to designate those general and somewhat vague speculations about the pattern and meaning of historical events in which historians, philosophers and even theologians occasionally indulge. As the term itself shows, this is a branch of human thought which has not yet emerged from the womb of philosophy; it has not yet become a separate science or intellectual discipline with its own concepts and its own rules. Like psychology a hundred years ago or physics before Aristotle, it has remained essentially a branch of philosophy, speculative rather than empirical in its approach, closely dependent on metaphysical presuppositions rather than on observations of fact.

The term 'philosophy of history' is also sometimes used to refer to the study of the nature of historical knowledge and of the methods of historical explanation.[1] This usage is similar to, and may have been formed in imitation of, the expression 'philosophy of science'; it covers what might technically be called historical epistemology and historical logic. This is a fairly recent development, however, and need not concern us here. For our purposes, we may confine the term to the older and more limited sense of general speculations about historical events—historical metaphysics, so to speak.

More often than not, philosophers of history have concerned themselves primarily with the problem of evil; their generalizations have had more the character of moral judgments than of

[1] For this distinction see W. H. Walsh, *An Introduction to Philosophy of History*, London, 1951, pp. 13–15.

I

plain statements about the inter-relationships of historical events. They have been prematurely anxious to answer the pressing question of man's place and destiny on this earth. Instead of patiently seeking for empirical evidence of regularities in the historical process, they have sought to prove at once that 'the Good' must triumph and that a happy future lies ahead for mankind. Tastes differ, of course, as to what constitutes 'the Good'. For St. Augustine it is the gradual realization of the City of God; for Marx the welfare of the average working-man. According to Gibbon, Civilization must eventually triumph over Religion and Barbarism; according to Toynbee, it is Civilization that is evil and destined to be swept away by some new synthetic religion. In recent years, 'Reason', 'Democracy' and 'Social Justice' have been the favoured candidates for the role of the historical force predestined to save mankind.

From an empirical point of view, however, these views are merely projections of the hopes and fears of their authors. They are no more to be taken seriously than some antique prophecy of a Saviour King on a white horse who will come riding out of the West. The fact that nowadays such prophecies are cast in abstract rather than anthropomorphic terms merely helps to obscure the fact that they are based on wishful thinking. No doubt, they serve some useful function in comforting and encouraging us in moments of despair; myths seem to be an essential part of the fabric of social life. But they should not be allowed to stand in the way of a more rational understanding of history, the utility of which scarcely needs to be demonstrated.

In recent decades some historians have adopted what they call a 'tragic' view of history, by which they mean the assumption, not only that the good need not triumph in the end, but that it can never be fully realized because of the inherent limitations of human powers and human nature. This has been a useful corrective to the overweening optimism of the liberal historians, to their tendency to see everything in terms of the predestined victory of Reason and Democracy, of Progress in its age-old battle with Reaction. But such a 'tragic' view is still a moral view; it still interprets history in terms of good and evil.

A little reflection would surely lead us to conclude that our personal preferences, even if expressed in the form of moral judgments, are poor guides to the understanding of anything whatsoever. The physical scientists are fond of citing the example of Kepler, the seventeenth-century German astronomer, who made eighteen successive attempts to prove that the planets revolve about the sun in circular orbits. Circles, he believed on the authority of Plato, are the most perfect form of motion so that God, in creating the solar system, must necessarily have assigned the best available orbits to the planets. In fact, God does not seem to have been guided by the human preference for circles; it was only by abandoning this basic assumption that Kepler was able to discover the fact that the planets move in elliptical orbits, a fact which has been amply confirmed by all subsequent observations. If moral judgments in the natural sciences had not come to seem to us absurd, we might call Kepler's a 'tragic' view of the solar system.

It is often argued, however, that moral judgments, though misleading in the natural sciences, are inescapable in the study of human affairs. Human beings, it is pointed out, are animated by purposes; they exercise free-will; they are guided by their preferences, their likes and dislikes, in every one of their actions. We shall examine the doctrine of free-will and the role which values play in history in later chapters. But it should be evident from our everyday experience in dealing with human beings that moral judgments can be equally misleading in the human sphere. If one man wishes to understand and predict another's behaviour, he does not consider his own preferences; he tries rather, in the common phrase, to 'look at things from *the other man's* point of view', to appreciate and sympathize with *his* likes and dislikes, rather than to project his own. It is only when some action is required that he finds it necessary to judge other men's behaviour, and his action is all the more effective if he has first understood this behaviour in as cold and rational a manner as possible.

So it must be with history. We shall never be able to understand it unless we first put aside all moral considerations. We must not seek for evidence of the truth or of the eventual triumph of Christianity or Buddhism, of Democracy or Communism, or whatever other system of beliefs may happen to embody our hopes and desires for ourselves and for mankind. A perfect objectivity is, no doubt, impossible but it must always be our goal, and we should do well to become fully conscious of our individual biases in order to be able to discount them ourselves and to help others to do so. It is not that we should cultivate an attitude of indifference towards historical phenomena; if we were indifferent, we should never study history at all. We must seek rather to adopt an attitude of universal sympathy, something of the enjoyment which the biologist finds in the variety of living forms or the chemist in the kaleidoscopic multiplicity of compounds which he is able to build out of his basic elements. Perhaps the best models we can find are those critics of art or literature who seek to understand each work in its own terms, without trying to prove the inevitable superiority of one particular form or style to another, of drama to the novel, say, or of Classicism to Romanticism. The best historians, of course, have always practised an active impartiality of this kind; it is one of the reasons why they have resisted the attempts of the philosophers to impose their moral systems. In Ranke, this universal sympathy took the form of an almost mystical self-effacement before the event; each epoch, he felt, was 'immediate to God' and should be judged in its own terms.

In the nineteenth century the great prestige of the physical sciences led certain historians to adopt the term 'historical science' to designate those more rational methods which they had devised for ascertaining the truth about historical events; the careful collation of documents, for instance, and the discounting of the prejudices of earlier historians and chroniclers. This interest in techniques of ascertaining historical truth can be traced back through Leibniz and Maubillon to Erasmus and the Italian Humanists, but it was only in the last century that it flowered and came to be called a 'science'. The expression 'historical science' is singularly inappropriate, however, for these methods do not constitute a science in any of the usual meanings of the word. Sciences are concerned *not* with establishing the facts about individual events, but with formulating general propositions about the patterned inter-relationships of such events. The chemist is, indeed, interested in what happens in his test-tube during the course of a particular experiment, but only in so far as these events exemplify or fail to exemplify chemical laws; the techniques of observation and measurement by which he ascertains the facts are not dignified with the name of 'science' or even of 'scientific method'. Just as 'science' refers to a body of general propositions or laws, so 'scientific method' refers to methods of obtaining those propositions. The historian's techniques for ascertaining individual facts are best designated by the term 'historical method', a method which is often highly rational but is not scientific.

Historians do from time to time formulate general propositions, usually of a rather tentative character, in the course of their work. But they do not attempt, as the scientist would, to prove these propositions by investigating all the available instances which might or might not confirm them. At most they will cite a few instances which seem to validate their generalizations, thus imitating the loose rules of common-sense reasoning rather than the more rigid and reliable rules of science. Moreover, general propositions, assumed though unproved are, as we shall see, implicit in all discussions of the causes or origins of historical events, and even in the terminology used to describe those events. For that matter, 'historical method' also involves the making of assumptions about the credibility of certain types of witnesses and certain types of evidence, assumptions which are general rather than particular propositions. But none of these assumptions has ever been fully justified; collectively they do not constitute an organized body of established knowledge to which alone the term 'science of history' might be applied.

It is true that some writers have put forward fairly elaborate systems of concepts in terms of which they believe that history should be interpreted. The names of Spencer, Marx and Spengler come to mind. Yet none of these systems has won general acceptance in the way in which the mechanics of Newton, let us say, or even some of the theories of Freud have done. There is no growing body of doctrine; there are no established positions and no progress; we do not even have an agreed definition of 'history'. Spencer and Spengler had few, if any followers and Marxism has become simply the banner of a political sect; we do not see anyone attempting to test or verify his propositions. And Marx's basic assumption that economic relations determine all other kinds of historical phenomena is demonstrably false. An Englishman or an American who seeks to understand history must choose between Collingwood's unregulated intuitions and Toynbee's religious fantasies.

It would be unjust then to blame the historians for continuing to use the loose sort of reasoning to which they have been accustomed. After all, their whole training has been to concentrate on individual facts and to produce coherent descriptions which are pleasing and inspiring as well as factually accurate. They have seen many brave attempts to launch historical 'laws', but all have foundered in the rough seas of historical fact.

Is a more systematic and rational understanding of historical phenomena then entirely impossible? Are the fluctuations of the sea of history too immense and too varied ever to submit to the rule of law? Many historians have thought so and some philosophers, like Croce and Collingwood, have supposed that only some 'unscientific' or, at best, semi-rational mode of thought, some sort of direct intuition, was suited to the understanding of historical events; I shall examine their views on a later page. We need not refute their arguments, however, to see that this is a question which cannot be settled by argument alone. It is as if we were to try to decide by pure *a priori* reasoning whether there is life on other planets or not. Clearly we can never be sure that there is no life until we have searched every nook and cranny of the universe and sifted the waters of a million million seas, a task which is manifestly impossible. So it is with history; we shall never be sure that a more rational understanding is impossible until we have tested and rejected all the infinite possibilities of order to which the phenomena might conform. The failure of a few dozen or a few hundred philosophers and historians to find any generally acceptable patterns proves nothing, one way or the other, except perhaps that understanding history is difficult. So early in the game there is no need for despair.

A fortunate historical conjuncture, as it happens, seems to make it possible at the present time to improve our understanding of history very considerably. The anthropologists in their studies of simple societies have developed a set of concepts and methods which, with some refinements and modifications, can be used in studying those more complex societies whose development constitutes the bulk of what we call history. It is these concepts and methods which we shall endeavour to examine in the following chapters, our purpose being to formulate a clear, coherent and intelligible conceptual system in terms of which many, or most, of the facts of history can be interpreted and general propositions can be formulated and tested. It would perhaps be too much to say that this is an attempt to create a science of history. The high degree of certainty and the mathematical precision which have been achieved by the physical sciences provide standards which it would be vain for the student of history to attempt to emulate. We cannot measure the past and it seems probable that, even if we could, exact measurement would contribute little to our understanding. We cannot experiment with human societies, though we can of course observe how they behave in varying sets of circumstances. It is not mathematical laws which we shall be seeking to formulate, but rather a more rational and systematic understanding which will approximate, as far as conditions permit, to the rationality of the physical sciences. Whether we call this a science or not, is really a matter of definition. For most of its long history, the word 'science' was used to denote any organized body of rational knowledge. It is only since the rise of physics that it has acquired the additional connotation of mathematical exactness. It is the older sense which we shall continue to use here; but whatever we may call this study, clarity and precision must be its goals, and a close adherence to the rules of logic, both deductive and inductive.

It is to anthropology then that we shall turn for help in understanding history. This science has in the last fifty years, in the English-speaking world at least, tended to fall apart into two separate disciplines: *cultural* and *social* anthropology. The studies of the cultural anthropologists, who flourish for the most part in America, centre around the concept of culture; that is to say, roughly speaking, the collective ways of life, the uniformities and regularities of behaviour, techniques and values which are found in primitive societies. Their cousins, the British social anthropologists, on the other hand, are primarily interested in the articulation of such societies, in the patterned inter-relationships between persons, groups and institutions; their discipline might be called a sociology of simple societies. There has been much unnecessary recrimination between the two groups of scholars; the Americans find the British narrow and limited, while the British find the Americans vague and unintelligible. It may be that these differences in outlook are due to differences in national temperament, though it is curious to note that Tylor, the founder of British anthropology, was primarily interested in culture, while Morgan, his American contemporary, had rather more sociological leanings—just the reverse of the present situation.

The two points of view are not mutually exclusive and, as we shall see, when I come to define the basic concepts, social structure may be looked upon as one aspect of culture. In these pages, however, I shall tend to rely rather more on the work of the cultural anthropologists. There are several reasons for this. First of all, they have always shown themselves more interested in the processes, the dynamics of cultures than their British cousins, whose studies have been primarily static in nature, more concerned with social structure in the present than with its development in time. Yet it is precisely the developments, the changes in the lives of many human beings over the course of centuries, which are of major interest to the student of history.

Moreover, since the cultural anthropologists concern themselves with ways of life, they are better able to content themselves with the study of such documents and artifacts as happen to be available and to do without that direct observation of social structure which seems to be essential to sociology and social anthropology and yet is impossible when we study the past. It is for this reason that the archaeologists—who may be regarded as a peculiar variety of anthropologist concerned with the past—have usually talked about culture rather than society. In their graves and refuse-heaps they find those physical objects—pots, weapons, ornaments and the like —which they call 'material culture' and which are the direct result of human actions. It is a relatively simple matter to infer from these articles the techniques used in producing them or even the values which they express, but much more difficult to infer those patterned relationships between one man and another which constitute social structure.[1]

The best reason, however, for making use of the work of the cultural anthropologists is the fact that the concept of culture has already obtained wide currency among historians and philosophers of history. Usually, the concept has been rather loosely formulated and often it appears disguised under other names, such as 'currents of ideas', 'customs', 'mores', 'values', 'national character', 'local colour', '*Geist*' and even sometimes '*Volk*'. Nevertheless, the central meaning of all these terms seems to be identical with that of 'culture' or one of the aspects of culture. In the last century and a half there has grown up a vast mass of culture-histories, of varying value, it is true, yet suitable for the sort of analysis which the cultural anthropologists make. And recent philosophers of history have tended to use 'culture' or a related concept as their guiding principle, thus providing a variety of speculative hypotheses which can be submitted to more rigorous verification than their inventors saw fit, or were able, to give them.

The same reasons which I have adduced for neglect of the work of the social anthropologists apply with equal force to the work of the sociologists. Their studies are static in nature, dependent on direct observation, and tend to neglect some of the important aspects of group life. In addition, while their science theoretically deals with the structure and functioning of all societies, in practice

[1] This point is well made by M. A. Smith, 'The Limitations of Inference in Archaeology', in *Archaeological News Letter*, Vol. VI, No. 1, 1955, pp. 3–7.

their studies have very largely been confined to European societies or those of European origin; their concepts and methods are therefore not on the whole designed for universal application. It is regrettable, however, from one point of view, that greater use cannot be made of the work of the sociologists and the social anthropologists in attempting to understand history. There is no doubt that their concepts are better defined, their studies clearer and their subject-matter often more definitely patterned than those of the cultural anthropologists. We do have sufficient evidence in history to make use of some of their concepts, such as 'class' and 'political structure'. But these, as I have already said and will later demonstrate, can be looked on as aspects of culture. Though vaguer, the concept of 'culture' is more comprehensive than the concept of 'social structure' and therefore provides a better basis for an initial attempt to make intelligible the complex and elusive processes of history.

What I shall be doing, then, may perhaps best be described as an attempt to formulate, by precise definition and logical argument, the conceptual background for a general theory of cultural forms and of culture-change and to show that many of the problems of historical regularity (or historical 'causation') can be formulated and possibly resolved in these terms. In the course of the following chapters there will inevitably be many rather tedious discussions of the meanings of words; our problem is very largely a linguistic one. As far as my general philosophic point of view is concerned, I have, almost of necessity, adopted in general that of British empiricism as it derives from Locke and Hume; not because I am convinced that this embodies the ultimate truth about the universe or about the sources of man's knowledge, but because experience has shown that it provides the most reliable, indeed, the only reliable method of obtaining propositions the validity of which is generally accepted. Empirical methods provide the only possible basis for any firm and systematic understanding of history; idealist and intuitive points of view are apt to lead to vague and unstable formulations whose only value lies in the absence of anything better. In particular questions of method, I shall have to rely, of course, very largely on the rules of inductive logic as they have been developed in the light of the experience of the natural sciences.

It may at first sight seem surprising that we should find ready to hand the tools which are needed to improve our understanding of history, but this coincidence, like so many others, is far from being an historical accident. Modern anthropology and the modern philosophy of history both have their source in the Romantic movement and more particularly in the discovery made by the earliest proto-Romantic philosophers in the eighteenth century that other societies and other periods were dominated by sets of values different from, and perhaps in some ways better than, their own. The Romantic movement is generally, and rightly, thought of as a reaction to the prevailing rationalism of the eighteenth century. Already two hundred years ago some of the inhabitants of the larger European cities had begun to find urban life too artificial and too restrictive. Its formality and variety, its stress on reason and sensation, seemed to them destructive of some precious part of human nature. Whether they turned like Rousseau to the 'noble savage', like Macpherson to the heroes of Celtic mythology, or like Herder to the European peasant, they were looking for a way of life at once simpler, more emotional and more satisfying than that of the upper classes in Paris, London and Berlin. Romanticism had of course other and perhaps more important aspects. It fostered individualism and favoured imagination and the emotions as against reason and order; but one of its cardinal principles was the high value which it gave to the exotic.

Movements of thought rarely begin abruptly and, no doubt, if we searched diligently, we should find traces of this point of view very much earlier. Leaving aside non-European or antique examples like Herodotus, we find that Montaigne, who is the precursor of so many later trends, continually stresses the relativity of customs in different times and places. At one point, he says: '*Il me semble que je n' ai rencontré guère de manières qui ne vaillent les nôtres,*'[1] a remark which might easily be echoed by many a modern anthropologist trying to combat ethnocentrism. Throughout the six-

[1] Montaigne, *Essais*, Book III, Chap. IX.

teenth and seventeenth centuries the reports of explorers and missionaries were accumulating, and providing the reading public with many accounts of strange habits and curious customs. Much of this early ethnographic material was impressionistic and inaccurate in the extreme, yet some of the missionaries made careful and thorough studies whose objectivity would be creditable in a modern trained ethnographer. It is curious to note that as early as 1724 a Jesuit, Father Joseph Lafitau, who had spent five years in Canada, expressed a number of the assumptions and conclusions of later anthropologists.[1] He held that contemporary savages reproduce the customs of early historical and pre-historic times, that they display virtues not excelled by civilized men and that much can be learnt from them, that their languages have peculiar beauties of construction quite different from those of Latin and Greek, that religion is found everywhere and that its variety represents the corruption of an originally pure monotheism. Some of these beliefs have now been abandoned, of course, but they all flourished during the nineteenth century and it is astonishing to find them expressed so early. Possibly even earlier instances could be found, for after all these beliefs derive partly from the nature of the facts and partly from the common background of the European tradition; they cannot be the property of any one man. There is no evidence, however, that Father Lafitau had much influence on his own or subsequent generations. The time was not yet ripe.

In 1725, a year after the appearance of Lafitau's book, Giambattista Vico, a half-educated Neapolitan literary hack, published the first version of his *Scienza Nuova*, which prefigures in a confused and ungrammatical manner many aspects of nineteenth-century historical thought. In it he demonstrated that the customs and institutions of the society portrayed by Homer expressed a set of ideas and values (a 'poetical logic') which he was the first to call 'heroic' and which more closely resembled the values of the European Middle Ages than those of Periclean Greece or of Europe in his own time. From this basic intuition he derived a theory of the

---

[1] *Moeurs des sauvages américains comparées aux moeurs des premiers temps, par le père Lafitau de la Compagnie de Jésus*, Paris, 1724.

regular development of civilizations in three stages, 'divine', 'heroic' and 'human'. His *magnum opus* was little read, however, until Michelet discovered and translated it into French a hundred years later.

Croce, who was Vico's chief exponent in this century, tried to set him up as a major philosopher, indeed, as *the* Italian national philosopher, and interpreted him as a precursor of his own 'historicist' variety of idealism. Vico's thought, however, is as muddled as his grammar and it is possible to find in his work unreconciled elements of idealism, empiricism and even pragmatism. From our point of view, he is chiefly interesting as the earliest European exponent of *systematic* cultural differences between different periods and nations and as the first European to see that these systematic differences might be arranged in regular developmental sequences. (I say 'first European' advisedly, as there are numerous Chinese and at least one Muslim example, Ibn Khaldun.) Vico's 'new science' then, prefigures very closely what we shall be trying to develop here.

Voltaire's visit to England may be taken as the next landmark in the development of a taste for exotic ways of life. He first expressed his liking for the rude vigour of Shakespeare in the preface to his play *Brutus* in 1731, and his *Lettres sur les Anglais*, in which he extolled the virtues of the English, appeared in 1734. What he chiefly appreciated in the English, however, was their reasonableness and the way in which the monarchy and the church in England were subordinated to the national welfare, or at least to the welfare of the aristocracy and gentry, a way of life which seemed to fulfil his own rationalist, anti-monarchic and anti-clerical sentiments. England was admirable not because it was different from France, but because it was what France might become. It was Voltaire, too, who first introduced into the writing of history the description of popular customs and institutions which developed into the cultural history of the next century. He provided a reasoned justification of this in his *Essai sur les moeurs et l'esprit des nations* which appeared in 1756. '*Les moeurs et l'esprit*', 'customs' and 'spirit', as we shall see, form the bulk of what is now meant by 'culture'.

Voltaire thus prefigures the Romantic historians, just as he prefigured the Romantic playwrights and novelists in his use of local colour. But he was never a true Romantic; he always remained faithful to the rationalist ideal, and even lived to regret the part which he had played in making Shakespeare popular in France.[1] It was Rousseau who first definitely asserted the superiority of a different way of life. One day, as he tells us, while on his way to see his friend Diderot in the prison of Vincennes, he read in the *Mercure de France* that the Academy of Dijon had offered a prize for the best essay on the subject: '*Si le rétablissement des sciences et des arts a contribué à rétablir les moeurs?*'[2] He wrote part of his essay in the coach before he finished the journey and when it was published in 1750, it won its author not only the prize but also an immediate popularity. In it he maintained that the simplicity of primitive life made possible an innocence and virtue quite beyond the capabilities of more civilized men. This sentiment, this paradoxical yearning of civilized men for savage simplicity, has provided one of the motivations, conscious or unconscious, for all ethnographic studies to the present day. Scattered here and there in the sober and technical products of contemporary anthropologists, we find little indications which show that many of them still believe primitive customs to be in some respects better than their own and hope by their science eventually to devise means of improving the world in which they live;[3] as Father Lafitau puts it, 'you can learn something to your advantage everywhere.'[4]

Voltaire might thus be called the father of cultural history, while Rousseau, in a sense, is the father of anthropology, though of course he never actually studied a savage tribe himself. A similar movement of taste, as might be expected, was taking place at about the same time in the other countries of Europe. In England we might take 1761 as the significant date. It was the year in which Macpherson's *Ossian* was published and obtained an immediate success. Like some new spice, the tenderness and passion, the Celtic

[1] Voltaire, *Lettre à l'Académie française*, Aug. 25, 1776.
[2] Rousseau, letter to Malesherbes, Jan. 12, 1762.
[3] For instance, Margaret Mead, *From the South Seas*, New York, 1939.
[4] Lafitau, *op. cit.*, p. 4.

soulfulness of these poems, which purported to be translations from the Gaelic, provided a welcome stimulus to jaded eighteenth-century palates. Like Van Meegeren's forgeries in a later day, they conformed so closely to contemporary conceptions of the past that people refused to believe that they were not genuine; Herder argued that, if they were false, it was a *'heiliger Schwindel'*.

The taste for the exotic continued to grow in England with such works as Bishop Percy's *Reliques of Ancient English Poetry*, which appeared four years after *Ossian*. It was in Germany, however, that the new point of view was first systematized. Already in Herder's first important work, *Fragmente über die neuere Deutsche Literatur,* which appeared in 1767, he expressed the idea that each nation, each people, had a unique character, which was manifest in all their customs and institutions, their works of art and literature, and which was intrinsically valuable in itself. In his *magnum opus*, the *Ideen zur Philosophie der Geschichte der Menschheit* (1784–91), he undertook a systematic survey of history, in which he tried to combine the notion of national idiosyncracy with a belief in the continual rational progress of mankind. It is in this work that the words 'philosophy of history' and 'culture' begin to be used in senses which approach the modern. Apparently, it was not Herder, however, but a certain J. R. Forster who in 1781 first used the term 'Völkerkunde', 'science of peoples', which is still the German term for ethnology or cultural and social, as distinguished from physical, anthropology.

It is instructive to observe Herder's explanation of his own motives. 'The feeling for sublimity', he writes, 'is the direction of my soul. How mightily distance works in me! What has appeared more touching to me than distance? Hence my liking for the shadow of antiquity and for distance in past ages.' We could hardly have a more frank confession of the taste for the exotic, the desire to escape from the present into an idealized past.

It was doubtless because of their anxiety to express their national individuality in opposition to the cultural and political predominance of France that the Germans took up this notion with the greatest enthusiasm; political nationalism is also a part of the

Romantic movement. It was in Germany (and to a lesser degree in Russia) that the philosophy of history chiefly flourished in the nineteenth century; *Kultur* was the German battle-cry as late as 1914. But the more general taste for exotic ways of life was a pan-European movement. From Marie Antoinette's pastoral games to contemporary films about life on Mars or in the Wild West, it has grown and flourished with the growth of the cities to which it is a reaction. From Beckford's Gothic castle to Heyerdahl's raft drifting across the Pacific, it is the same search for a different and more satisfying way of life which motivates us. In art and literature, in fashions of dress and fashions of thought, in the annual holiday and the round-the-world cruise, wherever we look we see evidences of a striving to escape from the restrictions and pressures of contemporary urban life, a striving which is now almost universal.

Toynbee, in a well-known passage, has distinguished Archaism and Futurism, a turning towards the past and a turning towards the future, as aspects of what he calls 'Schism in the Soul'.[1] But this dichotomy oversimplifies the historical process. We may seek salvation by displacements in space as well as in time, by going to Mexico or the South Seas rather than to Medicean Florence or Periclean Greece. We may even seek for escape in the life of a different stratum of our own society, in imitating the ways of peasants or film-stars or gangsters.

It is with the consequences of this search for history and anthropology, however, that I am concerned here. I cannot trace the developments in every detail. It was in the first decades of the nineteenth century with the triumph of the Romantic movement that the new point of view began really to predominate. Germany produced a flood of philosophers of history of whom Hegel is the most famous; he saw the universal spirit manifesting itself through history in a variety of forms of which the Prussian State was the culmination. At the same time, both in Germany and France, the actual writing of history took on more and more of a cultural tone; 'customs' and 'spirit' become legitimate and even necessary subjects of inquiry for the practising historian. We may think of

[1] Arnold Toynbee, *A Study of History*, London, 1934–54, Vol. V, p. 383 et sqq.

Niebuhr in Germany and Thierry in France as outstanding early examples. At first of course these cultural histories were inserted into the more conventional narrative histories and they tended to be of an impressionistic, intuitive character. But all the while the techniques of historical research were improving and the standards of historical accuracy being raised.

It is in the latter half of the century that we begin to get culture history as an independent undertaking. And here it is the art-historians who play an important role: Burckhardt and Ruskin; they were trying to illuminate and explain works of painting and sculpture from the Renaissance and the Middle Ages which in the eighteenth century had been considered merely rough and primitive. In their attempts to revivify the past, it was no idle curiosity which motivated them; as Burckhardt confesses, he was consumed 'by a great longing for the golden age, for the harmony of things'. Since his time the culture-histories: histories of art and thought, of customs and 'morals', of religion and economics, have poured from the presses in ever increasing numbers, until today as much as half of most conventional histories is devoted to the cultural and social background, and many histories deal with that background alone. Meanwhile, new worlds have opened out for the historian: China and India, the Arab countries and Byzantium, while the archaeologists have uncovered still others: Egypt and Babylonia, the Assyrians, the Hittites and the Cretans. The philosophy of history as such, however, has rather flagged. The nineteenth century attempts to explain all history in terms of some general principle: race as in Gobineau, environment as in Buckle or the conflict of classes as in Marx and his followers, have been consigned to the dust-bin or the library shelf (except of course by the Russians, who in this, as in other matters of taste, seem not to have outgrown the Victorian Age). Of those writers who have tried to generalize about the development of culture, Spengler is thought of as an erratic genius with occasionally valuable intuitions; Rückert and Danilevsky have never even been translated into English or French; and Toynbee, quite rightly, is considered too vague, inaccurate and prophetic to be taken seriously by the historians. Today's historian eschews broad generalizations, but in writing cultural and social history he may well be preparing the data which will make such generalizations possible.

The development of anthropology was somewhat slower. Accounts of primitive tribes continued to accumulate, sometimes highly romanticized, for their authors were amateurs, not specialists. It was perhaps again a German, Gustav Klemm, who, in his *Allgemeine Kulturgeschichte* in 1843, first envisaged the systematic study of primitive life. He took up Herder's suggestion that contemporary savages might reproduce earlier stages of man's development and proposed the formation of museums of anthropology which would contain collections of primitive artifacts from all over the world to illustrate the different stages of cultural development, an arrangement which is followed even today by some of the older anthropological museums such as the Pitt-Rivers in Oxford. Like Klemm and indeed like Herder, the anthropologists of the second half of the nineteenth century—Tylor and Morgan, for instance—were principally interested in showing that a necessary process of development, something similar to orthogenesis in biology, had led primitive man through various stages to civilization. Towards the end of the century a reaction set in; British and German schools of diffusionists argued that the process was not unilinear and that cultural improvements had originated in a single or a few centres and thence spread outwards. It was to resolve this dispute that Franz Boas, the German who is the ancestor of most modern American anthropology, insisted on the precise and intensive study of individual tribes, both in the present and the past. 'Historical reconstruction' thus became the watchword in America in the first three or four decades of this century.

It is important to notice that this development had two aspects. One was a stress on the necessity for accurate empirical research which we may think of as beginning with Boas's expedition to the North Pacific at the turn of the century; the other was an interest in individual tribes. More and more the American anthropologists came to feel the unique character of the culture of each tribe and thus gradually lost sight of the original goal of anthropology: the establishment of general principles of social development. Today the prevailing interest in America is in separate cultural units and more especially in their psychological dimensions, a line of research which is particularly associated with the name of Ruth Benedict. Only here and there do signs appear of a renewed interest in regularities of cultural or social change.

Meanwhile a rather similar development was taking place on the other side of the Atlantic. The same new concern for accuracy begins to appear with the Cambridge expedition to the Torres Straits, in which Haddon, Rivers and Seligman participated; it was roughly contemporary with Boas's first field-trip. At about the same time in France, a philosopher and sociologist, Durkheim, began to take an interest in primitive tribes. He was not so much concerned with their historical development, however, as with the general principles exhibited by the organization or structure of individual societies. It is from him, through Malinowski and Rad-cliffe-Brown, that the modern British social anthropologists derive.[1]

The search for accuracy in the description of primitive tribes is the development in anthropology which corresponds to the increasing sophistication of historical method. In both instances scholars were trying to give a sound empirical basis to what had originally been the intuitions of the Romantic philosophers. The Romantic reaction against reason had served to reveal an aspect of experience which the rationalists now sought to reconquer, to assimilate into the rational picture of the world. In much the same way the Romantic interest in abnormal psychological states has contributed to the foundation of modern dynamic psychology. The ancestry of modern sociology, on the other hand, is almost entirely rationalist or positivist, except where it has learned from anthropology.

The anthropologists, it should be noted, have gone one step further than the historians; they have sought to make their studies not only accurate but scientific, to formulate a clear and coherent

[1] This sketch of the history of anthropology is largely based on Robert H. Lowie, *The History of Ethnological Theory*, London, 1937.

system of empirical generalizations. No doubt, a scientific approach has been made easier for them by the small size of the societies with which they deal. Whether they are cultural or social anthropologists, whether they are intellectual descendants of Boas or of Durkheim, they try to see their societies as distinct wholes. Even if he is focusing on only one particular feature of the life of a tribe, the anthropologist knows that he must keep in mind the social structure, the economics, the technology, the law, the religion, the customs and the pervading *ethos* of the people he studies. Moreover, while the historian buries himself in the study of a single period of a single nation, the anthropologist is forced to keep in mind the immense variety of differing societies which cover the earth. He is not so easily tempted then to make generalizations from a single or a few instances, and the generalizations which he does make are designed to be valid for all societies, civilized as well as primitive, historical as well as pre-historical. It is the great variability of primitive life as well as the small size of the individual units which ensure that the theoretical formulations of the anthropologists shall have something approaching universal validity. For this reason, a future science of history must at first rely heavily on anthropology both for concepts and methods.

We must naturally not suppose that everything in anthropology is already perfectly clear and well-established beyond a doubt. No anthropologist would make so sweeping a claim. On the contrary, there is much that is still obscure and doubtful even in some fundamental questions. As we shall see, there is considerable disagreement about the very definition of culture. Nevertheless, the improvement both in the accuracy of the primary data and the clarity of terminology since the days of Klemm has been immense. The present-day standards of the anthropologists (and the other social scientists) seem as far superior to the loose reasoning of the historians as they are inferior to the mathematical precision of the physical scientists. Whatever its defects, the science of anthropology is already far enough advanced to serve as a useful guide to those who wish to attain a rational understanding of history.

The studies of the culture historians, of course, provide one of the necessary foundations for such a science of history. In France, in particular, under the influence of Durkheim, a whole school of economic and social historians, among whom Marc Bloch and Lucien Febvre are the most notable names, has been working along lines which seem to prefigure the approach which we shall advocate here.[1] In addition some anthropologists in recent years, notably those interested in the psychological aspects of culture, have begun to undertake the study of contemporary civilizations.[2] Professor Kroeber has studied the clustering of geniuses at particular times and places as an index of what he calls the 'cultural climaxes' of the great civilizations.[3] There are undoubtedly unnumbered opportunities for research and analysis in the field of comparative history, nor can we hope that at this stage any one theoretical formulation will prove to be definitive. In this work I shall chiefly be concerned with the analysis, refinement and adaptation of certain primary concepts to our new tasks. I shall discuss the meaning of the word 'history' and how in practice histories are written. I shall describe and analyse with care the concepts of 'culture', 'society' and 'civilization', of 'culture-trait' and 'culture-complex', of 'a culture' and 'a civilization', as well as other related concepts. I shall describe how cultures are articulated and integrated and how they may be analysed and characterized. I shall pay particular attention to the questions of causation and explanation in culture and in history, which have been the subject of much metaphysical and even theological argument. And finally I shall show how these concepts may be used to understand and to explain historical events.

In all this I shall have one primary end in view, one particular problem which I wish to attempt to solve. It is the same problem which has chiefly engaged the attention of recent philosophers of history such as Spengler and Toynbee, that is, whether there is any regularity in the development of civilizations, in their slow growth and their sometimes rapid decline. It is a problem which seems to

[1] Marc Bloch, *Métier d'historien*, Paris, 1949; tr. by Peter Putnam, New York, 1953.
[2] For instance, Ruth Benedict, *The Chrysanthemum and the Sword*, London, 1947.
[3] A. L. Kroeber, *Configurations of Culture Growth*, Berkeley, Calif., 1944.

be of particular urgency in our own times, for a cold wind has blown across Europe, an intuition that European civilization is doomed to go the way of Egypt and of Rome, of Nineveh and Tyre. The loss of faith, the stagnation of the arts, the shattering of the Liberal dream, the catastrophic character of recent wars, all these have seemed to betoken an imminent decline.

Is such a decline inevitable? It is only by interrogating the past that we can hope to answer this question. But the failure of the philosophers of history to find any clear answer up to the present day must be at least partly due to the lack of a precise terminology in which to formulate the question. It is the provision of such a terminology which is my purpose here. The answering of the question must be the subject of future investigations.

The anthropologists sometimes talk as if their science necessarily included as subsections all the other disciplines which happen to deal with human beings: sociology, history and even psychology. They have at least an etymological justification for this since 'anthropology' does mean 'the science of man' and thus seems to have a general character. It was in this general sense that Kant used the word. In the past, however, the studies of anthropologists have been confined to primitive societies and this still remains their principal concern. In the same way, the sociologists would like to embrace every discipline concerned with human groups, but in practice they too have limited themselves; they have concentrated their efforts on the structure and functioning of society in Europe and America and have tended to neglect earlier or non-European societies. The historians, too, have not been lacking in ambition. While in practice they have concerned themselves principally with recounting the sequence of events which occurred in or affected literate societies (that is, those for which documents were available), it is certainly possible and desirable to study the sequence of events in other societies and even in inanimate nature; this too can be called history. Few people would agree with Croce, however, that the historical dimension (that is, the temporal sequence) of events is the only significant one and that all the branches of knowledge may be included in history.

In so far as these manifestations of academic empire-building portend an interpenetration of the various disciplines they are useful and desirable developments. We cannot hope to resolve the terminological dispute, however; the entrenched positions which the various parties happen, for historical reasons, to occupy are too strong. I shall therefore continue to use the various terms in their narrower rather than their broader sense. What I shall be doing here is an attempt to provide a basis for generalizations about history in the narrow sense. This undertaking might be thought of as belonging to anthropology or sociology in their broader senses; I have also used the term 'science of history'. But a more exact description would be 'the comparative study of civilizations', where by 'civilizations' is meant those large, complex, urbanized (and usually literate) cultures, whose development embraces most of the events described by the historians. This matter will become clearer in the course of the following chapters.

2

THE NATURE OF HISTORY

OUR first task must be to identify and define our subject-matter. We must focus our searchlights on the particular area of this dark universe of ours which we now propose to explore. What is it that we mean by 'history'? The word has been on human lips now for something more than two thousand years and, if we look in a dictionary, we see that it has acquired a variety of closely-related meanings, not all of which are relevant to our purpose. Perhaps the most satisfactory mode of inquiry will be to investigate the origin and development of its uses in the present day. In so doing, we should be able to disentangle the central meaning or meanings from those which are merely metaphorical or extended.

The word 'history' can be traced back to the Greek word: ἰστορία, which originally meant 'inquiry' or 'research' or, by a natural extension of meaning, 'knowledge obtained as a result of inquiry'. This latter sense still survives in English in the old-fashioned but not quite obsolete expression 'Natural History'. When Herodotus, in the middle of the fifth century B.C., came to write his great work on the wars between the Greeks and the Persians, he called it the 'Histories of Herodotus'. By this he meant simply the results of his inquiries or researches into the events of the Greco-Persian War and the events leading up to it. Had he been an astronomer or a biologist, he might still have used the word 'histories' to describe the results of his labours.

Herodotus' 'Histories' was the first of a long line of distinguished works of the same kind. His followers imitated him by also using the word 'history' to describe their writings. We cannot be sure precisely when it acquired a more specific meaning, but certainly by the time of Polybius, let us say, in the second century B.C., it was no longer used to refer to any kind of inquiry, or report on an inquiry. It had come to mean a written account of certain kinds of events, the same kinds of events that Herodotus had described.

Now Herodotus pursued his inquiries, as we have seen, not only into the incidents of the Greco-Persian War (although some scholars believe that this alone was his original intention), but also into the various events leading up to them. He described the rise of the Persian Empire, the diplomatic intercourse between the various states concerned, the factional struggles inside those states, and the lives and deeds of rulers and statesmen. About a ninth of his work is devoted to what we should now call anthropology or cultural history—descriptions of the customs and manners of the various peoples of the ancient world.

The central idea in all this seems to be that these were events which involved or affected large numbers of people. And in a rough way, it is similar matters which have been the concern of all those who have called themselves historians ever since. Accounts of wars and diplomacy, of revolutions and the more peaceful forms of political strife, of the deeds of kings, presidents, their ministers and opponents—these have formed the bulk of historical writing to the present day. Even where historians have introduced into their works new subjects not treated by Herodotus: the climate and terrain, for instance, of the countries where the events took place, they appear to be guided by the belief that in some way these facts affected the lives of a great many people. The focus, the centre of interest, is the life of one or more communities.

So also with the histories of particular organizations and institutions or of various aspects of social life—of religion, of art, or of law, for instance—it is because these deal with aspects of the lives of many people or are presumed to affect them, that they are of interest. Events involving or affecting only a single person are not history, but biography. The life of a herdsman or peasant would not interest historians unless he later became king or prime minister, or unless his life could be taken as typical of the lives of herdsmen and peasants in that part of the world at that time. Even in the life of a ruler or statesman, the more discriminating historian would tend to neglect those details which, he felt, had not affected the public at large or were not typical of the times.

One of the earliest and still one of the principal meanings of 'history', then, is 'written accounts of events involving or affecting a large number of people'. An equally common and important meaning is obtained by a simple shift of focus. 'History', as it is often used, means, not written accounts of certain kinds of events, but the events themselves. In sentences such as 'History reveals the continual struggle of mankind towards freedom' or 'The history of Scotland is full of murdered kings' we have ceased to talk about the works of historians, and are discussing the subject-matter of those works instead. The earliest example of this usage that I have been able to find is in Polybius,[1] but on the whole it is rare in Greek and Latin writers. It is only in relatively modern times that it has become one of the principal meanings of the word.

To confuse the word and the thing, the idea and the reality, is a common human failing; it is by no means confined to primitives and children as some ethnocentric psychologists have maintained. Indeed, the whole subject of history has become one of the favourite stamping-grounds of idealist philosophers partly because the ambiguity of the concept—which reflects and is reflected in the actual practice of historians—helps them to perpetuate their comfortable confusion. In reading Croce it is often impossible to tell whether he is using the word 'history' to refer to the events themselves, the accounts which historians have given of those events, the conceptions which historians have of those events, or perhaps all three together. Most sensible people would agree, however, that ideas and things must be clearly distinguished; in this book I shall do my best always to make clear when I am speaking about events and when about accounts of events.

One of the ways in which this distinction can be made clear is by the use of the article, definite or indefinite. In common usage, '*a* history' almost always means a written account; '*the* history' almost always means the events themselves. We say that Momm-

---

[1] Polybius, *Histories*, I, 3, 4.

sen wrote '*a* history' of Rome, but that he wrote about '*the* history' of Rome. The same is true of the indefinite plural, 'histories', and of the definite plural, '*the* histories'. 'Histories of England' are books, but 'the histories of France and England' are two different series of events. Occasionally we find an exception, as when some one speaks of 'the history of Rome which I lent you last week', meaning a particular book. For the sake of clarity let me make this rule absolute; in these pages I shall always use the indefinite article for written accounts of historical events and the definite article for the events themselves.

When we come to the general or mass-noun, 'history', the ambiguity in common usage is complete. We are always forced to guess from the context whether a writer means by 'history' a particular branch of literature or a particular kind of event. Does a student of American History study certain events or the accounts given of these events by historians? It is impossible to say—perhaps the most accurate answer would be that he studies the events as they are reflected in the works of historians.

It is this inherent ambiguity of the word which makes possible such paradoxes as the statement that 'before writing was invented there could be no history'. At first reading, this sentence seems to mean that there were no events involving or affecting large numbers of people before the invention of writing. Interpreted in this way, the statement is simply not true; there must have been many wars and migrations, not to mention the invention and diffusion of speech, of fire and the wheel, the domestication of plants and animals, and so on, before writing was invented. If we reject this meaning, we are left with the meaning that there could be no written accounts of important human events before writing was invented, a statement which approaches the tautologous. Actually, the German nineteenth-century historians and philosophers who were fond of repeating this paradox probably meant that there could be no awareness of the great sweep or direction of historical events over long periods of time until writing had been invented and more or less accurate records could be preserved.

Even in this sense, the statement does not seem to be universally true. The Polynesians, for instance, have handed down relatively accurate accounts of their great migrations through many centuries by word of mouth alone. In the light of this and similar phenomena among other non-literate peoples, we might have expanded the first meaning of 'history' to include oral as well as written accounts of events. But the narrower meaning is the more familiar one and we had best confine ourselves to it. *Ipso facto*, the meaning I have just noted above, 'awareness of the direction of historical events', had best be disregarded; it is not to be found in any dictionary.

Our two principal meanings, 'events involving or affecting many people' and 'accounts of those events' are even more closely fused in the word 'pre-history', which was first used by the Scottish antiquarian, Sir Daniel Wilson, in 1851,[1] to designate those historical events which took place before our written records began. 'Pre-history' is before history, if 'history' means 'written accounts', but it is part of history if 'history' means a certain kind of event. Now that a great mass of evidence has been uncovered as to what happened before writing was invented, it is quite possible to write a 'history of pre-history' or a 'history of pre-historical man', absurd and self-contradictory as that may seem.

As a matter of practice, of course, historians have limited their investigations to those times and places for which written records are available. They are trained in the use of texts and feel lost when there are no texts available. A separate discipline, archaeology, has developed in relatively recent times which studies those periods for which the written evidence is slight or entirely lacking. The distinction between the two disciplines, however, is essentially one of technique rather than subject-matter; the historian digs in archives and the archaeologist in the soil, but both are concerned with what happened to large groups of men and what they did in the past. Some periods, such as Roman Britain or Ancient Greece are best studied by the archaeologist and the historian in conjunction, the relative roles of each being determined by the amount of documentary evidence available. The archaeologist may even, like

[1] Daniel Wilson, *The Archaeology and Prehistoric Annals of Scotland*, Edinburgh, 1851.

Breasted, uncover a large number of inscriptions and write up his results in the literary fashion set by historians; while, *vice versa,* a historian like Collingwood may feel sufficiently skilled to use archaeological materials.

'History', then, can mean either certain kinds of events or written accounts of those events. The more literary historians, in so far as they are artists, take pleasure in such ambiguities, which are one of the essential features of poetry; but if we wish to study historical events as rationally as we can, we must do our best to draw clear distinctions. One possible device is to invent a new word for one of our two meanings, and in this instance a new word has already been found. 'Historiography' is used, occasionally in English and more frequently in the other modern European languages, to refer to historical writing in general. As far as I have been able to discover, the first known use of this word in any language was by the unknown author of an interpolation in the earliest surviving manuscript of Josephus' *Contra Apionem*.[1] Its invention therefore took place not later than the eleventh century and possibly not much earlier. The formation seems to be unknown in Classical Greek or Latin, although it is a natural one and the analogous form 'historiographer' was quite common. Presumably the Greeks and Romans did not feel the need for such a word since 'written accounts' was still for them the primary meaning of 'history'.

We might agree to adopt 'historiography' to refer to written accounts of historical events and reserve the word 'history' for the events themselves. Unfortunately, 'historiography', like most neologisms, is ugly and rather awkward. A writer who uses such terms too frequently, as modern sociologists are notoriously inclined to do, makes his works unreadable for the general public and difficult even for the specialist. It is true that in the more precise sciences the use of novel technical terms is inevitable, but we should err if, in seeking to give an air of precision and learning to our studies, we make them incomprehensible. Wherever possible, an ordinary word or phrase, which may if necessary be somewhat refined in meaning, is to be preferred to a new one. Let us then use

[1] Josephus, *Contra Apionem*, I, 19.

'historiography' sparingly and substitute for it, wherever possible, the less offensive phrases: 'historical literature', 'books about history' or 'historical writings'.

I have now, I hope, succeeded in distinguishing two important meanings of the word 'history' and in limiting the use of the word to one of these meanings. This is all that is needed for our purposes here. The definition of a field of study should enable us to distinguish some particular class or classes of events from those which we do *not* wish to study. When I say that 'history' means 'events involving or affecting a large number of people', I have satisfied this criterion, although, as we shall see, there is another criterion which I have left unsatisfied. For the present, however, let us be content with this definition inasmuch as it reflects the actual practice of historians.

There are, in addition, a number of subsidiary uses of the word which we might briefly note in order that we may be in a better position to disregard them. One of these is 'history' as 'conceptions of historical events'. It is in this sense that we may say that 'history is in the mind of the historian' or that 'history changes with every generation'. Here, 'history' indicates a body of knowledge of a particular kind of events, much as a science is a body of knowledge of a particular kind of recurrent regularities. For idealist philosophers, like Bradley and Croce, this is the primary meaning of 'history', since they believe that external events have no real existence apart from our knowledge of them.

Another use of 'history' is to mean 'the activity of historians', that is to say, the study and writing of accounts of historical events. Here 'history' is an art, an occupation or a discipline. The word 'historiography' is also often, and perhaps most properly, used in this sense, and the Germans have invented a special word for it: *Historik*, on the analogy of *Technik*. To avoid both confusion and the use of neologisms, I shall express these meanings by circumlocutions, such as 'conception of history', 'knowledge of history', 'the art of history-writing' and so forth.

Perhaps the most important extended uses of the word derive from the fact that historians usually give their accounts of historical events in chronological order. Thus 'history' has come to be used to refer to any series of events or any account of them, whether the events concerned involve one or more human beings or none at all. We may speak of 'the history of a love-affair', 'the history of my dog', 'the history of the stars', or even 'the history of my dining-room table'. (In French, the word *histoire* has been stretched even further, it can mean simply an anecdote or an incident, as in '*j'ai raconté une histoire*' and '*il s'est passé une histoire*'.) No doubt, these extensions of the word are quite useful in ordinary speech—there is no other term which will quite replace them —but they would be confusing for the sort of systematic treatment which we are undertaking here. Some philosophers of history have gone so far as to argue that to recount facts in their temporal sequence involves a special mode of understanding (also to be called 'history') which must be distinguished from the modes of understanding which are used in science. I shall examine this view in the next chapter, but it suffices to point out here that there appears to be no necessary or intrinsic connection between this method of describing a large body of events and the sort of events that are described. We must confine our use of the word 'history' to a particular category of events, however they may be described.

The methods used by historians are not, however, entirely irrelevant to our inquiry. By examining them we may be helped to understand why it is that no systematic and rational understanding of historical events has as yet emerged. It cannot be denied, moreover, that our methods of describing or analysing events inevitably influence our conceptions of what those events are, and to this extent we must agree with the idealist philosophers, without sharing their belief that the events only exist in our minds. These methods, however, can best be understood if we see them in the light of the purposes of historians, since it is to fulfil these purposes that their methods have been devised.

First and foremost the historian seeks to *inform*. He wishes to provide us with accurate information as to what took place. Indeed, one of the primary uses of writing in early times was to preserve accurate accounts of memorable events, whether in the form of annals, chronicles or inscriptions. Accuracy has always been one of the historian's goals. Herodotus, for instance, is usually careful to mention his sources, which include personal observation, inscriptions and the reports of eye-witnesses;[1] while Thucydides tells us that he investigated 'with the greatest possible accuracy' every detail of the events he recounts, comparing the conflicting reports of eye-witnesses and trying to establish the truth.[2] In the nineteenth century, when the writing of history underwent a great flowering in Europe and especially in Germany, historical method was developed, as we have already observed, into a highly refined technique. It became an instrument of great delicacy and produced an astonishing wealth of relatively reliable results. But only relatively reliable; as we shall see, there are certain inherent limitations to the accuracy of historical knowledge as it is ordinarily conceived.

Occasionally, one finds a historian expressing the naïve view that to inform is all that he seeks to do. The most notable of these was Ranke, at least if we take literally his famous formula: '*wie es eigentlich gewesen*'.[3] But if the historian sought only to inform he would have no means of deciding which events to inform us about. Unless he selects a few significant events from the vast material at his disposal, he will soon find himself bogged down in a morass of disconnected facts and details. His task will exceed his powers and at the same time become meaningless. 'History', it has been said, 'to be accurate must be thick enough', but all the bookshelves in the world would not suffice if accuracy were the only criterion. In order to choose which events to describe, the historian must have some other purpose in mind besides the simple one of giving information.

The dangers of attempting to make 'history thick enough' are well illustrated by that earnest and ingenuous researcher who has recently published a whole book on *The Day Lincoln Was Shot*.[4] Obsessed by what he felt to be the fateful consequences of that day and anxious to understand how the murder could have come

---

[1] Herodotus, *Histories*, I, 1; I, 5; I, 140; II, 59; IX, 16.
[2] Thucydides, *Histories*, I, xxii.
[3] Leopold von Ranke, *Sämmtliche Werke*, Leipzig, 1877, Vol. 33, p. vii.
[4] Jim Bishop, *The Day Lincoln Was Shot*, London, 1955.

about, the author spent twenty-five years trying to collect all the information about it, even keeping a separate notebook for each hour of the day. And yet, he tells us, he does not 'believe that this book presents all of the facts, nor anywhere near all of the facts'. Indeed, how could it? His undertaking was by its very nature impossible of execution.

At times, it is true, some workers in the field of history will undertake to gather together and publish all the documentary evidence of a particular kind which happens to be available for a particular period, without regard to the purposes for which it may eventually be used—the State Papers of Queen Elizabeth, for instance, or the despatches of Venetian ambassadors at the French Court in the seventeenth century. Such publications, however, are usually considered to be aids to historiography and not historiography proper. The historian must decide what to write about and then sift the evidence, compare it with other evidence, and judge its reliability before he begins to write. And in so doing he will be guided by other purposes than simply to provide information.

Let us leave aside these other purposes for the moment and examine a little further the methods used by the historian in his attempts to inform us of the facts. As we saw in the first chapter, the historian tells us about particular events and this fact suffices to distinguish his work from that of the scientist who seeks to inform us about general truths—patterns, configurations, regularities which recur as the great river of individual events flows past us. It is true that some of the disciplines usually described as sciences also attempt to establish the facts about particular events. Geology, the various kinds of palaeontology, a large part of astronomy and meteorology are all concerned with what happened in the past or is happening now. For this reason, these sciences are sometimes called 'historical', though in procedure they differ from the study of history in the strong emphasis which they place on the explanation of events in accordance with well-established general 'laws'.

It is sometimes said that the historian seeks to describe the events with which he deals in their full uniqueness and particularity. But here again the historian would never be able to make his work 'thick enough', if he really sought to describe every detail of the particular events which interested him. Every event on the level of human action and interaction is almost indefinitely complex and the number of things we can say about it is limited only by the range of our interests and the fineness of the distinctions we wish to make. Perhaps if we could record the movement of every electron, we would have reached some sort of practical, if not theoretical, limit of discrimination but even a description of the movements of the electrons in a grain of sand during one second would fill all our libraries. Here again the historian must be guided by some ulterior purpose in choosing which features of an event to record.

These points might be illustrated by considering the famous, though probably apocryphal, anecdote of Newton's being hit on the head by a ripe apple while lying under a tree and thus discovering the law of gravity. The story was first told by Voltaire who claimed to have it from a nephew of the great physicist's; it may very well be false. But it is important to note that, even if the story is true, Newton did not bother to record it. As a scientist, he would not have been interested in the particularity of the event; he would have concerned himself only with such features as the mass of the apple, its speed and direction of fall, etc., which he could compare with similar features of other moving bodies. Voltaire, the historian, is interested in the particular event; he tells us when and where it took place, what position Newton was in, and that the apple was 'ripe'. But he too is not interested in every detail of the event; he does not tell us the precise time of day, or what species of apple was involved or what its colour was. He confines himself to those features which interest him.

In their attempts to give accurate descriptions of particular events, historians have usually relied, of necessity, on accounts given by others, either oral accounts by first-hand witnesses such as were used by Herodotus (and possibly by Voltaire in this instance) or contemporary documents which themselves rest on oral accounts. Only occasionally has the historian, like Polybius or Churchill or Caesar, himself participated in some of the events he describes; for the most part he must rely on the accounts of other witnesses, which he often receives at second or third hand. We all know how variable and unreliable even the accounts of first-hand witnesses can be; sometimes it seems to be more difficult for a court to establish the truth about a street-corner accident if there have been many witnesses rather than only one. Human beings appear to perceive the most straightforward events quite differently. Apparently the historian is condemned, therefore, in spite of his most ingenious efforts, to a partial or approximate accuracy. He sees the events through the eyes of others; he can never go back and re-examine the events themselves.

Fortunately, in certain spheres we do have evidence which is more reliable than that of witnesses. We have the actual products or by-products of men's activity in the past: their artifacts, their art and architecture, even their rubbish. These mute testimonials are all the more reliable because they were not intended to convey information; they were not left in the ground purposely to convince someone of the validity of a particular partisan point of view. Even documents may be considered in this fashion, not for the information which they are intended to convey, but for what they can reveal, quite unintentionally, about the thought, the purposes and the prejudices of their authors and the sort of world in which they lived. We shall never know whether the incident of Newton and the apple actually took place or not, but the fact that Voltaire wrote the story tells us something about him and about his readers.

For the most part, of course, such evidence gives us more information about the cultural development of peoples, their *moeurs* and *esprit*, than about the particular kind of incidents which historians in the past have been interested in recording. But this need not always be the case. If the actual text of a treaty has survived, we have a by-product of an historical event which is often more informative and certainly more reliable than any contemporary account of how the treaty came to be negotiated. By and large, however, we can say that our knowledge of the sort of large-scale events or aspects of events with which cultural history deals is potentially more accurate, in spite of the loose way in which it has often been formulated, than our knowledge of the small-scale events which have so often been laboriously described by the historian. This will be an important point in our argument in later chapters.

One of the purposes of historians, then, is to provide accurate information regarding particular historical events in the past. This cannot be their only purpose, however, since if it were, they would have no means of selecting which events or which features of events to describe. Let me now attempt to distinguish and examine these other purposes.

One of these emerges when we look more closely at our definition of 'history'. I have said that history is 'events involving or affecting a large number of people', and I arrived at this rough definition by attempting to cover the kinds of events which historians have in fact described in the past. But the word 'affect' introduces the notion of causality or of explanation. Apparently, the central interest of the historian is in events in which a large number of people have participated, but in order to explain those events he also describes other events which are presumed to have played the role of causes, even though they may not intrinsically involve a large number of people. Herodotus, as we have seen, described not only the Greco-Persian war but also the events leading up to it. Explanation, then, is one of the purposes of the historian and to some extent guides his selection of historical events.

Let me go deeper into this question and try to make my meaning clearer. The actions of individuals belong properly to biography and not to history, since they are events involving not many, but only one or at most a few individuals. Nevertheless, historians have included a great many biographical details regarding monarchs, statesmen, generals and other important individuals in their works. If they were asked why they did so, they would reply that these individual actions affected a great many people and therefore were worthy to be considered as history. Let us suppose, for instance, that some historian of the French Revolution has given us an account of Marie Antoinette playing at being a shepherdess in the Petit Trianon. If we were to ask him why he bothers with a fact which seems to be purely individual or bio-graphical, he would reply, apparently quite reasonably, that Marie Antoinette's behaviour was typical of the frivolity of the French Court at that time and that this frivolity, leading as it did to the mismanagement and bankruptcy of the French treasury and to the disgust of the French people with the absolute monarchy, was one of the contributory causes of the revolution. In other words, Marie Antoinette's private amusements affected a great many people and therefore were historical events.

It is important to note that the causal assumptions made by his-torians do not rest on any well-tested generalizations about how historical events are inter-related. Such generalizations do not exist; if they did they would form a science of history. In the ab-sence of such a science, historians are forced to make use of the vague, untested and highly unreliable generalizations which con-stitute what is usually called 'common-sense'. These 'common-sense' generalizations are formed like those of science by induction, but it is induction based on a few roughly-observed examples. They are often sanctified by repetition through generations, but their validity is frequently not much greater than the explanations of physical events given by primitive tribes. In the example of Marie Antoinette, for instance, it is highly questionable whether her frivolity was not more a symptom than a cause, an expression of the general loss of faith and purpose in the upper classes at that time, or perhaps even a reaction to a sense of impending disaster. It may seem natural to suppose that subjects will react unfavour-ably to frivolity on the part of the sovereign, but we must re-member that many other sovereigns, notably Charles II and George IV of England, have lived frivolous lives in rather similar circumstances without such catastrophic consequences.

Let us consider some other examples. Historians regularly in-clude accounts of great earthquakes, droughts and epidemics in their works, as these events seem clearly to affect many people. Few writers would deny that the Black Death is a legitimate part of English history. But until recent times it was also customary to include accounts of strange or unusual natural events. The early annals of most countries are full of mentions of comets and eclipses. Livy is fond of recording the birth of two-headed calves and the perverse behaviour of lightning. Such events can be justified as a part of history on the grounds that there was an immediate and noticeable popular reaction to them. But the reason why they were included by ancient historians is not so simple. They were thought of as omens and portents, as signs of the intentions of the gods towards mankind. An angry deity, it was thought, would send a comet as a warning before he let loose the horrors of plague or war. Unusual meteorological or biological phenomena were thus held to be indications of alleged causal factors in the historical process; they were included because they were believed indirectly to affect mankind. Modern historians, rightly or wrongly, no longer believe in divine intervention and so they omit accounts of omens unless there is a popular reaction to them; but even by omitting them they are expressing one theory of historical causality and rejecting another. Here again their choice of historical events depends on their individual opinions about causal interrelations.

It is not only in their choice of subject-matter, but also in their arrangement of it, that historians show that they are attempting to explain historical events. As we have seen, they usually give their descriptions of events in chronological order, and this narrative form in itself constitutes a naïve method of explanation, the method most commonly used in ordinary discourse. The historian tells us not only *what* happened, but *how* it happened, and this *how* includes both *what* and *why*. Although he often uses expressions of causal relationship, such as 'since', 'because', or 'possibly due to', he does not need to do so. The mere fact of recounting one event after another at once suggests that the earlier event is the cause of the later one, especially if the succession of events corresponds to some common assumption as to how events do succeed each other. If Voltaire tells us that the apple was ripe and then that it fell, we immediately assume that it fell *because* it was ripe, and that he intends us to make that assumption. Unless the historian is a mere annalist, then, what he presents to us is not simply the facts about individual events, but rather these facts immersed in a sort of causal nexus, where even the choice of which events or which features of events are to be described is dominated by presuppositions, conscious or unconscious, as to their inter-relationships.

I might add that similar naïve or common-sense assumptions about causation are used by the historian even in establishing what he regards as the facts. As long as he must rely on the accounts given by others, he must make assumptions as to how likely the sequence of events described may be, what motives the author of the document may have had for inventing, suppressing or distorting certain information, and so on. Needless to say, these assumptions are often of questionable validity, and the accuracy of historical researches that rest on documentary evidence is thereby even further diminished.

One of the methods favoured by historians in their attempts to explain the events they describe is to speculate about the thoughts and feelings, the purposes and motives of the individuals involved. Here, too, they are following the procedures of ordinary narrative. Often, in telling a story, we mention in passing what we assume to have been the thoughts and feelings of the people concerned and this seems to give an extra psychological dimension to our narrative, to clothe the bare bones of observable fact with the rich garments of human emotion.

Many historians pride themselves, as Ranke did, in being able to 'penetrate' into the innermost souls of the great historical personages they describe and to exhibit all their motives, even the most shameful and petty, even those which are hidden from the actor himself. Yet to a coldly critical eye, this 'historical intuition', or whatever it may be called, is often no more than the crudest, the most naïve guesswork.

We do, of course, habitually understand and explain human behaviour in terms of individual purposes and motives, that is to say, in terms of thoughts and feelings, whether conscious or unconscious. But these thoughts and feelings are never directly observable and we are apt to assume that other people would have the same thoughts and feelings as we might have in similar circumstances. There is a certain justification for this assumption since, to some extent, all human beings have a common psychological structure; they share in what is generally called 'human nature'. The thoughts and feelings of members of the same family or residents in the same town resemble each other even more closely; each man's innermost life is partly organized in imitation of his parents and neighbours. Nevertheless, even within a single society or a single family, human beings vary considerably and in daily life we often make wrong guesses as to the motivations of others.

The historian is even more likely to fall into error when he makes such speculations since, as is well known, the whole structure of individual thought and feeling is apt to vary considerably from country to country and from age to age. It is quite unsafe to suppose that Caesar, in crossing the Rubicon, was motivated in the same way as a twentieth-century general might be in the same circumstances. It is even less likely that his thoughts and feelings would correspond to those of an academic scholar who has spent most of his life in his study.

As a matter of fact, the historian is apt to base his assumptions not so much on his own psychological peculiarities as on the popular psychology of his day, as it is expressed in novels, plays and current sayings. No doubt, the historian who has immersed himself in a particular period often acquires a great knack for understanding the ways men thought and felt at that time. We can never be sure, however, that his speculations are accurate, since he almost never makes his reasoning explicit.

One result of this practice of speculating about motives is that the historians tend to make events seem much more the result of conscious intentions than in fact they are. Political and military events are thought of as the result of careful and conscious planning by statesmen and generals. If success is obtained, it is very much to their credit; if failure is the result, it is due to their folly or stupidity. Certainly, in retrospect political and military leaders are apt to take credit for whatever success may occur, just as in ordinary life rich men think that rises in the stock market are somehow due to their own foresight. A little experience of the actual practice of government, however, would lead historians to see how little of what happens is the result of conscious planning and how much is due to diverse and ever-shifting pressures which able politicians can foresee, but no one can control. When things go badly, statesmen and generals are always eager and able to demonstrate that in fact they had no control over events and were unable to act otherwise.

Historians, then, customarily attempt to explain historical events by presenting them in a sort of causal nexus, in narrative form, and enriched with speculations as to the motives of the characters involved. This is perhaps one of the reasons why 'history' (that is, conceptions of history) may be said to change with every generation. Our assumptions as to what are legitimate explanations and our customary modes of thinking and feeling do indeed change with each changing generation; and when we project these into the past we naturally get a rather different picture from that which is revealed to the historians of a previous generation. These differing pictures are not necessarily false, but they are necessarily one-sided and they lack the element of consistency and continuous growth which is characteristic of the pictures of the physical world offered us by the scientists in *their* successive generations.

There is another sense in which the historian's task is one of explanation. He seeks not only to explain the events which he describes but also the events of his own day—and this in two different ways. History may be looked on as a continuous causal process leading up to the present and any information which the historian uncovers may be thought of as a contribution to a full explanation of current events. Thus Polybius in recounting the Punic wars was explicitly trying to explain the rapid rise of Rome to world-hegemony in his own day. A vast number of modern historians have sought to explain the contemporary predominance of liberal democracy and parliamentary government by delving into the past of the European nations. Inevitably, many writers have been inclined to give rather more emphasis in their researches to what seem to be the remote origins of important contemporary move-

ments than to events which were important at the time they
happened. Thus much more attention has been paid to the first
stirrings of liberal thought in seventeenth-century England than
to the numerous justifications of monarchical absolutism and
'squirearchy' which occupied a considerably more important place
in the thought of those times. Yet liberalism can scarcely be understood if it is not seen as, at least partly, a reaction to other types of
political theory and practice. In this respect, the historians often
resemble those romantic travellers who find the source of a river
in some remote fountain rather than in the watershed which it
drains.

The same concern for explaining important present-day phenomena is one of the reasons why historians of different nationalities
tend to confine themselves each to the history of his own nation.
Historians of other nations than their own do exist, but they are
relatively rare. Indeed, the whole historical movement of the nineteenth century may be looked on as part of the growth of nationalism, as an attempt to justify the claims of diverse linguistic and
cultural groups to political independence or predominance over
their neighbours. As Schopenhauer said, 'Only through history
(that is, historiography, in our usage) does a nation become completely conscious of itself.'[1] In thus encouraging the growth of
national self-consciousness, the historians have inevitably distorted
the past by projecting into it the nationalist goals and aspirations
of the present day. Moreover, they have given an exaggerated importance to the rude and barbarous origins of the European nations
which now dominate the world and have consigned to relative
neglect the rather more glorious pasts of China, India and other
nations which are now looked on as colonial and backward. Only
ancient Greece and ancient Rome have benefited from the same
minute attention which has been paid to the early histories of the
European nations, and this because we see in them (perhaps in-
correctly) the source of several aspects of our own civilization.

There is another, though somewhat rarer, way in which the
historian makes use of the past to explain present-day events. In-

[1] Schopenhauer, *Die Welt als Wille und Vorstellung*, III, 228

stead of looking for the source of contemporary conditions or tendencies in the past, he may look for models or examples of something that is happening in his own time. From these earlier instances he often seeks to derive general truths which can be applied to the present. Thus modern English-speaking historians of Greece have usually sought, in the conflicts between oligarchy, tyranny and democracy in the Greek city-states, for certain lessons about the nature of democracy which can be applied to modern times. The Germans, Mommsen and Droysen, on the other hand, in studying the deeds of Caesar and Alexander the Great, were more interested in understanding the nature of imperialism and the state. Although these attempts at explanation resemble science in that they seek to arrive at general truths, they must be looked on as pre-scientific rather than scientific. The generalizations thus obtained are never very precisely formulated; they are derived from a few instances, sometimes only from one. No historian has ever attempted to cover all the examples of a particular phenomenon; no one has tried to validate generalizations about democracy derived from the history of the Greek city-states by testing, for example, their application to the history of the Italian city-states in the Middle Ages. Historians have continued to operate with the rough and unreliable methods of 'common-sense' induction rather than with the more refined rules of scientific method.

Explanation, then, of historical events both past and present is one of the purposes of the historian. Another is simply to give pleasure to his readers. Historiography, after all, is an art, one of the branches of literature, and some of the greatest literary artists have been historians. Occasionally, we find a writer like Bury denying that it is any part of his task to clothe the facts 'in a literary dress',[1] yet Bury himself did not neglect to write up the results of his researches in a manner agreeable to the public. For most historians, the presentation of the facts in an easily digestible literary form is an essential aspect of their undertaking. Thierry, for instance, tells us that he wanted to *'faire de l'art en même temps que de la science, d'être dramatique à l'aide de matériaux fournis par une érudi-*

[1] J. B. Bury, *An Inaugural Lecture*, Cambridge, 1903, p. 17.

tion sincère et scrupuleuse.[1] The patient and humble labours of those who merely grub in archives are rarely dignified with the name of historiography; they are historical researchers, not historians, and the results of their efforts lie buried in a thousand learned journals until they are unearthed and vivified by the skilful pen of the true, the artist-historian.

In his role of literary artist, the historian does not confine himself merely to describing the facts in clear and harmonious language. On the contrary, he borrows many of the tricks of the novelist and the dramatist. To divert his readers, he stresses the unusual or the amusing incident. He quotes the apter sayings of historical personages and not their duller every-day remarks. He pads his works with local colour, but only where it is agreeable or exciting. Often he uses vague and highly-coloured language, seeking to stir his readers' emotions rather than merely to satisfy their curiosity. In all this he panders to that prevailing taste for the exotic, that love of other places and other times which, as we have already seen, is one of the characteristic aspects of modern urban life. And in so doing, he inevitably gives us a distorted picture of the past, one composed primarily of the brighter colours, omitting the dull workaday greys and browns. In Descartes' words: 'Even the most faithful histories, if they do not alter or enhance the value of things to make them more readable, at least nearly always omit from them the baser and less notable circumstances.'[2] No wonder, then, that the past seems happier and more enjoyable than the present; the historians teach us to feel and to enjoy the Elizabethans' taste for finery and ceremony, but we hear little of the discomfort of their palaces or the misery of their hovels.

Another way in which historians seek to please their readers is by giving them many colourful biographical details about historical personages. Sometimes, like Marie Antoinette's frivolity, these details can be justified as a part of history, but they are often completely irrelevant to the central purpose of the work. In this the historians cater to what the psychologists would doubtless call

[1] J. N. A. Thierry, *Lettres sur l'histoire de France*, 7th ed., Paris, 1842, Chap. II.
[2] Descartes, *Discours de la Méthode*, in *Oeuvres*, Paris, 1897–1910, Vol. VI, p. 6.

the universal tendency to megalomania. We all like to imagine ourselves as kings and queens or great men. We like to think that we might be able to control and dispose of the fortunes of whole peoples and, after many struggles, finally win the well-deserved admiration of the multitude. This is an innocent failing, and perhaps does not lead to as much distortion by the historian as might at first be imagined. Even though great men in their individual capacity probably have little effect on major historical events, nevertheless much of political and military life is actually conducted through individuals who serve as the symbols and agents of great popular movements. Through the descriptions of individuals, we may often discern the larger currents which they symbolize and serve.

Perhaps a more serious way in which the artistic preoccupations of historians distort their subject-matter is due to the necessity which most of them feel of giving a sort of dramatic unity to the incidents with which they deal. A historian will usually organize his work around some compelling theme, the conflict between two leaders, two nations, two factions or two opposing systems of thought. His choice of what facts are relevant is very largely determined by this need for unity; it is expressed in a thousand diverse modes of shading and emphasis. Usually the historian will identify himself with one side in the conflict and subtly lead his reader to do the same; writer and reader will rejoice and mourn together the triumphs and defeats of their chosen heroes. Nor is this entirely a harmful practice; the historian can argue with some justice that history is composed of conflicts between individuals and groups and that he does not reproduce the facts correctly unless he conveys to his readers something of the emotions and passions which were felt by his protagonists. He must present the facts in all their immediacy, hot with the passions of living men. It was on these grounds that Droysen complained that Ranke had 'the objectivity of a eunuch'.

There is certainly much to be said for this argument and yet in practice it cannot but lead to a distortion of the facts. After all it is only our own emotions which can make us hot. We may be able to describe more or less objectively the behaviour or even the motives of others to which we are indifferent; if we wish to *feel* their emotions, we must inevitably project into them something of ourselves. For this reason, our knowledge of human beings in the past, and for that matter in the present, is necessarily limited. We are inevitably outsiders and must resign ourselves to that fact; what we gain in accuracy we lose in freshness and immediacy. An objective study of history must, in the nature of things, be somewhat superficial, while dramatic histories, on the other hand, are necessarily inaccurate.

The dramatic character of historical literature has another function; it serves not only to please the reader but to inspire him, and thus we are brought to consider the last of the purposes of the historian. As the psychologists often point out, verbal communication is a substitute for action, a means of inducing others to act. The historian would not be human if he did not secretly hope to influence through his readers the political events of his own day or the near future. In presenting to his fellow-countrymen the noble deeds of their ancestors he hopes to inspire them to rise to equal nobility. Or where, as so often happens, it is a tragic failure which he must recount, he hopes that this will serve as a salutary warning to his contemporaries. The historians not only make nations conscious of themselves, they urge them on to further deeds of glory.

It is not only in the light of national aspirations that historians judge the past and seek to inspire their contemporaries. They are often deeply involved emotionally in some one of the currents of thought of their day, some movement for political or social or even religious reform. Gibbon and Voltaire were among the chief propagandists of the 'Enlightenment'. More recently, Tawney in his studies of the fifteenth and sixteenth centuries has sought religious justifications for socialism today. Most commonly, among English and American historians in the last hundred years, it is liberalism which has provided the motive force and the unifying moral vision. History is seen as the 'Story of Liberty',[1] as a long and ultimately successful struggle between the forces of liberal

[1] Benedetto Croce, *History as the Story of Liberty*, tr. by Sylvia Sprigge, London, 1941.

democracy and those of tyranny and reaction. That this view of history is inspiring to those who seek to advance or defend the cause of political freedom in our own day there can be no doubt; but that it leads to distortions of the facts is also unquestionable, and has been ably demonstrated by Professor Butterfield in a penetrating study.[1] He himself, if I have not misunderstood him, seems to advocate another moral attitude; the constant failure of men's political aspirations should lead us back, he feels, to religion.

It is this desire to inspire which explains the moralizing tone of much historical writing, the lengthy discussions as to whether Charles I was a good king or Caesar a wise statesman. In its extreme form as expressed by Acton, moral and didactic purposes are placed foremost in the historian's scale of values. 'I exhort you', he says, 'never to debase the moral currency or to lower the standard of rectitude, but to try others by the final maxim that governs your own lives, and to suffer no man and no cause to escape the undying penalty which history has the power to inflict on wrong.' While most historians would not agree with these prophetic thunders and would subordinate the need for moral judgment to the need for accuracy, nevertheless explicitly or implicitly moral judgments or recommendations for action are almost always to be found in their works. Even Burckhardt, as he fled back in time to the golden age of Renaissance Italy, must have hoped that his writings would induce his fellow countrymen to restore some order and harmony to their affairs.

On the whole modern writers tend to follow the more devious practice of Machiavelli as described by Hobbes: 'Digression for instruction's cause, and other such open conveyances of precepts (which is the philosopher's part), he never useth, as having so clearly set before men's eyes the ways and events of good and evil counsels, that the narration itself doth secretly instruct the reader, and more effectually than can possibly be done by precept.'[2]

When these moral points of view become fully explicit, when they are used to order, evaluate and explain the whole past of the

---

[1] Herbert Butterfield, *The Whig Interpretation of History*, London, 1931.
[2] Hobbes, *English Works*, London, 1839-45, Vol. VIII, p. xxii.

human race, we are dealing with the philosophy of history in its most common form. All historical events are seen as leading to the ultimate triumph of the Good. But the moral ends of historians need not find so sweeping and systematic an expression; they may be confined to the assumption, never openly expressed, that, for instance, the Welsh are a fine and badly-treated people or that rural life and simple faith are to be preferred to the pleasures and scepticism of cities. In contrast, the approach to history which will be advocated here is essentially aesthetic rather than moral. It involves a sympathy with things as they are, rather than as they ought to be. It is the point of view of the scientist or the saint as opposed to that of the political or religious reformer.

I have now described four of the principal purposes of historians and have pointed out some of the methods which they use to achieve these ends. We have seen that they seek not only to inform, but also to explain the events of the past. And at the same time they wish to please their readers and to inspire them to action in the present. They give us not simply the facts about the past, but certain selected facts, arranged in a chronological sequence which exhibits their supposed causal inter-relations, and illuminated by a unifying aesthetic and moral vision. All four of these purposes must be present; if they are not, then what we are dealing with cannot be called historical literature. Pure information exists only in the form of documents, annals or chronicles; pure explanation would be the task of a science of history which does not yet exist; while it is the historical novelist or dramatist who devotes himself primarily to entertaining his readers. In theory perhaps, the moral purposes of historians at least might be absent. Certainly many historians would deny possessing such purposes, and their presence is often disguised. Yet psychology teaches us that every human activity must find its origin in present human needs, and if we examine the works of historians, we almost invariably find, if only in the preface, some reference to contemporary problems.

It must be admitted, however, that I may have distorted the work of the historian in thus dissecting and analysing his motives.

In practice they are fused; often he himself is unable to distinguish between them. In ordinary life when we observe some physical object we see it, not isolated, but in its relations with other things; at the same time we enjoy its appearance and consider what should be done about it. And all this we do together and instantaneously; in the act of perception, the moral and aesthetic values are as much present and part of the object as its sensory qualities and its relations to other objects. So the historian gives his readers the past, not as it might be dissected by a student of society, but as his readers might have perceived it, instinct with moral and aesthetic values, enriched by guesses as to causes and motives, dominated by a few great symbolic figures. What he reveals to us is *not*, it should be noted, the past as it would have been perceived by men living at the time; this would be of no immediate interest to his readers. On the contrary, he presents the past in the light of the present, illuminated by the tastes and preoccupations of his contemporaries. It is primarily for this reason that 'history' must constantly be re-written. Each generation must find its own interpreters, the historians who will show how the past can be related to the new needs and problems of the day.

The historians thus play the same role in our society as the bards of less-developed peoples. They revivify and remould the past in order that it may serve as an inspiration for the present. We need not condemn them, as Aristotle did,[1] for imitating the tragedians and the epic poets. After all, the poet is as necessary and useful as the scientist. He tries to express the facts of experience in their full intensity and actuality as transformed by the emotions and preconceptions of the observer, and in so doing he brings richness and order into our emotional life. The pure sense-datum of the scientist and the empirical philosopher is perhaps no less a fiction than the glorified human figures of mythology and history—experience always involves the observer as well as the observed. But both are useful fictions. The historian and the poet serve to strengthen our purpose, the scientist to ensure that these purposes are not rendered ineffective by ignorance and wishful thinking.

[1] Aristotle, *Poetics*, XXIII, 1, 1459a21.

The writing of history, then, as it has been practised up to the present, is only a semi-rational activity. It takes place at the level where knowledge is not separate from judgment, where the demonstrable qualities and inter-relations of objects have not been abstracted from their moral and aesthetic values. Yet if, in my account of the practice of historians, I have stressed their lack of rationality it is only by contrast with a more rational, a more 'scientific' approach to historical events which does not yet exist and which we can as yet only dimly envisage. After all, in the last few pages I have followed very much the same procedure as the historians. I have generalized from a few instances, made use of ordinary literary techniques of description and argument and judged the work of historians in the same breath that I used to describe it. All rational understanding, indeed, must begin with loosely-formed observations of this kind. It is only at a later stage that we can refine our terms and test them by a re-examination of the facts.

The irrationality or semi-rationality of historians will only, then, seem reprehensible in the light of our desire for a more rational approach. As we have seen, they have a most useful and valuable function to play in society, and there will undoubtedly be literary historians as long as there are literate societies. The historians are the guardians of tradition, the priests of the cult of nationality, the prophets of social reform, the exponents and upholders of national virtue and glory. They are as deserving of honour as Homer or Taliesin.

The historical movement of the nineteenth century, of which we are now enjoying the fruits, is distinguished by its increased concern for accuracy, the wide range of its interests and its growing emphasis on the facts of group life and thought, rather than on the deeds of a few important individuals. In each of these characteristics it seems to prefigure, to be developing towards, the sort of science of the life of peoples which we shall be trying to formulate in later chapters. At the same time a certain resistance towards the formulation of a science of history has developed—a fear that the historians by becoming more scientific might find their function in society sadly diminished, might cease to communicate with their readers in the direct and human manner to which they have become accustomed. Numerous arguments have been put forward to prove that a scientific approach to history is impossible or undesirable, and it is these which I shall examine in the next chapter.

3

THE UNDERSTANDING OF HISTORY

As we observed in the first chapter, *a priori* arguments as to whether any systematic and rational understanding of historical events is possible cannot of their very nature carry very much weight. They are based on metaphysical presuppositions or subjective insights for which the evidence is necessarily very slight. Whether a science of history is possible or not is really an empirical question which can only be decided by attempting to create such a science.

Nevertheless, the many arguments which have been put forward against the possibility of a science of history may be looked on as at least indications of the difficulties and pitfalls involved. If only for this reason, we shall do well to examine these arguments and attempt to estimate their validity.

Let us consider the more naïve ones first of all. It is often argued that historical events, unlike physical events, are unique—that 'history never repeats itself'. But physical events are also unique; each grain of sand, each drop of water in the sea differs from its neighbour—differs from it in some respects and resembles it in others. (Some physicists, it is true, have argued that the sub-atomic particles and the quanta of energy resemble each other exactly, but it is questionable whether these terms refer to anything more than hypothetical entities which help us to order our perceptions. Whatever reality underlies them may well be as variable as the objects of sense.) What the scientist does is to neglect the differences between the events and to study the similarities. It is essentially these similarities which he attempts to express in the form of classifications of objects or as hypotheses, theories and laws—terms and general statements, that is, which describe the common elements in certain classes of events or in relationships between them.

Historical events, in this respect, do not differ from physical events. Each one is different from the rest but at the same time resembles some others. They fall into classes and categories to which we give names. If they did not do so, we should not be able to describe them at all, for description is nothing more than a pointing-out of the resemblances between the event we are describing and other more familiar events. Every noun classifies and every adjective compares. When the historian uses such terms as 'city', 'nation', 'king', 'war' and 'revolution', he is saying that the objects or events he describes fall into certain familiar categories. It is true that each city differs from every other city but, nevertheless, all cities exhibit certain common features which enable us to classify them under the term 'city'. Each has a large number of dwellings concentrated within a relatively limited space. As used by the historians, terms like 'city' are, it is true, rather loosely defined, but there is no inherent reason why they should not be defined more closely. In the case of 'city' even a quantitative definition would be possible. We might set a lower limit for the number of dwellings or the number of people and an upper limit for the relative amount of space per dwelling or per person. It is precisely such resemblances as these among the features of the physical universe which has made the physical sciences possible.

These resemblances in the objects of sense (among which, naturally, human beings must be included) form the basis, not only of science, but also of ordinary conversation and of that form of loose reasoning which is known as common sense. If someone says 'I saw a purple cow today', each one of his words refers to some recurrent feature of the universe. 'Seeing', 'purpleness', and 'cow' are all terms of experiences which recur and to which we are able to give a label precisely because they do recur. Even 'I', that is, the speaker's self, is known as a common element in consciousness; babies must learn to distinguish between themselves and the world. If there were no such resemblances in experience we should be unable to communicate with each other and also unable to function in our daily lives. There is a famous and much-quoted passage in H. A. L. Fisher's *History of Europe* where he declares with masterful modesty that he has been denied the pleasure of finding patterns in history.[1] He must have meant *general* over-all patterns; if he had meant no patterns at all, he would have refuted himself with every word he wrote.

There is, of course, no possibility of telling in advance how close or how precise the resemblances which we shall find between historical events will be. Certainly the common experience of students of human affairs, whether they are historians, psychologists or sociologists, indicates that these resemblances are either less frequent and less precise or more difficult to find in the world of human events than they are in the world of inanimate objects. This fact of experience has led to the argument that a science of history is impossible because the causal relations of human events are too manifold and too complex ever to be disentangled. Here we must distinguish, however; difficulty is not the same thing as impossibility, and the failure of previous attempts to deal with history scientifically need not lead us into counsels of despair.

The difficulty of finding recurrent patterns in history has undoubtedly been somewhat increased by the historians' habit of focusing their attention on a few important individuals whose unique characters and influence on the lives of others are placed in the forefront of their works. It is, indeed, impossible as a practical matter to trace all the influences which have led to the formation of the character of an individual in the past. The evidence is simply not available. And similarly, when we seek to trace one man's influence on his fellow men, we need evidence, not only as to all his conversations and interactions with them, but also as to all the other (perhaps conflicting) influences to which they were subjected. The task of tracing individual interactions anywhere but in the very recent past far exceeds our powers.

If, however, we raise our sights and attempt to deal, as for instance economic and social historians do, not with the actions of individuals as such, but with the common elements in their acti-

[1] H. A. L. Fisher, *A History of Europe*, p. vii.

vity we find ourselves on a level of large-scale events for which the evidence is much more readily available. It seems not inconceivable that the situation in the world of human affairs may resemble that now generally held to prevail in the world of physics. Individual particles, electrons, protons, etc., and even individual molecules and atoms may vary considerably, it is believed, in their behaviour. Such random individual actions, however, cancel each other out and the mass effect of the behaviour of millions of individual particles is found to be regular, predictable and even measurable or quantifiable within limits. Similarly, when dealing with human events, we may suppose that, although the actions of individual men vary, the net effect of their group activity may well be regular. On the other hand, since human societies never contain anything like as many individuals as even very small chunks of matter, it may be that such regularities as they do exhibit are less precisely definable or measurable than those of physics.

The remarks in the last paragraph, it must be stressed, are only speculations based on analogies which may or may not be valid. Nevertheless such speculations are useful if they indicate to us possible lines of research. In this case they would indicate that if we wish to find regularities in history we must look for them in the mass action of large groups of individuals and in the common elements of their behaviour. Fortunately, as we saw earlier, it is events involving large groups of people that have always been the major focus of interest. The study of individuals has been justified only on the assumption that what these individuals did affected large numbers of their contemporaries—an assumption which I shall attempt to disprove in a later chapter.

Some of the earlier and more ingenuous enthusiasts for a science of man, such as Condorcet and Comte, in their anxiety to prove such a science possible, fell into the opposite error of supposing that every detail of every natural event, whether physical, biological or human, was fully determined and that, if we knew all the laws of the universe, we could predict every movement of everything in it, including every human action. Traces of a less rigid point of view can be found in these authors, but nevertheless their works as a whole give the impression that they believed in universal determinism. So for that matter, do the works of the early idealists, such as Kant and Hegel, in spite of their insistence on the freedom of the will. Freedom becomes for them a metaphysical principle which itself determines, strange as that may seem, the whole of human life, much as 'reason' and 'progress' do for the early empiricists.

This universal determinism, it is clear, is deeply rooted in anthropomorphic theology; it derives from the belief in an all-powerful Creator whose might and majesty would be diminished if it were supposed that anything happened without His foreknowledge. Its most noted Christian proponent was St. Augustine; we find it expressed in its traditional form as late as Bossuet. With the decline of religious belief in the eighteenth and nineteenth centuries, various secular divinities were substituted for the Christian God. 'Nature' was the favourite cult-object of the physical scientists, while the philosophers preferred 'Spirit'. The philosophers of history, for their part, devised various historical forces to take the place of the abdicated ruler of the universe. But in every case these novel deities retained the compelling anthropomorphic power of the Almighty.

Indeed, as Croce has pointed out in one of his most perceptive passages,[1] if a philosopher believes that everything is determined, he is almost forced to invent an all-powerful metaphysical principle to support his causal system. And, *vice versa*, if a philosopher believes in some all-powerful metaphysical principle, it follows that every actual fact will be pre-determined. In Croce's terminology, the transcendent generates the immanent, and the immanent the transcendent.

From our empirical point of view, we can simply disregard these hypothetical metaphysical principles, these all-determining powers standing outside of experience. But do we not feel that there are forces operating within the flow of events? That behind every event there stand others which somehow force it to happen?

---

[1] Benedetto Croce, *Theory and History of Historiography*, tr. by Douglas Ainslie, London, 1921, pp. 64 et sqq.

This is certainly a common supposition. As early as the eighteenth century, however, Hume showed that no necessary connection between cause and effect could ever be empirically demonstrated. This arises from the fact that in empirical reasoning we make use of clear and *distinct* ideas. We are therefore forced to divide up the flux of experience into discrete events and what has once been clearly distinguished cannot later be joined together. In the course of the present century Hume's view has become widespread among scientists. They no longer hold that some compulsive force binds the cause to the effect, but rather that events simply do happen in certain recurrent patterns, which experience has shown are the more likely to recur again the more frequently they have recurred in the past. It is no longer necessary to show that a cause is contiguous in space and time with its effect or that the effect *always* follows the cause; any recurrent pattern will serve as an explanation. The causal and other types of order observed in the universe become matters not of necessity, but of statistical probability. There may well be some necessity underlying them— some connection between cause and effect—but its existence is not empirically demonstrable.

If we wish to study history empirically, then, we must exclude from our considerations every form of necessity, whether it be called 'God', 'Nature', 'Spirit', 'Law', 'Progress', 'Dialectical Materialism', or even 'Causality'. We shall merely be observing recurrent patterns or regularities—types of order into which the phenomena happen to fall. Anyone is free, of course, on the basis of the empirical evidence, to speculate as to the meaning or purpose of history, the direction in which the vast mass of historical events seem to be tending. They are free also to postulate transcendental principles or divinities which ensure that the events will go in some particular direction. But these can only remain speculations; they have nothing to do with science. The singular uniformity with which such speculations in the past have turned out to provide reinforcement for the varying moral preferences of their authors is fairly good evidence that they are little more than myths.

What we study in science, then, is recurrent patterns or regularities and this fact has two rather interesting logical consequences, which have not, so far as I know, been noted by philosophers. The first is that some order, some recurrent features, must occur in any homogeneous and inter-related field of events. The other is that such a field of events cannot be fully ordered; there must be some features of it which are arbitrary, undetermined and inexplicable. These consequences arise from the very notion of comparison, which requires both similarity and difference. Absolute similarity would reduce all differences to identity and leave us nothing to compare. Absolute difference would eliminate all possibility of comparison.

This can be understood more clearly by a practical example. Let us put three pennies on a table and attempt to arrange them in some fashion which will be fully ordered or not ordered at all. It can easily be seen that, whatever position we place the coins in, they will form either a straight line or some kind of a triangle. Straight lines and triangles are recognized forms of spatial order which have been extensively analysed by mathematicians. On the other hand, if we attempt to make this order perfect we cannot do so. We may choose, let us say, to put them so that each coin will be at an equal distance from both the others, thus giving us an equilateral triangle. But, even so, the fact that there are only three coins, the position of at least one of the coins and the distance between any two coins must be arbitrary decisions. It is only the fact that the last of these arbitrary features is repeated which constitutes the order in our arrangement.

It is true that the order exhibited by any field of events may be more or less precise in its definition. It may provide for greater or lesser limits of variation. But even chaos is a sort of order. When we decide to exclude certain types of regularity we automatically include others. History, therefore, we may be sure, exhibits some patterns but is not determined in every detail. What patterns it exhibits and how precisely these can be defined remains to be discovered.

If there is anyone who still doubts that the behaviour of large numbers of human beings exhibits at least some fairly well defined regularities, he should study the evidence provided by vital statistics and voting behaviour. Not only do these show that behaviour is fairly uniform in widely separate areas within a single nation, but they also show that such behaviour changes uniformly over a whole nation. Dr. Gallup and other students of public opinion (or psephologists, as they are now called) have more frequently than not been able to predict how a whole country will vote from the investigation of a small but well-selected sample. It is only by stubborn disregard of the facts that some historians are able to go on asserting that human events show no regularity at all.

Another feature which, it has been alleged, differentiates the realm of history from that of the physical sciences is our inability to experiment with human beings. This appears to be more of a practical than a theoretical problem. In contemporary Western society at least, the prevailing belief in the value of the individual human being prevents us from treating him as a mere object. He must consent to the experiment, while damage to his life or health must be avoided. In a more autocratic society, however, somewhat more ruthless experimentation would be possible. An excellent example of this is given by Herodotus; he recounts how the Egyptian King Psammetichus devised an experiment to reveal the origin of human speech. He had two new-born children reared in solitude by a shepherd who was instructed never to speak to them. At the end of two years the children began to repeat something that sounded like 'Bekos', and this upon inquiry turned out to be the Phrygian word for 'bread'. Psammetichus then concluded that Phrygian was the oldest language.[1] His conclusion was incorrect because his assumptions were incorrect, but the experiment was a well-devised and successful one. Even now it can be cited as evidence in support of the generally accepted theory of the 'babbling instinct', i.e. that children of all nations at an early age instinctively emit ill-defined sounds, often bisyllabic, like 'ba-ba' and 'ma-ma', which they later learn to transform into words in imitation of their elders.[2]

---

[1] Herodotus, Histories, II, 2.
[2] Otto Jespersen, Language, London, 1922, pp. 154–60.

There is one feature of experimentation with human beings which, while again only a practical difficulty, seems to exclude any possibility of obtaining results as accurate as those of the physical scientists. Individual human beings are phenomena on the same scale as the experimenter. The mere fact that they are being observed is a new causal factor sufficiently important to influence the results of the experiment. Only in a few very rare instances can we inveigle someone into the special conditions of an experiment without letting him know that he is being observed. In most cases, we can never be sure how he would react when *not* being observed. The situation is analogous to that which takes place when we wish to observe the movements of an individual electron. The light or other electromagnetic waves which we make use of in observing the results of the experiment are sufficiently important factors to influence those results.

It is this fact which gives rise to Heisenberg's famous Principle of Uncertainty, which states that it is impossible to specify or determine simultaneously both the position and velocity of a particle as accurately as we wish. This is not, as some hopeful idealists have claimed, a statement about the fundamental character of elementary particles and therefore of nature, but a statement about the limitations of precise observation in the physical sciences. Similar limitations undoubtedly exist with regard to the observation of human beings. In another respect, however, our difficulties with human beings are not as great as our difficulties with elementary particles; we *can* observe human beings directly, even though we cannot do so with accuracy under controlled conditions.

On the still larger scale of historical events it is obviously almost impossible for the individual experimenter to set up controlled conditions. If he wished to hold a nation-wide experiment in, let us say, the social effects of the prohibition of alcohol, even the most autocratic despot would require the willing participation of his subjects and this willing participation would itself be a new causal factor likely to influence the results. All these difficulties that we have mentioned are merely practical difficulties, however; nothing is changed in the character of the events we are studying. As we have seen, similar difficulties may arise in the physical sciences: we cannot argue that historical events are, for this reason, intrinsically different from physical events. Fortunately, the whole recorded past of the human race and the many artifacts which survive provide a rich variety of combinations of conditions under which we can observe individual and social behaviour. History, it has been said, is a social laboratory and this fact, though it cannot remove, somewhat mitigates the difficulty of experimentation.

Neither the uniqueness nor the complexity of historical events, then, nor our difficulties in experimenting need discourage us in our hopes to render history intelligible. There is one difference, however, between historical events and physical events which seems to be intrinsic to their character and which has often been used by philosophers and historians to argue that entirely different modes of understanding are required for the two types of events. This is the fact that many, perhaps most, human actions are the result of human purposes. They are not simply automatic reactions to external pressures as we conceive physical events to be. Human beings, before acting, very frequently contemplate in imagination some goal which they would like to attain as well as the means of attaining it. Sometimes they contemplate a variety of different goals or different means of attaining the same goal and choose between them. Freud—and this is perhaps his greatest contribution to human thought—has argued rather convincingly that *all* human actions are preceded by some such process of purposeful choice, even when the actor himself is not aware of his motives. Many types of actions which previously appeared to be unmotivated and unintelligible can now be understood if we assume that they are the result of invisible processes taking place in a hypothetical realm known as the sub-conscious—processes analogous to those which we are aware of in our conscious minds.

The evidence for Freud's hypothesis of the sub-conscious is weighty and convincing, but whether we accept it or not it is certainly clear that purpose or motivation provides an extra dimension of intelligibility in human behaviour which physical events are usually thought to lack. A few vitalist philosophers such as

Whitehead,[1] it is true, have thought that physical events were also the result of some sort of semi-conscious or pre-conscious motivational processes, but certainly in conventional discourse, as in science, this possibility is usually disregarded. We think of physical events as behaving in a 'mechanical fashion', reacting automatically to events external to them. Human actions and their products, however, we regard habitually in the light of their *intended* effects. We even classify them in terms of these intentions rather than in terms of their observable sensory qualities. A knife is something to cut with and a chair something to sit in. If we say that a man 'pushes his way' into a room we do not distinguish whether he uses his hands, his shoulders, or even his knees, but rather the effect which the use of any part of his body is intended to have on the other people present. If we say that a woman has a 'kind' expression this is not so much a description of a certain arrangement of her facial muscles as an account of the effect which this muscular action has or is intended to have on others. Normally we even *perceive* human behaviour in the light of its intended effects; it requires a very considerable effort to disregard these effects and to observe only the discreet sensible characteristics of behaviour. The behaviourist psychologists, of course, have made this effort, but the poverty of their results will hardly encourage us to follow their example. Most, if not all, human action is motivated and we shall be seriously limiting our possibilities of understanding it if we disregard this fact.

We must accept the fact of human motivation, then, but we need not accept the consequences which many philosophers and historians have drawn from it. It does not follow from the fact of motivation that human action cannot be subject to empirical investigation or logical reasoning. Often we find it argued that, because they are motivated, human actions are free (in the sense of undetermined), that they are due to final not efficient causes, and that they are not open to direct observation, but can only be understood by a mysterious power known as intuition. Let us consider each of these arguments in turn.

[1] Alfred North Whitehead, *Process and Reality*, New York, 1941, p. 35.

We have already seen, from our example of the coins, that no system of events can be fully determined or fully ordered. There must be some events or some features of events which are undetermined, inexplicable, random or arbitrary. In this sense, some human behaviour (and some historical events or aspects of events) are undoubtedly free, but the events which are free in this sense are unintelligible and can barely be described, much less discussed. It is not this sort of freedom that is meant when it is said that human beings have freedom of choice or of will. Human beings do indeed choose between alternative goals or alternative means of attaining a single goal, but they choose what they prefer. Their preference is not inexplicable or unintelligible. It is by no means unrelated to their biological and psychological endowment, their individual temperaments, their prior experience, their training and the circumstances with which they are confronted. In ordinary discourse we often enquire why someone made a particular choice in the same way that we enquire why a certain physical event took place. And in our replies we explain these choices, just as we explain physical events, in terms of regular patterns of relationship with prior or contemporaneous events.

Freedom in this sense is not the same thing as absence of determination; it is rather self-determination, freedom from immediate external pressures, freedom to do what *we* want and not what someone else wants or what circumstances dictate. Such freedom is of course not incompatible with empirical investigation and rational argument. We do in fact seek to explain our friends' motives and we do so in the same way that we seek to explain physical events, that is, by demonstrating that their behaviour is related to other events in recurrent and familiar patterns.

Let us suppose, for instance, that a man murders his wife. His friends, his enemies, the police, the courts and the newspapers will all be interested in explaining why he did so. First of all they will try to establish his motives. Perhaps his wife nagged him habitually and nagging, it is well known, often throws men into murderous rages. Or perhaps he had many and pressing debts and his wife's life was insured for a large sum of money. A psychologist might study his early life and decide that he had violent aggressive feelings towards all women which derived from unsatisfied dependency needs in early childhood. A believer in Dr. Sheldon's somatotypes might point out that he had the physical characteristics of a man inclined to violence. A follower of Lombroso might indicate that the murderer had no lobes to his ears; while a genetecist might argue that his father and grandfather had both been soldiers and that perhaps he had a hereditary inclination to violence. An anthropologist might add that the murderer was Irish and had been drinking. In all these cases, however, the arguments would consist of showing that his action in murdering his wife fitted into a familiar and recurrent pattern of events. The fact that some elements of this pattern are presumed to have taken place in the mind of the murderer does not alter their familiar and repetitive character nor does the fact that he undoubtedly *chose* to murder his wife rather than, let us say, to desert her.

So it is with historical events. In studying the causes of the recent world war we shall undoubtedly wish to consider the motives of the German people in allowing the Nazis to come to power and in carrying out Hitler's monstrous and rapacious designs. We may talk about the injustice of reparations, the ineffectiveness of the Weimar Republic, mass unemployment in the early thirties, the pattern of authority in the average German household, the Prussian tradition and a thousand other possible causes, but, whatever explanations we may suggest, we shall be relating the behaviour of the Germans to known and familiar psychological patterns.

Sir Isaiah Berlin in a recent pamphlet entitled 'Historical Inevitability' has restated with striking eloquence and force the old argument in favour of the freedom of human choice and against any sort of historical determinism. What he has not seen, however, is that this opposition between free-will and determinism only arises if we adopt the old-fashioned view of determinism as involving some sort of theological or metaphysical necessity, some force flowing through the cause and controlling or compelling the effect. Of course, when we make choices we do not feel these choices to be subject to any controlling or compelling force, we do not feel them to be determined in this old-fashioned sense. But, if we assume that determinism and other forms of explanation only involve recurrent regularities, no opposition to free-will arises. The necessity of the process is only semantic, not metaphysical. We choose what we prefer; it is meaningless to say that we can choose what we do not prefer.

Indeed human choices are only interesting and valuable if they *are* determined in the modern sense of the word. We do not praise or blame people for their random actions but rather for those actions which show a consistent disposition or tendency. The most obvious function, in fact, of this process of choosing is to permit us to act in accord with our fundamental tendencies, rather than at random or in automatic response to external stimuli. In so far as history is the result of human choices it will probably reflect fundamental and common human needs and we may assume that whatever regularities we find are at least partly explicable in terms of these needs. Vico stated this point, in his own typically obscure way, in his eleventh axiom.[1] 'Human choice,' he said, 'though by its nature most uncertain, makes itself certain and determines itself through the common sense of men regarding human needs and utilities, which are the two sources of the natural law of nations.' We may agree with Croce, then, that history is 'the Story of Liberty', without sharing his anti-empiricism. It is the story of how men have pursued their own goals, at first severely limited by external conditions, but then more and more learning to exploit those conditions, and discovering different possibilities of satisfaction. But it is not 'free' in the sense of being unintelligible. It must exhibit some order in the very nature of things and the order which it does exhibit will derive from the fact that it is a pursuit of *human* ends.

Part of the confusion over this question is due, it seems to me, to a misapplication of Aristotle's theory of the four causes. It is thought that because human actions are purposeful they must be explained teleologically and not mechanically, in terms of final and not of efficient causes. But what Aristotle meant by a final

[1] Giambattista Vico, *Scienza Nuova*, Milan, 1946, Vol. I, p. 175.

cause was something objective, the goal or end of action; thus, in his favourite example, health is the final cause of exercise.[1] This notion has almost completely dropped out of modern thought; what we now mean by purposes or motives are prior events, thoughts and feelings, in the mind of the actor which determine the action much in the same way that Aristotle's efficient causes did. The goal of an action is not thought of as being outside or beyond it but rather as having prior existence in an inner mental world; for us, it is the *desire* for health that is the cause of exercise. Since this desire precedes its expression in action, this modern notion of purpose fits nicely into ordinary explanations in terms of cause and effect.

It is certainly true, on the other hand, that, unlike physical causes, these purposes are not open to direct observation. Each man can only observe his own purposes, not those of others. In seeking to interpret the actions of others he must attempt to reconstruct their purposes, partly on the evidence provided by their other actions and partly on the basis of how he himself would have felt and thought in similar circumstances. It has sometimes been argued that this reconstruction of motives is a procedure quite foreign to science. In fact, however, similar procedures are frequently used even in the physical sciences. Entities such as electrons or electromagnetic waves are assumed to exist, even though they can never be directly observed. The use of these 'hypothetical constructs', as they are called, is justified by the fact that they serve to unify and explain large areas of phenomena which *are* observable. In this respect, the position of the student of human actions is actually stronger than that of the physical scientists, for he is at least able to observe his *own* mental processes and he can be fairly sure that something analogous takes place in other people. His constructs are not entirely hypothetical. On the other hand, as we saw in the last chapter, he runs the danger of assuming too quickly —without sufficient evidence—that other people's motives are identical with his own. But whether he falls into this error or not, he is still attempting to explain human actions in terms of recur-

[1] Aristotle, *Physics*, II, 3.

rent regularities and his procedure does not differ fundamentally from that of the physical sciences.

In ordinary life we make these assumptions about other people's motives very quickly and only half-consciously, or perhaps even unconsciously. We seem almost to see what they are thinking while they are acting. It is this faculty for rapid judgment, especially of motives, which is usually referred to as 'intuition'. Sometimes indeed it is claimed that intuition involves a direct and immediate perception of the contents of other people's minds; but in any particular case we can almost always show that a so-called intuitive judgment is based on the evidence of the senses and the analogy of our own mental processes. Even the most intuitive of historians will bring forward evidence to justify his insights. If he did not do so, there would be no means for his readers or other historians to judge whether they were true or false. Everyone would be free to assert that he and he alone had penetrated directly into the minds of his predecessors and there would be no possibility of argument or of agreement.

It may well be that some direct perception of the mental processes of others does occasionally occur. We cannot disprove its existence and the experiments of the parapsychologists have certainly given us strong reasons for believing in it. But their experiments have also shown that this faculty, if it exists, is extremely haphazard, inaccurate and liable to error. It may serve to pierce the barriers of sense under the pressure of some urgent need, but it can hardly provide knowledge of other men's motives in a way which will be generally acceptable.

Even if we did assume, then, that historians occasionally exercise a faculty for extra-sensory perception, which we might call 'retro-cognition' on the analogy of 'pre-cognition', we would still have to ask them for evidence to bolster their insights before we could accept them. In so far as intuition is a valid means of understanding it must be based on, or confirmed by, empirical evidence available to everyone. We cannot accept the position associated with the name of Dilthey which divides the sciences into *Naturwissenschaften* and *Geisteswissenschaften* and bases the latter on some direct, mysterious and uncontrollable power of understanding. Such understanding, since it could not be validated empirically, would be merely private and serve no common human purpose. Indeed experience shows that those historians who have relied on their own loose and rapid judgments and not on the evidence very rarely agree with one another. Their works tend to become towers of confusion.

It scarcely needs saying, then, that an even further degree of confusion would result if historians took literally the contentions of these idealist philosophers, such as Croce and Collingwood, who hold that historical events (and everything else) only exist in the human mind. Idealism is even more dangerous than intuitionism. For it would follow that, not only the motives of human beings in the past, but also their actions and any events which affected them only existed in the mind of the historian. Anything which he chose to think or to say would be true. Evidence would be irrelevant unless he chose to make use of it and there would be no possible basis for reconciling different views or even for choosing between them. Of course, in practice, even idealist philosophers do consider the evidence; their idealism is not to be taken as an absolute dogma but rather as an attempt to emphasize the subjective element in human understanding and human behaviour. It permits them to lay additional stress on whatever moral values they may happen to prefer and to indulge in occasional flights of fancy without regard to the facts.

It is not surprising, then, that the followers of Croce are notorious for their high-handed treatment of historical evidence and Croce himself is not entirely free of this fault. Collingwood too, in his practice as a historian, exhibits the defects inherent in his idealistic theories. In his work on Roman Britain,[1] he shows a thorough mastery of the evidence and great skill in interpreting it. But he also indulges in extensive flights of the imagination, of which the most notorious—and, let it be said, the most readable— is his chapter on King Arthur. Here, out of a minimum of facts,

[1] R. G. Collingwood and J. N. L. Myres, *Roman Britain and the English Settlements*, Oxford, 1936.

he creates a new Arthurian legend, worthy to stand beside the inventions of Tennyson and Geoffrey of Monmouth.[1] Direct insight into the minds of others, then, whether it is called extra-sensory perception or intuition or something else can never be a valid method for obtaining conclusions which are generally acceptable. Any such conclusions must be based on evidence which is open to examination by everyone.

We need not, however, disparage the value of the intuitions and insights which have been shown by many historians. In the absence of a more systematic manner of approaching the facts they have done well to express whatever guesses and speculations have emerged from their studies. All science, after all, is based on the refinement and systematic verification of similar intuitions. The philosophers of science have been in almost unanimous disagreement with Bacon's theory that the facts, once collected, will simply speak for themselves. The scientist *must* make guesses; often he must make many wrong guesses before he finds one that can be empirically verified.

On the other hand, the guesses remain guesses as long as they are not verified. To set up intuition as a mode of understanding, opposed to and perhaps superior to reason, is to misunderstand the functions and the inter-relations of both. They are not opposites, but two forms or two stages of the same process. Intuition is looser, vaguer, more immediate and more subject to error, while reason is tighter, more precise, more indirect and more reliable. Reason grows out of intuition and depends upon it; but intuition without reason is mere groping in the dark. Both are necessary whether we are dealing with material objects or with human beings.

One of Croce's arguments against the empirical approach to history (and to everything else) deserves more serious consideration. He points out that the logico-experimental method of the sciences inevitably divides things into separate and distinct categories, while reality itself appears to be a continuous process in

[1] See also Mortimer Wheeler's review of *Roman Britain* in *The Journal of Roman Studies*, Vol. 29, Pt. 1, 1939, pp. 87–93.

which the phenomena are not distinct but merged in a sort of unified flow. (He considers this process to be 'ideal' or 'spiritual', but we can accept that it is continuous without accepting this second point.) Empirical thought, he says, divides what is united in reality, while ideal thought distinguishes and at the same time unifies. He is perfectly willing to accept that empirical thought is useful as a means of ticketing and cataloguing experiences so that they can be set aside for future use. But it is dead; it does not present to us the living reality.[1]

There is certainly some justice in this argument. We have already seen that empirical thought cannot express the flow of energy which we feel to take place between cause and effect. But Croce's 'ideal' thought lands us in even greater difficulties. He is forced to use words; and words, after all, stand for distinct concepts or features of process. Much of Croce's historical writing can be taken as an empirical analysis of how sets of ideas or values held by human beings in successive periods may be related in a regular pattern somewhat similar to Hegel's famous dialectic. There is nothing unempirical in this procedure. When, however, he seeks to express the living reality, the unity of things, he makes use either of the ambiguous and evocative language of poetry or of the language of mysticism in which everything is identified with everything else. Thus history, he says at one point, is philosophy and, at others, that it is spirit, thought, life, and value, not to mention culture, civilization, and liberty. Many of his passages read like verbal cocktails; he mixes together a lot of fine words and gives them to you to drink off in one great draught.

Inspiring and stimulating as mystical and poetical language may be it does not provide any basis for a common understanding of phenomena. Empirical thought, while it may not be able to express some aspects of reality, nevertheless does provide such a basis. It may be 'dead', but it is certainly useful. We shall do well to continue to use it, then, as Croce himself does, while recognizing its limitations.

As we have seen, then, there is little or no justification for sup-

[1] Croce, *op. cit.*, pp. 117–27.

posing that the events of history are, by their very nature, refractory to scientific study. Their uniqueness and complexity are not intrinsically different from those of material objects and we may hope to surmount our difficulties in experimenting with them. The fact that they are the result of human purposes does, indeed, serve to differentiate them from the entities of the physical universe, but it does not make them any less subject to the ordinary canons of intelligibility. They can and must be intelligible in the light of the normal procedures of science. The principal difficulty has probably been our failure so far to make the right guesses, to find the unifying concepts in terms of which we can order at least part of the vast assemblage of facts. As I indicated in the first chapter, however, it seems likely that these unifying concepts have already been developed and applied in another field. The systematic interpretation of culture as developed in anthropology is most likely to provide the concepts and methods necessary to illuminate the dark jungle of historical events. It is, therefore, to the examination of the concept of culture and other related concepts that I shall turn in the following chapters.

4

THE CONCEPT OF CULTURE

IN the physical sciences, little or no progress was made until certain very general aspects of the physical environment had been abstracted from the confusing mass of impressions which make up our experience. These abstractions were then investigated in and for themselves without regard for other aspects of that experience. Among the abstractions of physics, for instance, are mass, momentum, and energy, all of which now seem to us familiar and even obvious, but whose discovery and clarification was the work of many minds and many centuries. It is probable that the difficulties which have hitherto been encountered in finding regularities in history are due to the absence of broad abstractions of this kind, in terms of which the phenomena can be ordered. As I have already suggested, the concept of culture and related concepts, which have proved so useful in the study of primitive societies, may turn out to be just what we need to clarify the larger field of events which we know as history. The idea of culture has fortunately already been made use of to some extent by historians and this fact should encourage us in seeking to use it even more extensively. Nevertheless, it is in anthropology—or rather in one branch of it—that the concept of culture has been most used and has acquired most precise definition; it has come to serve as the basis of a whole system of theoretical formulations and it is to the anthropologists, therefore, that we must turn if we wish to use the concept as the foundation of a science of history.

Like all abstract notions, the anthropological concept of culture has only come to be formulated very gradually. No doubt men have always been aware that the habits and customs, the ways of life, of neighbouring peoples differed from their own; they have chosen to express this observation in various ways. The Greek distinction between φύσις and νόμος, which we might translate as 'nature' and 'convention', undoubtedly expresses something similar to our distinction between the biological and cultural sources of behaviour. We have already seen that Voltaire used the expression '*moeurs et esprit*'—customs and spirit—which seems to cover the same range of phenomena as 'culture' in its contemporary anthropological use. In its first appearance in the European languages the word 'culture' had not yet acquired the meaning which we give to it today. In Latin and in Middle English it usually had the literal meaning of 'cultivation' or 'tillage of the soil', which survives in the words 'agriculture' and 'horticulture'. Cicero already used it in a transferred or figurative meaning; he spoke of '*cultura mentis*' which he identified with philosophy.[1] This use is rare, however, in Latin and the *Oxford Dictionary* gives 1510 as the date of its first appearance in English. 'Culture' in this sense means any deliberate effort to develop the qualities of some object. We must always speak of 'the culture of wheat' or 'the culture of the arts'; we cannot speak of 'culture' alone. As late as 1852, a purist like Newman made use of the terms 'mental' or 'intellectual culture', but not 'culture' alone.[2] At the present time we are more apt to use the word 'cultivation' in both of these senses, the literal and the figurative.

It was in France in the eighteenth century that such authors as Vauvenargues and Voltaire began to use the French word '*culture*' in an absolute sense; for them it meant the state or result of training (or refinement) of the mind (or of thought or taste)—but not, it should be noted, of plants—rather than the process of training or refinement. Very quickly the word came to be applied to the actual attainments of an educated person. Good manners, literature, the arts, and the sciences—all these were called '*culture*' and were looked on as objects which might be acquired by education. Ac-

[1] Cicero, *Tusculan Disputations*, 2, 5, 13.
[2] John Henry Newman, *The Idea of a University*, Cambridge, 1931, pp. 88–90.

cording to the *Oxford Dictionary* this sense does not appear in English until 1805. It was popularized by Matthew Arnold in his work *Culture and Anarchy* and survives today as the most common literary use of the word; we speak of 'acquiring culture', 'a cultured person', and so on.

All these meanings are fairly remote from the modern technical use of the word in anthropology. It is only with Herder and his contemporaries in Germany towards the end of the eighteenth century that we see the first beginnings of the modern usage. For Herder, culture is still a meliorist notion; it means the improvement of the individual, or the skills, techniques and learning which the individual acquires in improving himself, but such attainments now include the technical as well as the intellectual side of life and it is recognized that different peoples may make different contributions to 'culture' in general or may even 'not have the same culture'.[1] It was not until the middle of the nineteenth century, however, that the connotation of improvement or development began to drop out. In the writings of Klemm, who was, as we have seen, the founder of the science of anthropology, there are still traces of the developmental connotations of the word, but its primary use now seems to be to cover all the aspects of the social life of a people: 'customs, arts and skills, domestic and public life in peace or war, religion, science and art'.[2] It was from Klemm that Tylor borrowed the word and first gave it the meaning which it has for English-speaking anthropologists today.

Before examining this meaning we should note that the word 'civilization' had a development almost precisely parallel to that of 'culture'. At first it meant a process of refinement of the individual, with perhaps more emphasis on the social graces than was implied by 'culture'. Thus Kant makes the distinction: 'We become . . . cultivated through art and science, we become civilized . . . to a variety of social graces and refinements.' The use of the verb 'civilized' in this sense has been traced back as early as the end

---

[1] Herder, 'Ideen zur Geschichte der Menschheit', in *Sämmtliche Werke*, Berlin, 1887–1909, Vol. 13, p. 109; Vol. 14, p. 275 *et passim*.

[2] Gustav Klemm, *Allgemeine Cultur-geschichte der Menschheit*, Leipzig, 1843–52, Vol. I, p. 21.

of the sixteenth century. In the latter half of the eighteenth century, 'civilization', like 'culture', came to mean a state rather than a process of refinement or, at times, the specific modes of behaviour, such as polished manners and a peaceful political life, which were the result of refinement. It is the word in this sense which Johnson deliberately excluded from his dictionary, as Boswell tells us, preferring to use 'civility' as the opposite of 'barbarity'. 'Civilization', like 'culture', appears to have been first used in this sense by the French. The Germans as we have seen, adopted the word 'culture' and extended it even further to cover all the aspects of social life, whether refined or not. In French, on the other hand, *culture* retained its developmental connotations until very recently and it was *civilisation* which, in nineteenth-century France, came to be used in the more general sense which *Kultur* had acquired in German.

Civilisation has continued to be used in this sense in France, both by anthropologists and more purely literary writers, until the present day. This meaning was also adopted in England and Tylor himself used 'civilization' at first before he borrowed the word 'culture' from Klemm. After Tylor, 'culture' came to be the preferred word in America; we may perhaps detect some influence from Germany as well in this preference. In England, however, as in France, 'civilization' continued to be used and as late as 1922 an English anthropologist, Goldenweiser, wrote a book on *Early Civilization*, though he preferred the word 'culture' in his later works. Even today we may occasionally find a reference to 'primitive civilizations' in English authors, like Toynbee, who are unaware of modern developments. In general, however, in recent decades both in England and in France—though somewhat more in England than in France—'culture' has tended to oust 'civilization', in so far as either word is used at all by the social anthropologists who prevail in both countries. 'Civilization' has tended to revert to something approximating its older meaning; it seems to indicate a higher or more developed form of culture, or more specifically, the culture of cities. Thus, writers speak of either 'Chinese culture' or 'Chinese civilization', but 'primitive culture' is preferred by almost every one to 'primitive civilization'. I shall attempt to clarify this distinction in Chapter VII.

It is curious to note that these technical uses of 'civilization' and 'culture', although they have been current in English for over eighty years appear only in the 1933 supplement to the complete *Oxford Dictionary* and not in the 1955 edition of the shorter version; the *Dictionnaire de l'Académie*, which is usually thought of as being excessively conservative, admitted them both in 1932.

It must not be supposed that the anthropological use of 'culture' was entirely clear from the very beginning, or even that it is perfectly clear today. As Freud puts it:

> The fundamental concepts and most general ideas in any of the disciplines of science are always left indeterminate at first, and are only explained to begin with by reference to the realm of phenomena from which they were derived; it is only by means of a progressive analysis of the material of observation that they can be made clear and can find a significant and consistent meaning.[1]

So it has been with 'culture'. Since Tylor's day understanding of it and its relationships to other phenomena has grown deeper and richer; at the same time definitions and descriptions have proliferated; Kroeber and Kluckhohn in their exhaustive study of the word have listed 161 definitions.[2] 'Culture', we read, is values; it is norms; it is learned or symbolizing or habitual behaviour; it is a stream of ideas or a social organism or any of a dozen other things. Sometimes, in writing about culture, American anthropologists seem to be singing a mystical paean of praise to their muse, in which a long series of diverse and often incompatible qualities are ascribed to her, much as in some litany to the Virgin. No wonder that the British social anthropologists should find the idea vague and confusing and should sometimes deliberately exclude it from their works!

Nevertheless, cultural anthropologists continue to use the word

---

[1] Freud, *An Autobiographical Study*, London, 1946, p. 106.

[2] A. L. Kroeber and Clyde Kluckhohn, *Culture, A Critical Review of Concepts and Definitions*, Cambridge, Mass., 1952. I have drawn heavily on this work for the historical material given above.

and appear to communicate with each other successfully; there must be a core of meaning which determines and justifies its use. If we wish to make our present studies as rational as possible we shall wish to define and delimit this central meaning as closely and as clearly as we can. We shall seek to construct a definition which will point, as a definition should, to some homogeneous realm of experience and distinguish it sharply from other realms of experience.

How are we to extract the core of meaning from the welter of definitions which are available? We have already used certain phrases such as 'ways of life' or 'all the aspects of social life', but these expressions are intentionally vague and cannot serve as definitions. Perhaps the best procedure will be to re-examine the sorts of objects or events which are usually described as culture. We cannot, of course, draw up an exhaustive list, but we can indicate the broader areas which have been covered. Among these there appear first of all the major departments of human activity: religion, politics, economics, art, science, technology, education, language, customs and so on. Any contemporary description of the culture of a particular tribe would attempt to cover some if not all of these areas. If we examine the realities behind these words, it seems clear that what we are dealing with primarily are modes of behaviour, ways in which human beings act. They worship gods, struggle for political power, buy and sell goods, paint pictures and so on; activities all of which may be described as culture.

But modes of behaviour are not all that culture includes. Anthropologists also refer to ideas, knowledge, beliefs, norms, values and other things, which would not normally be described as behaviour. Some of the areas of human activity which we have mentioned above can also be thought of as including features which are not, strictly speaking, behaviour. Religion, for instance, includes religious beliefs and religious experience as well as religious practices, while science covers a body of knowledge as well as the activities involved in acquiring that knowledge. In part, at least, these non-behavioural kinds of culture can be described as modes of thinking and feeling; they are features of that inner 'mental' activity which we can observe only in ourselves and must presume to exist in others. Modes of thinking and feeling, then, as well as modes of behaviour in the narrow sense, are among the objects included in the class of objects we call 'culture'.

Quite often, of course, we conceive of beliefs, values and so forth as entities somehow apart from the actual thoughts and feelings or the external behaviour in which they are said to be 'expressed'. These entities, according to a common spatial metaphor, seem to be buried deep inside our heads or breasts or even to float in the air above our heads. A man's belief in political liberty may, we feel, lie dormant and unobserved inside him until some act of tyranny causes it to issue forth in strong emotion and positive asseveration. The exact locus of these entities seems to vary from society to society. Thus, for the Trobriand Islanders' intelligence resides in the larynx while memories are stored in the belly.[1] Nevertheless, mankind is generally agreed that they are somewhere inside.

It is one of the great puzzles of psychology—and, for that matter, also of philosophy—how to deal with these popular and useful concepts. On the one hand it seems doubtful that we really do carry around inside us a whole population of invisible little beings that determine our thoughts, feelings and actions; on the other hand, some, at least, of these entities can probably be justified as hypothetical constructs analogous to electrons in physics and genes in biology. Certainly, if we tried to do without them entirely, our descriptions of human beings would be much impoverished. Psychologists have attempted to dispose of the problems which the use of these concepts raises by labelling them with certain vague, ambiguous and general terms—'attitudes', for instance, or 'cognitive and affective orientations'. Recently a distinguished philosopher, Professor Ryle, has pointed out that many of them can be regarded as 'dispositions' or tendencies, that is, as probabilities that human beings will think or feel or act under certain circumstances in some particular fashion.[2] But even he

[1] Bronislaw Malinowski, *Argonauts of the Western Pacific*, London, 1922, pp. 408–9.
[2] Gilbert Ryle, *The Concept of Mind*, London, 1949, pp. 116–35.

often tends to speak as if a probability were something existing apart from the observers who judge it probable, though he would doubtless deny that this is his intention. We seem to be dealing here with a problem similar to that of the connections between cause and effect, which we feel to exist, but the existence of which we can never prove.

These involved philosophical difficulties can hardly be resolved here. But in the interests of clarity and in line with our general empirical approach we might agree to exclude these highly questionable entities from our definition of culture. This is not to say that we must exclude such terms as ideas, beliefs and values from our vocabulary altogether. On the contrary, we shall be able to go on using them but we shall take them as referring not to any hypothetical internal mechanisms and not to opinions about the probability of future behaviour, but rather to the previous recurrence of certain modes of behaviour—the same behaviour that from another point of view we should take as evidence for the existence of these entities or as a basis for our judgments about probabilities. In practice, it will be found that this alteration of focus makes very little difference in our ordinary habits of speech. Thus an historian might write that personal loyalty was one of the most important values in Western Europe in the Middle Ages. He would go on to cite various writings of the time and various institutions which he would hold to be expressions of this value and proofs of its existence. But if we take the value of personal loyalty to be, not some unobservable internal entity, but simply the common element in certain kinds of actions and in statements approving those actions, we shall have to change very little in what the historian has written. To say that certain people value loyalty will be simply to say that they have acted loyally and spoken in praise of loyal actions.

Many readers will doubtless find this procedure excessively behaviouristic. They are of course at liberty to retain attitudes, or orientations, or dispositions, or whatever they would like to call them, as one of the categories of objects to be included in the definition of culture; but they will do so at the expense of clarity.

The definition will no longer be homogeneous. It will cover entities of different orders and will for that reason be unwieldy and awkward to use.

Let us agree, then, that culture includes modes of thinking and feeling and modes of behaviour, but not any of the invisible entities, whatever they may be, which determine these modes. Shall we go further and reduce the thoughts and feelings to the behaviour which expresses them, just as we have previously reduced the attitudes and dispositions? For my part I do not find this necessary. There is no question that thoughts and feelings exist; we have direct experience of them ourselves. They may be looked on as a kind of inner behaviour. Some philosophers—most notably Spinoza—have held the doctrine known as psychophysical parallelism, that is, that to every thought or feeling there corresponds some physiological change or activity in the body. Professor Ryle even maintains that thoughts and feelings *are* such changes or activities; his view might be called psychophysical identity. We need not go so far, however; we can still agree that thoughts and feelings must be regarded as a particular variety of the activity of the total human being. In conformity with this point of view, we can transform the expression: 'modes of thought, feeling and behaviour' to read 'modes of behaviour, mental and physical' or 'internal and external' or 'observable and unobservable'. In this way, we can stress the common element in, or the homogeneity of, the various categories of objects included in culture. They are all activities of human beings.

There is still a further category of objects which writers sometimes refer to as 'culture', or more specifically, as 'material culture'. These are the physical objects which are the products of human activity: tools, weapons, pots, buildings, works of art and so on. For obvious reasons, it is the archaeologists and the keepers of anthropological museums who are chiefly interested in these objects; 'artifacts' is another generic term often used to describe them. It is not difficult to see, however, that it is not the physico-chemical structures of these objects in and for themselves which concern the scholars who study them. Artifacts are interesting simply and solely because of the activities of the people who made and used them. There is no need then to obscure our concept of culture by including physical objects as one of the categories to be covered; art and technology, which are the principal interests of the students of 'material culture', are already included in our expression: 'modes of behaviour, internal and external'.

Since Aristotle, it has been generally agreed that a definition must have two parts; it must indicate both genus and species, both the larger category within which the objects or events that interest us fall, and the limitations of the smaller field which is our main concern. So far we have established the genus; our phrase, 'modes of behaviour, internal and external', points to a fairly large segment of the universe of experience which we must now delimit more precisely. If we did not do so, we should be unable to distinguish the domain of culture from the events studied by psychology and physiology.

If we examine the 161 definitions given by Kroeber and Kluckhohn, we find that there are two principal ways in which this delimitation has been achieved. One is to describe the causal origin, the way in which the particular modes of behaviour that interest us come about. In accordance with whatever terminology may be favoured by a particular writer or with the fashion of the times, cultural modes of behaviour are said to be learned, or handed down by tradition, or socially inherited, or transmitted through symbols; they are developed as solutions to problems or as adaptations to the environment. The purpose here seems to be to distinguish culture from the domain of general, or as Windelband calls it, nomothetic, psychology, as well as from the domain of physiology. We would not wish to regard the fact that all men eat (or try to eat) when they feel hungry, or the fact that all men become angry when they are frustrated, as cultural facts; they are looked on rather as physiological or psychological functions, as parts of 'human nature', inherited by the individual from his parents in accordance with the usual biological mechanisms. It is particular customs of eating: diet, table-manners, and mealtimes, and particular styles of expressing anger, which concern the anthropologist; inherited modes of behaviour he leaves to the psychologist or the physiologist.

There is one obvious difficulty in this manner of separating culture from the rest of behaviour. If we mention the causal origins of culture as part of our definition, we are answering in advance some of the questions which it will be the task of our science to discover; and, as our science progresses, we shall have to change our definition to fit the new theories of causality which have been developed. It is already clear, indeed, that some of the terms used by the authors of the definitions we have mentioned are no longer adequate. Some kinds of culture, such as styles of gait and posture, for instance, are clearly transmitted, not through the mediation of symbols, but by imitation and example; others, such as art and religion, are by no means clearly adaptive to the environment; most anthropologists would like to include in culture those new styles of behaviour which are invented as well as those that are learned.

Yet there must be some phrase in the definition of culture which will serve to distinguish it from the subject-matters of physiology and general psychology. Perhaps the best way of doing this will be to evade the question of causal origins by using a negative phrase; let us say that culture is those modes of behaviour, internal and external, which are *not* clearly hereditary in origin. No doubt, this leaves the boundary between culture and human nature somewhat uncertain, but in so doing it conforms to the actual state of affairs as regards the two sciences of anthropology and psychology. Language, for instance, is a universal human phenomenon, and is usually regarded as one of the aspects of culture; but we do not know how far some of the regularities of language, the laws of sound-change, for instance, or the general capacity to use intelligible speech, are hereditary phenomena, that is, part of human nature. Until this is decided, the behaviour in question may legitimately be studied either by psychologists or by students of linguistics. The latter science, of course, may be considered one of the branches of anthropology in the broadest sense of the word.

By excluding from this definition those modes of behaviour

which are clearly hereditary, I have distinguished culture from the subject-matters of physiology and general psychology, but I have not yet distinguished it from the subject-matter of individual, or as Windelband calls it, 'idiographic' psychology. Psychologists study not only those general aspects of human nature which seem to be inherited, but also those regularities of individual behaviour which serve to differentiate one individual from another and which are usually considered to be the result of prior experience or interaction with the environment rather than simply the product of inheritance. These personality-traits, as they are usually called, are also modes of behaviour which are not clearly hereditary, and would be included in our definition if we made no further distinction.

The anthropologists who have drawn up definitions have attempted to make this distinction by referring in some manner or other to society. Sometimes they have fused this notion with that of the causal origins of culture; culture, we read, is tradition, or social heritage or, in Tylor's lapidary phrase, is 'acquired by man as a member of society'.[1] Other writers speak simply of the behaviour characteristic of a group of people rather than of an individual, or use vague expressions similar to our 'ways of life' or 'all the aspects of social life'. The central idea here seems to be that, while personality-traits are modes of behaviour which recur in the life of an individual, culture is modes of behaviour which recur in the different members of a group or society. Thus, in our society it is a matter of indifference whether a man puts his right or his left shoe on first; if some individual regularly does one or the other, we would regard this as a private habit or personal idiosyncrasy. But all the men in our society, or very nearly all, have the buttons on the right-hand side of their jackets and this is a feature of our culture.

Recurrence or regularity in the diverse features of our experience is what renders them intelligible, as I have already pointed out in a previous chapter; it is their regularity that makes them capable of scientific treatment. We should have expected then that

[1] E. B. Tylor, *Primitive Culture*, London, 1871, p. 1.

culture would turn out to be some kind of regularity, and this has proved to be so. We can now complete our definition by saying that 'culture' is 'regularities in the behaviour, internal and external, of the members of a society, excluding those regularities which are clearly hereditary in origin'.

The word 'society' may seem ambiguous, but it can be taken in its simplest sense as a number of people who, in certain respects and at certain times, interact more with each other than they do with outsiders. It thus covers all the varieties of human associations, large or small, from tribes and nations, or even groups of nations, down through social classes, institutions, clubs, and families to the simplest case of two people conversing momentarily on a street-corner. Even in such a minimal society there may well be a phrase or trick of speech used by one person and repeated by the other, similar to the private vocabularies which are usual in families. If so, that peculiarity of speech would be a feature of the culture of that evanescent street-corner society. In plain language, 'a society is composed of people; the way they behave is their culture.'[1] This meaning of 'society' should be clearly distinguished from several others which are current either in popular or technical uses: 'the upper classes' (as in 'presenting her daughter to society'), 'social organization' (as in 'a student of society'), and 'an organized group' (as in 'primitive societies').

The word 'regularities' also requires further comment. It has come into use in recent decades in the physical sciences to replace the older term 'laws' with its implication that the universe is governed by the absolute *fiat* of an anthropomorphic law-giver. If we say that science is the study of observed regularities, we avoid all the difficulties involved in a belief in absolute determinism. 'Patterns', 'configurations', 'features of order' are other expressions with identical, or nearly identical, meanings. A regularity need not be universal or quasi-universal in its occurrence as the 'law' of gravity is; it may be restricted to a local habitation. From a strictly empirical point of view, the objects of ordinary discourse, tables and chairs, for instance, are regularities of this narrowly

[1] M. J. Herskovits, *Man and his Works*, New York, 1948, p. 29.

limited variety. The persistent recurrence in the dining-room of a flat wooden surface resting on four legs is what we call 'the dining-room table'. That circular brightness which keeps recurring in the sky is 'the sun'. The class of regularities we call culture is similar; cultural regularities need have no broader scope than a single society: they may or may not also be found in other societies.

It is important to note that cultural regularities need not recur in the life of a single individual; what is important is whether they recur in the behaviour of more than one member of the society. The word 'the', for instance, recurs many times a day in the speech of almost all members of our society; the ceremony of marriage occurs only once in the lives of most members and in some lives not at all; yet both the word 'the' and the marriage ritual are features of our culture. So, for that matter, is the coronation ritual in a monarchical state, even though it occurs on the average only once a generation.

Should we go on to say that a regularity must hold for all the members of the society? Ideally, perhaps we should. We need not insist that the behaviour of each member should be identical; the definition of a regularity may allow for a greater or lesser degree of variation, and the range of variation which can actually be observed is an important feature of the culture of any society. Nor need the behaviour even be similar; the regularity may consist in the fact that the members of one section of the society behave in one way and the members of another section in another; the men wear trousers, for instance, while the women wear skirts. There may even be cases where the behaviour in question is exhibited by only one individual. In some societies, for instance, only one man, the king, wears a crown. But the regularity consists in the fact that all the other members of the society do not wear crowns (except in certain well-defined situations, such as on the stage); it is this regular distribution of 'crown-wearing' and 'not-crown-wearing' which is the cultural fact; otherwise, 'crown-wearing' would be a mere personal idiosyncrasy.

Ideally, then, the full description of any cultural regularity should cover the behaviour of all members of the society; differences in behaviour should be correlated with membership in well-defined segments of that society, such as age- and sex-groups; social, economic and occupational classes; religious or political factions and so on. A full description should point out the degrees of variation observed in each of these segments. It should also provide for all exceptions by correlating the absence of the behaviour in question with some unusual feature of individual physique or temperament or with individual contact with (that is, partial membership in) some other society. For instance we may say that all Englishmen shake hands on being introduced to a stranger, except if they are small children, or if they are physically incapacitated, or if their hands are very dirty, or if the stranger is an Indian and the Englishman is acquainted with the Indian method of salutation, and so on. We may also enumerate the variations of the handshake and their occurrence, from extending the fingertips to vigorous squeezing. In practice it is very difficult, if not impossible, for the student of culture to list all the variations and exceptions to any particular regularity; he must content himself with observing that *most* of the members of a society (or of well-defined segments of it) behave in a particular fashion. If we seek for cultural regularities in the past, it is always impossible to determine their application to all the long-dead members of some extinct society. But it is well to remember that this is the desired goal, however far we may be from achieving it.

In our failure to achieve it, we shall differ only in degree from the physical scientists. Physical and chemical regularities also have their ranges of variation and their unexplained exceptions. A measurement can be exact only to a certain number of decimal points, and the measurements obtained in identical physical experiments often vary to a considerable degree. Anomalous and inexplicable exceptions, too, are more frequent in science than is generally admitted. The public hears about the experiments that succeeded, not those in which 'something went wrong'. An embarrassed silence has covered the fact that the famous Michelson-Morley experiments, on which the theory of relativity is allegedly based, did *not* demonstrate the constancy of the speed of light, but showed anomalies which have yet to be explained.[1] The precision and general validity, then, of any scientific observation, whether in the natural or the social sciences, can be only a matter of degree, even though it must be confessed that social scientists are forced to accept a considerably lower degree of accuracy than the standard set up by their *confrères* in the physical sciences.

Another possible way of looking at cultural regularities is to conceive of them as emergent forms of order, beginning in one small segment of the society and gradually spreading through all the other segments, though never perhaps achieving complete universality. This process can most clearly be observed in the case of language, where the rules of grammar often approach but rarely attain a universality which knows no exceptions. In English, for instance, the regular plural suffix '-s' was once rather less common than the suffix '-en'; it is now almost universal and all plurals of new words, other than those of foreign origin, are formed with '-s'; there are only a few exceptions to this universality, all of them in familiar words like 'mice', 'teeth' and 'deer'. Nevertheless, we shall wish, if we can, to explain each of these exceptions by showing that it belongs to some definite category: names of the broadest divisions of mankind ('men', 'women' and 'children'), names of familiar animals which end in a sibilant ('geese', 'mice', 'fish', and 'oxen') and so on. The linguists have developed refined and ingenious, though not always convincing, explanations to fit each one of these exceptional plurals, even those which do not fit into categories, such as 'deer' and 'sheep'. Here too then, even when the order is thought of as emergent, an ideally complete statement of the regularity as it holds at any given time would cover all the exceptions. We must think, then, of a cultural regularity as ideally applying to all the members of a particular society.

Here some one might ask: 'What of the plays of Shakespeare? Are they not part of English culture, even if we take "culture" in an objective and not an evaluative sense? And yet they are the

---

[1] Michael Polanyi, 'From Copernicus to Einstein', in *Encounter*, Vol. V, No. 3, Sept., 1955, pp. 59-61.

work of one man.' The apparent difficulty here lies in the fact that we use the word 'plays' to cover several different categories of reality: the books in which the plays are printed, Shakespeare's activity in writing them, their reproduction on the stage and so on. For each of these categories, we must give a different answer. The books are not 'culture': they are physical objects; it is how they are made and used that interests us. Shakespeare's activity in writing them is a part of culture in so far as it resembles the writing of other dramatists of his time or country. What is purely individual in his ideas and style (which has usually been considered the 'best' part) is not a part of 'culture' taken by itself. The cultural regularity lies in the fact that what he wrote has frequently been reprinted, much read and often reproduced on the stage, and very generally admired by literate Englishmen. The idiosyncrasies of some obscure Elizabethan dramatist, no longer read or played or admired today, would not be a part of English culture today. It is the reading and playing and admiring of the plays, or their similarity to other plays, which are the cultural facts, not the plays themselves.

Culture, then, is a particular class of regularities of behaviour. It includes both internal and external behaviour; it excludes the biologically-inherited aspects of behaviour. Cultural regularities may or may not recur in the behaviour of individuals, but, to be called 'culture', they should recur (or fail to occur) in a regular fashion in the behaviour of most of the members, and ideally in that of all the members, of a particular society.

If culture is a class of regularities, how then shall we name the particular regularities of which that class is made up. The customary term in anthropology is 'culture-trait', formed on the analogy of 'personality-trait'. Several culture-traits which are regularly found together in association are called a 'culture-complex', again on the analogy of the 'complexes' of psychology. 'Complex' and 'trait' are only relative terms, however; in practice, almost any trait can be analysed into further separable entities. The plural-suffix '-s', for instance, has two written forms, '-s' and '-es', and three spoken forms, the sounds represented by '-ez', '-z' and '-s'. A minute phonetic analysis would undoubtedly enable us to make even further distinctions. Any trait then may be regarded as a complex; it is merely a question of the fineness of the distinctions we wish to make in any given context; there are no atoms of behaviour, either psychological or cultural. Identical or similar culture-traits and complexes, may, of course, be found in more than one society. Here writing or the making of pots are good examples. A particular trait may even sometimes be found in all societies, though these cases are rare. Speech is perhaps the most notable example, since it is found in all societies with the minor exception of deaf-and-dumb associations, and even in them a manual substitute for speech is used. But it is essential that a culture-trait or culture-complex be found in the behaviour of most of the members of at least one society for it to be a cultural regularity at all.

The emphasis which we have laid in our definition on the presence of culture in *particular* societies reflects the relativistic and comparative approach of contemporary anthropology. As we saw in the first chapter, nineteenth-century anthropologists and nineteenth-century philosophers of history tended to look on all of human history and pre-history as exhibiting a single continuous process of development. This view was closely related to the rationalistic values of the eighteenth century and the belief in inevitable progress. In accordance with this view, culture was looked on as somehow the property of mankind as a whole, a good which accumulated under its own momentum, like money left in a savings account. The studies of anthropologists were principally directed towards establishing a necessary sequence of stages of culture and, in the latter part of the century, in showing the wide diffusion through the world of individual culture-traits and complexes.

As more was known about the actual course of events, however, it became clear that this line of approach was not particularly profitable. Different societies with substantially differing sets of culture-traits had developed at different times in relative isolation from one another. The progress of mankind as a whole might not be an entirely invalid conception, but it could only be stated in the most vague and general terms. The absence of any other rational animal whose cultural development might be compared to that of man made it difficult to find valid terms in which our observations of man's development might be expressed. For these reasons, and doubtless also for others, in the first decades of this century, the attention of anthropologists on both sides of the Atlantic shifted to the analysis of behaviour in particular societies. Here comparisons were possible and a whole wealth of new data could profitably be collected, ordered and understood. A similar development in the philosophy of history may be observed in Spengler. In his violent rejection of the idea of progress and in his insistence that civilizations are entirely autonomous entities, he expresses, though with much exaggeration, the same relativistic trend which is evident in anthropology. At the present time only a few authors, Toynbee and Gordon Childe in England, Leslie White in America, are willing to express opinions about the cultural development of mankind as a whole. Here we shall continue to emphasize the place of culture in particular societies, simply because it makes comparisons possible. Without comparisons, without the possibility of a calculus of similarities and differences, no valid generalizations, that is, no science is possible.

The reader will doubtless have found this prolonged discussion of the definition of culture tedious and excessively abstract. Yet without precise definitions we shall have no clarity and no precision in our science. To get definite answers when we examine the data, we must be able to ask definite questions. We must be able to point to some feature of the universe of experience and say definitely whether or not it is what we are looking for. The utility of the distinctions I have made in the preceding pages will become clear in later chapters where I shall apply them to the elucidation of particular phenomena.

We can already use our definition to clear up one or two problems. It is often said, for instance, that culture is an abstraction, and that therefore it is not real, not a matter of experience; only individual human beings are real. Now it is quite true that the word 'culture' (or the concept for which it stands) is an abstraction, in the sense that it points out certain features of experience (in this case, certain kinds of regularities of behaviour) and disregards the other features with which they are closely enmeshed. But in this sense, all words stand for abstractions, 'cows' and 'horses', 'tables' and 'chairs', even 'human beings' as much as 'culture'. A human being is constantly interacting with neighbouring portions of the environment, breathing in and out, perspiring and eating. To some extent, when we speak of a human being, we falsify our experience by isolating one aspect of that experience, the human being, from all that surrounds it. But here it will be objected that we can see and touch human beings, and cows and horses, and tables and chairs; they are concrete objects, while regularities of behaviour are invisible, at least at any given time. This is certainly largely true: some of the regularities of experience, such as tables and chairs, are continuous in time and contiguous in space; if we cannot see all their sides at once, at least we can see a definite outline which persists in time. Cultural regularities, on the other hand, are inherently discontinuous in time and space. Only in the most exceptional circumstances, such as a tribal ceremony in which all the members are present, can we take in the regularity of their behaviour with a glance. This discontinuity, however, does not make culture any less a matter of experience.

In addition, some kinds of cultural regularity, such as those of thought and feeling, can only occasionally be observed directly. If lack of visibility is the criterion, however, we would have to say that the wind is unreal. We can never see it; occasionally we can feel it as coolness and a pressure on the cheeks; more often we infer its existence from the movement of clouds and trees. Is the wind then an unreal abstraction? No, it is a regularity in the movement of certain air molecules, just as culture is regularities in the behaviour of certain human beings. Both are equally abstract and equally real. Similarly, the solar system is a regularity in the movements of the planets about the sun. We can never observe all these movements at any one time; many of them have to be inferred; yet it would be wrong to say that only the sun and the planets are real and that their movement or the regularity of their movement does not exist.

Culture, then, as we have defined it, is perfectly real, though it is not real in precisely the same way as physical objects; it resembles rather more closely their common properties, movements or relationships. Just as we can verify the presence of a table in the dining-room by going to look at it, so we can verify the presence of the culture-trait, writing, in China by going to China and watching Chinese write. If we had included in our definition of culture those hypothetical entities to which such terms as 'beliefs', 'ideas' and 'values' are usually taken to refer, we might justly incur the reproach of having made culture unreal, or at least of having put its reality in question. Even here the unreality of these entities would lie, not in the fact that they were abstractions, but in the fact that they were hypothetical, that they had been constructed to explain behaviour and could never themselves be observed. As it is, we have deliberately taken these terms to refer to features of behaviour, and thus the reality of culture has been preserved.

Another problem which our definition will help us to resolve is that of the relationship between culture and social structure, the respective subject-matters of cultural anthropology, on the one hand, and both social anthropology and sociology, on the other. Many writers have assumed that culture and social structure were two kinds or levels of abstractions made from the same underlying reality.[1] If we examine the notion of social structure, however, we shall see that it covers some of the same sort of abstractions as are covered in our definition of culture. Evans-Pritchard, for instance, speaks of 'structural relations between persons'[1] and Radcliffe-Brown uses the expression 'the forms of association amongst human beings'.[2] Max Weber uses the term 'social relationship' for his most fundamental concept and says that it denotes 'the behaviour of a plurality of actors in so far as, in its meaningful content, the action of each takes account of that of others and is oriented in these terms', though later he adds that the relationship consists in the *probability* of such behaviour.[3]

[1] See, for instance, E. E. Evans-Pritchard, *Social Anthropology*, London, 1951, pp. 17–18.
[2] A. R. Radcliffe-Brown, 'White's View of a Science of Culture', in *American Anthropologist*, Vol. 51, 1949, p. 510.
[3] Max Weber, *The Theory of Social and Economic Organization*, tr. by A. M. Henderson and Talcott Parsons, New York, 1947, p. 118.

What seems to be meant by all these expressions is that in given societies certain classes of the members act in regular ways towards the members of other classes. For instance, men who have children will feed, teach, punish, fondle and otherwise behave towards their children in regular and specified ways characteristic of the particular society of which they are members. This complex of regularities in the behaviour of fathers towards children would be called by sociologists the *rôle* of the father in a particular society; the roles of father and child would together, presumably, form a relationship in Weber's sense; a set of inter-related roles forms an institution such as the family and the whole complex of inter-related roles and institutions in a given society would be its social organization or social structure. In fact, then, social anthropology and sociology deal with regularities in the behaviour of men towards each other. Moreover, sociological regularities are characteristic of groups rather than of individuals and are not hereditary. In other words the regularities of social structure are, by definition, included among the regularities of culture as we have defined them. Culture, indeed, is a wider concept; it includes not only regularities in the behaviour of men towards each other, but also regularities in their behaviour towards non-human objects, animate and inanimate, as well as towards supernatural beings. Art, technology, religion and so on are all to be included along with social structure under the heading of culture. When sociologists and social anthropologists wish to avoid the word 'culture', they refer to these non-structural regularities in the behaviour of groups as 'forms' or 'aspects' of social life; Durkheim uses the expression *'faits sociaux'*. 'Social life' and *'faits sociaux'*, indeed, might be accepted as terms identical in meaning with culture.

Although culture is more comprehensive than social structure, this is not to say that social structure is lacking in interest or importance. Indeed, almost every human action is at least partly directed towards other human beings; the way in which human interactions are related to each other is often an integrating factor which greatly helps to make the rest of the culture intelligible. We might think of the social structure as the skeleton and the remainder of culture as the flesh with which it is clothed. We should be wrong however to think of them as two entirely different aspects of, or abstractions from, human behaviour.

We have now obtained a fairly precise and homogeneous definition of culture, and one which in addition is empirical, that is, which can be verified by reference to experience. Furthermore, by referring to the behaviour of members of particular societies we have made it possible to adopt a comparative approach, that is, to formulate scientific generalizations by observing the similarities and differences between different occurrences of culture-traits and complexes.

I need not argue that this is the only possible definition or even the only useful one. Other somewhat different definitions may prove useful in particular contexts. Thus the archaeologists may find it convenient to continue to use the term 'culture' to designate the man-made objects which they disinter and study. But if so, they would do well to use some other word to describe the regularities of behaviour which they infer from these objects. Similarly an anthropologist is at liberty to define culture as norms or standards of behaviour, as probabilities regarding behaviour or even as expectations regarding behaviour if that is what he wants to emphasize; but his definition will be less comprehensive than ours and more difficult to verify empirically. The utility of the definition we have adopted here can only be demonstrated as we proceed to use it to clarify our chosen field of study. In the next chapter I shall examine and define the concepts 'a culture' and 'the culture'.[1]

[1] Some of the ideas in this and following chapters have previously been expressed in P. H. Bagby, 'Culture and the Causes of Culture', in *American Anthropologist*, Vol. 55, 1953, pp. 535–54.

5

CULTURES

WE have now defined culture as 'regularities in the behaviour, internal and external, of the members of a society, excluding those regularities which are clearly hereditary in origin'. 'Culture' here is a general or mass-noun; it points to a class of elements in our experience, just as 'milk' and 'wheat' and 'mankind' do. How then shall we define the singular noun, 'a culture' or 'the culture', as used in such expressions as 'the culture of the Eskimos', 'Chinese culture', 'a primitive culture', 'the cultures of Southeast Asia', 'middle-class British culture' and so on? At first sight this seems quite easy; we might say that 'a culture' is the sum or aggregate of the culture-traits and complexes found in any particular society. Substantially similar definitions have been given by some writers, notably Linton.[1]

Unfortunately, the usage of anthropologists, as well as ordinary literary usage, is by no means so clear as this. It varies considerably and seems to contain at least two unresolved criteria. It will be recalled that we defined a society as a number of people who interact, in certain respects and at certain times, more with each other than with outsiders. It is doubtful, however, if the various Eskimo settlements, which are scattered from Greenland to the eastern tip of Siberia, do form at the present time a society within the scope of our definition. Some settlements probably have more extensive relations with the white officials, traders and missionaries in their particular areas than they do with other settlements. Some groups of settlements may well be cut off from the rest of the Eskimos entirely. It would require, indeed, a careful

[1] Ralph Linton, *The Cultural Background of Personality*, New York, 1945, p. 32.

sociological study to determine just where the lines of interaction fall.

What do we mean by 'the culture of the Eskimos' then? Apparently we mean a distinctive set of culture-traits and complexes found in a number of societies. Indeed, it is because they exhibit a large number of closely similar cultural traits, such as wearing fur garments of a peculiar make, speaking closely-related languages and so on, that we identify the members of all these societies as 'Eskimos'. No doubt, we assume, in addition, that at some distant point in the past the ancestors of the present-day Eskimos did form a single society, and archaeology tends to confirm this assumption.[1] But at the moment what strikes the eye of the observer is the distinctive character of a certain set of culture-traits, and it is this that leads him to call that set of traits Eskimo culture. The same is true of Chinese culture. It is not only the fact that the Chinese form, or formed until very recently, a single society, that leads us to isolate their culture as a particular entity, but also the distinctive character of that culture, the fact that certain culture-traits and complexes regularly appear together. Often we identify a Chinese by his culture rather than by the society in which he participates; his dress, speech, customs and so forth are more important than whether he lives in Formosa, Singapore, San Francisco or China proper.

We might then define a culture as a distinctive assemblage of culture-traits and complexes regularly found together, and this is what archaeologists usually do.[2] A certain style of pottery, certain kinds of weapons, house-types and methods of burial, when found together in a number of neighbouring sites, will be identified as a particular culture. But this would not cover all the uses of the word. When Malinowski went off to study the culture of the Trobriand Islanders, he did not trouble himself with how far their culture-traits and complexes formed a distinctive assemblage *vis-à-vis* those found among their neighbours, the Amphlett Islanders or

[1] Henry B. Collins, Jr., 'The Origin and Antiquity of the Eskimo', in *Annual Report of the Smithsonian Institution for 1950*, Washington, 1951, pp. 423–68.

[2] Irving Rouse, 'The Strategy of Culture History', in *Anthropology Today*, ed. A. L. Kroeber, Chicago, 1953, pp. 57–76.

the Dobu. He was interested in what he found in a particular group of villages and that was all. This group of villages formed an interacting society in our sense and so we might say that for Malinowski, 'the culture of the Trobriand Islanders' was simply the cultural regularities found in that society, whether distinctive or not. Many anthropologists study the culture of a single village which may resemble closely the culture of a village next door.

The terms 'a culture' and 'the culture', then, it would appear, may be used to refer either to a distinctive assemblage of culture-traits and complexes or to the set of such traits and complexes found in a particular society. There is a further difficulty, however, in the use of these terms. As we have seen in Chapter IV, a society according to our definition may vary enormously in size and character from groups of nations down to two men talking on a street-corner. It may include families, clubs, and associations of all sorts as well as villages, towns, cities, tribes and nations. All these are groups of people who interact with each other more than with outsiders. Technically speaking, if its presence in a particular society is what characterizes a particular culture, then there must be a culture for each society. Anthropologists do often speak in this way, more particularly when they have specified the particular group of people to whom they refer. Thus we find them speaking of 'the culture' not only of a particular village, tribe or nation, but also of a church, factory or political party and even occasionally of a family or club. There have been studies of the cultures—and more particularly of the social structures—of hospitals and adolescent gangs.[1] Often the term is used of segments of a society: classes, professions and age-groups; we speak of 'middle-class culture' or 'adolescent culture'. It might be argued that the members of these groups do interact with each other more in certain respects than they do with outsiders and that therefore they could be called 'societies', but it is as segments of larger societies that we usually think of them. Perhaps it is because their behaviour does show dis-

---

[1] For instance, George Devereux, 'The Social Structure of the Hospital as a Factor in Total Therapy', in *American Journal of Orthopsychiatry*, Vol. XIX, 1949, pp. 492–500, and William Foote Whyte, *Street Corner Society*, Chicago, 1943.

tinctive regularities that we isolate them; we are all conscious of class-differences in speech, dress and manners. But we identify them by their presence in a certain segment of society, not by their distinctiveness.

The use of the definite article 'the' with the word 'culture' seems to imply that the particular society or segment of society in which the cultural regularities are to be found has been identified, or, as in the case of the Eskimos, that the principal regularities which serve to distinguish their culture are already known. The expression 'the culture' is usually followed by a proper name, such as 'of the Eskimos', or the word 'culture' may be preceded by that name, as in 'Eskimo culture'. There is no great difficulty then in using the term 'the culture' of all societies, large or small, or even of segments of societies. But when anthropologists use indefinite expressions, such as 'a primitive culture', 'any culture' or 'all cultures', they do not intend to include the cultures of all societies, large or small, as well as the cultures of all segments of societies. They wish to limit themselves to the cultures of certain large-scale societies such as tribes and nations, perhaps because this is the level at which cultural differences are most marked.

Is there any way in which we can characterize these large-scale societies? They seem to be composed of groups of local communities, such as villages or bands, although in rare cases a single village, such as Zuni in New Mexico, is thought of as having a culture of its own. The word 'nation' suggests that political unity might be the criterion, but many tribes lack any form of central political power. Malinowski's Trobriand Islanders would be a good case in point here; the principal chief now has no power outside of his own district.[1] It might be argued that such groups of local communities do interact with each other more than they do with outsiders and thus constitute a special kind of society. I have used this argument in the case of the Trobriand Islanders, but in many cases it would be tedious and sometimes impossible to prove that such interaction takes place among a number of local communities before ascribing to them a culture of their own. It looks very much

[1] Bronislaw Malinowski, *Argonauts of the Western Pacific*, London, 1922, pp. 69–70.

as if we shall have to fall back on the criterion of distinctiveness, with an additional proviso that we are only interested in those distinctive cultures which are found in groups of local communities or occasionally in a single local community.

To make matters worse, anthropologists have discerned certain broad similarities in groups of neighbouring cultures and these groups of cultures, which share a number of elements, may also be referred to as cultures. For instance, a large number of tribes in the grass-covered plains of the Central United States showed a marked resemblance in their cultures in the last few centuries before their final subjugation. Technologically, all these cultures centred around the hunting of bison on horseback, but they shared many other elements: dancing societies, medicine-bundle purchases, a peculiarly formalized kind of warfare, a deliberate seeking for supernatural visions and so on. These common elements, or rather the cultures of the tribes which share them, are called Plains culture, an entity generally recognized by anthropologists alongside of the cultures of the Cheyenne, the Arapaho, the Blackfeet and so on. Similarly, the culture of Zuni is only one among the Pueblo cultures of the Southwestern United States; we may also speak of 'Pueblo culture' in the singular.[1] Among more developed peoples, the nation seems to be the locus of the most markedly distinctive cultures, but the nations of Western Europe and those nations which have been heavily influenced by them have many common cultural elements which every one recognizes under the name of Western European culture. On the other hand, where the area of a culture is a large one, we may have local and regional variants which are also called cultures: the cultures of the Eastern and Western Eskimo, for instance, or of New England and the Southern United States.

So far I have spoken of cultures as if they existed only at a moment or for a limited span of time; the introduction of the time-dimension will involve us in further difficulties. A culture in

---

[1] A. L. Kroeber, *Cultural and Natural Areas of North America*, University of California Publications in American Archaeology and Ethnology, Vol. 38, Berkeley, Calif., 1939, pp. 76–84 and pp. 34–5.

fact may exist for many centuries during which many of the regularities which make it up will change. The culture may spread from one society to another; it may develop into two distinct cultures or it may merge with another culture. It may disappear and another culture take its place. How then can we identify the enduring entity in all this change? How can we delimit it in space and time? How can we be sure that we are dealing with distinctive entities at all?

It might seem tempting at this point to give up the attempt to define a culture at all, to admit that we are dealing only with certain vaguely discernible ever-shifting uniformities like patches of colour on the surface of the sea.[1] Yet anthropologists and cultural historians do use the term with a certain amount of assurance; they may disagree in a few cases, but more often they agree as to the identity and boundaries of their cultures. There must be some isolable features of reality to which they refer, something to which we can point and say: 'That is a culture.' Perhaps we shall be able to understand the problem better if we examine how cultures come into being and how they are connected with the groups of interacting human beings which we call societies.

No human being can live entirely alone all his life. In order to grow up, to procreate, to defend himself against animal and human enemies, to exploit his environment effectively, he needs the co-operation of others. Even a single family is insufficient; a man needs other men to join him in hunting parties, in war expeditions or in clearing the soil. For this reason, as we may suppose, and perhaps for other reasons which we do not discern clearly, all over the world among undeveloped peoples we find groups of families living close together and co-operating in the various spheres of human activity. These are the local communities to which I have already referred. Among settled agricultural peoples they take the form of villages; among wandering hunters and nomads they are more apt to form bands which travel about together. We might distinguish them from the other kinds of society, not only by the common residence or travels of their mem-

[1] As is held, for instance, by A. L. Kroeber, *Anthropology*, New York, 1948, pp. 261-5.

bers, but also by the fact that their members interact with each other, not only in certain respects and at certain times, but most of the time and for most of the purposes of life. They are general-purpose, full-time societies. This might be called the primary mode of social integration on a primitive level.

Perhaps in the very earliest stages of man's development such local communities were entirely self-sufficing and independent; this seems to be the case among man's nearest relatives, the apes and monkeys. But among all the primitive peoples we know, the local communities are not isolated. They intermarry, they trade with other such communities and they co-operate with them in defence. It is among small groups of such communities that the isolable assemblages of cultural regularities which anthropologists call cultures usually appear. Indeed, it might be argued that they always have their origin in groups of local communities rather than in single communities. The exception we have mentioned, Zuni, is clearly a case of the reduction, through war and attrition, of what was once a much larger and more scattered population to a single large village. The same may be true of other cases where a distinctive culture is limited to a single village.

Why cultures should appear in groups of communities and not in single communities is not entirely clear. As many anthropologists have pointed out, if men are to co-operate effectively, they must be able to know what sort of behaviour to expect from others. Hence there must be a common language, common customs, common ways of doing things in the circle of people with whom a man usually co-operates. But this does not explain why cultures should be differentiated so clearly between groups of communities and not so clearly between individual communities or indeed why they should be clearly differentiated at all. Perhaps we should postulate a universal human need for social solidarity which operates among groups of this size under primitive conditions, which makes individuals want to identify themselves with some society and to pattern their behaviour on that of the other members of the society. There is no generally accepted psychological theory of needs, however, and, in accordance with the ancient empirical rule known as Occam's Razor, we should not multiply entities unnecessarily, especially not invisible entities. Let us then just take it as a matter of fact that, on the primitive level, distinctive cultures are usually found among groups of local communities.

It is these groups which the anthropologists identify as tribes. Undoubtedly the communities of which they are formed do cooperate more with each other than with outsiders, and thus they come under our definition of societies, but it is the uniformity of their culture that strikes the eye of the observer. Usually they are fairly sharply differentiated by language, dress and custom from their neighbours. Any member of such a tribe can identify his tribe as well as the members of neighbouring tribes. The tribe is the society to which he feels he *belongs*; his membership enters into his conception of himself. Though individuals do occasionally migrate from tribe to tribe, ambiguities and transitional states are relatively rare. We can now say that, under primitive conditions, the tribe is the *secondary* mode of social integration; it is the *primary* mode, however, of cultural integration. It is in these societies at this level, in groups of local communities, that we find the most clearly differentiated sets of cultural regularities and our definition of 'a culture' must take account of this fact.

It can easily be understood that in urbanized literate societies, where travel and communication are easier and political power serves to unify large areas, cultural uniformity will be found covering much larger numbers of local communities than under primitive conditions. In the world with which my readers are familiar, it is at the level of the nation that the most marked cultural differentiation takes place. It is to the nation that we feel that we belong; we seek to imitate the customs and manners of our fellow nationals and we distinguish quite easily between Frenchmen, Englishmen and Americans and between their modes of speech, their customs, their styles of dress and so on. Thus in the civilized world as we know it, it is the nation rather than the tribe which is the secondary mode of social integration and the primary mode of cultural integration. Although we may find considerable variation between the customs of local communities within a nation, the differences here are not so sharply defined. All the local communities have extensive relations, political, economic and otherwise with other communities and with the capital. Priests, schoolteachers and other officials often come from outside and almost always receive their training somewhere else within the nation. Thus under civilized conditions the distinct cultures of tribes break down into mere local or regional variations of the national culture.

There have of course been other modes of social integration larger than the local community and yet differing from the tribe or the nation. The best known of these are the city-states of Classical antiquity and the religious communities which were prevalent in the Near East during much of the last two millenia. If you had asked an inhabitant of the Turkish Empire: 'What are you?' he might have replied that he was a Greek, or a Jew, or an Armenian, or a Druse, indicating by this his religious affiliation rather than his place of residence or the political authority whom he obeyed. Local communities were formed of groups of co-religionaries and the most sharp cultural differentiation was between groups of such local religious communities. Only a Muslim would have felt it necessary to indicate his place of origin, his tribe, or the speech-community to which he belonged.

At this point it should be somewhat clearer how we can define 'a culture'. A culture, we can say, is the aggregate of cultural regularities found in a group of local communities; the size of the group of communities, however, and which communities we choose to include in it will be determined by their sharing a number of cultural features which neighbouring communities do not possess, in other words, by the distinctive character of their culture. This procedure may seem circular. The society serves to define the culture, while the culture, or rather some features of it, serve to define the society. Yet it is in accordance with the actual practice of anthropologists and not unlike the procedures of other branches of science. For instance, a biologist will study the anatomy, that is, all the features of bodily structure, of some animal or plant species. Nevertheless, he will define his species and decide which animals or plants to include in it by their possession of certain common anatomical features. In the same way a chemist may wish to examine the properties of some chemical, but whether the stuff in his test-tube is sulphur or iron or mercury can only be decided by observing some of its properties. The existence of uniformities in nature is an empirical fact; we must recognize them first before we can study them.

If we had defined 'a culture' simply as those traits and complexes which serve to distinguish a particular tribe or nation from its neighbours, rather than all the traits and complexes found in a society of a particular kind, we should have severely limited the scope of our inquiry. Similarities will interest us as much as differences; otherwise there would be no hope of comparison. It is true that anthropologists and culture-historians often tend to limit themselves to what is novel or unfamiliar in the cultures they describe. They point out the unusual features, taking for granted those features of the culture which are like our own. In this they do not differ greatly from psychologists, novelists and even ordinary people when they are trying to describe an individual personality. Here again it is the salient differences which receive the most attention, while the features of behaviour which a man may share with the common run of humanity are often overlooked. The effect of such descriptions of individuals, whether they are of human beings or of individual cultures, often resembles caricature; nor is this a fault, if it is differences that primarily concern us. But a full, thorough, 'scientific' study of culture must deal with *all* the behaviour in its chosen field and hence with similarities as well as with differences. For this reason we must define a culture as all the cultural regularities found in a certain human group, though we recognize the culture—and the group which displays it—by its differences from other cultures.

If the term 'a culture' is limited to a group of local communities, how shall we designate the cultural regularities found in smaller societies or segments of societies? Here the anthropologists sometimes make use of the expression 'a sub-culture'. We might adopt this useful term, defining it as the aggregate of cultural regularities found in any society or class of human beings smaller than the group of local communities which serves to define a culture. Such are local and regional groups of communities, individual communities, classes, age-groups, professional groups, and associations of all kinds. There can be no objection, naturally, to the use of the term 'the culture', or simply 'culture' preceded by an adjective, to refer to a sub-culture, as long as the society or group meant is clearly indicated so that no confusion can result. Here we can simply take 'culture' to mean 'cultural regularities'. But it must be clearly understood that 'a culture' is more restricted in its meaning than 'the culture'. The culture of Britain is *a* culture; the culture of the British middle-class is a *sub-culture*. Other indefinite expressions such as 'any culture', 'all cultures' or simply 'cultures' will also have the restricted meaning of 'a culture'.

When we come to delimit the society or segment of a society which defines a sub-culture, the actual individuals to be included may often turn out to be defined by common elements in their behaviour, that is by the distinctive features of their sub-culture. Thus the middle-class or the professional group of clergymen are known by their behaviour, by what they do. We do at times define the area of a sub-culture geographically, as in the cases of New England or the Southern United States, but even here the cultural differences are often clearer than the geographical boundaries.

To correspond to the term 'sub-culture' a new term 'super-culture' might be invented which would cover the cultural regularities of those groups of tribes or nations, such as the Plains Indians, or the Western European nations, which we perceive to share a number of distinctive common elements. These common elements will define the larger society or group of societies, all of whose cultural regularities will constitute the super-culture. This neologism may be offensive to some ears; if so, they can substitute some phrase such as 'comprehensive culture' or 'higher-order culture'. Although further distinctions could undoubtedly be drawn, these three terms: 'culture', 'sub-culture' and 'super-culture' will probably suffice to make clear our meaning in any particular case. Thus we can speak of the regional Scandinavian sub-culture of the Western European super-culture or of the sub-cultures, also parts of Western European super-culture, of Catholic monastic orders, of modern painters, or of psychoanalysts. Where the distinction is of no importance, we may go on referring to a super-culture as a culture.

In most cases, the communities in which we find a culture, and the larger groups of communities in which we find a super-culture will exhibit internal interaction and thus form a large-scale society. Indeed, it is necessary that they should do so at the time that the culture or super-culture was formed and diffused; otherwise the formation and diffusion could not have taken place. The exceptions, such as the Eskimos—whose culture is properly speaking a super-culture—we shall explain on the grounds that what was originally a society has later become fragmented. But whether they form societies or not need not enter into our definition; it is the distinctive features which serve to define them.

Obviously the key to the identification of a culture as I have defined it lies in the choice of those distinctive culture-traits or complexes which serve to set apart the group of local communities all of whose regularities of behaviour constitute the individual culture. If it were *any* shared trait or complex that could serve to set apart such a group of local communities, we should have an endless multiplication of individual cultures of extremely varied size and character. Thus, if the use of a phonetic alphabet were the distinguishing criterion, we should be able to speak of an 'Alphabet super-culture' including all contemporary literate societies except for a few in the Far East. Similarly, on the basis of the favourite beverage we might have a 'Tea-drinking super-culture' including such scattered cultures as the British, the Chinese and the Arab cultures of North Africa, contrasting with a 'Coffee-drinking super-culture' which would include the cultures of the United States, France, Italy and most of the cultures of the Near East. The use of tobacco by at least some members of the society is a cultural trait which is probably found in very nearly all contemporary societies as large or larger than a local community, the only exceptions being a few isolated tribes in the Amazon basin, the highlands of New Guinea and similar out-of-the-way spots. Obviously, individual traits of this kind do not suffice to distinguish cultures which we feel to be meaningful and equivalent entities.

In practice we are most likely to use either language or political unity as the distinguishing criterion; yet neither of these is completely satisfactory. No one would deny that Britain and the United States have clearly distinguished cultures in spite of the fact that the members of these two societies speak fairly close variants of one language. The fact that Germany is at the moment politically divided does not prevent us from thinking of a single German culture as continuing to exist. If we wish to have criteria which will correspond to the general opinion as to how cultures are differentiated we must find others besides language and political unity.

The difficulty here seems to be that some features of culture change more rapidly than others. Technological features such as the phonetic alphabet or the use of tea and coffee can spread very rapidly from one society to another and be adopted without our feeling that the 'basic culture', that is, the differentiating features of the culture, have changed. The lines of social interaction may also change very rapidly. Portions of a tribe may break off and join other tribes; whole tribes may be conquered by their neighbours. On the national level, similar alterations in the boundaries of individual sovereignties also frequently take place. It is true that if the boundaries of social interaction, which on the national level are primarily political boundaries, remain in the same place for several generations, minority groups will tend to assimilate the culture of the majority, or the cultures of disparate groups such as the conquerors and conquered will tend to fuse into a new common culture. For instance, the French culture imported by the Normans when they conquered England was fused in a few generations with the Saxon culture of their subjects to form a new English culture. The conquest of the Welsh at a later date was followed very gradually by an assimilation of English culture in Wales which is not yet complete. On the other hand, when a nation is divided politically into two, cultural differentiation will also eventually result. Such has been the case with Britain and the United States.

and such is likely to be the case with Germany if the present political division persists for a century or more. In general, we might say that the lines of social interaction change more rapidly than the rest of culture, although the rest of culture will follow in time.

What then are the common elements which underlie all these changes? What can we identify, for instance, as the distinguishing features of all English culture? Often we seem simply to be able to recognize a culture without analysing its features, much as we recognize the face of a friend, the style of a painting or the make of a motor car. Such objects seem to have complex and indefinable qualities which immediately leap to our attention; perhaps the best general word for these qualities is 'style'. Cultures, too, may be said to have styles. Running through the great variety of traits and complexes of which they are composed, we seem to perceive common qualities—an elusive something which we recognize as English or American, or as Navaho or Eskimo, but which we would find it difficult, if not impossible, to describe.

Fortunately, the art-historians have shown that the styles of works of art are not absolutely indefinable. Indeed, if they were indefinable, how should we be able to recognize and to identify them? In works of art, style appears to consist of certain 'underlying' ideas and values which are felt to be 'expressed' in certain observable features; according to one definition, it is 'a system of forms with a quality and a meaningful expression through which the personality of the artist and the broad outlook of a group are visible'.[1] First of all, apparently a student of art begins by feeling that there is a common quality in the works of an artist or a group of artists. He goes on to analyse what it is that gives him this feeling, the observable features: qualities of line, colour, form and composition, the kinds of objects represented, the techniques used, the organization of space and so on. Then he tries to describe the ideas and values which these observable features 'express', the underlying attitudes of that artist towards the world of experience. Something of the same kind is done by the anthropologist and

---

[1] Meyer Schapiro, 'Style', in *Anthropology Today*, ed. A. L. Kroeber, Chicago, 1953, pp. 287–312.

the culture historian. He too feels a common flavour in the diverse features of a culture or a period; he too tries to point out the observable qualities which give rise to this feeling and to analyse them in terms of ideas and values, and apparently it is just precisely these ideas and values which serve to distinguish one culture from another. If you wished to explain the difference between American and English culture, you would refer to the differences in their attitudes towards authority, towards tradition and class-distinctions, to the emphasis on quantity rather than quality in America, the British love of nature, and so on. And you would illustrate these observations by referring to particular regularities of behaviour, political, social and economic. You would mention the monarchy and aristocracy in Britain, the written constitution with its checks and balances in the United States, the height of American buildings, mass-production in American factories, the relatively greater frequency of English gardens and parks and as many other culture-traits and complexes as you felt necessary to convince your interlocutor. In choosing which features of culture in the two countries to call to his attention, you would be inclined to take those which have endured for a considerable time, which are important in the sense of covering a whole area of human activity, and which are most clearly differentiated, that is, have differences which are easily perceived. You would neglect the more subtly differentiated areas, such as English and American literary usage or styles of dress, even though these differences would undoubtedly be revealed as significant on close analysis. But above all you would choose features of culture which demonstrate the differences in ideas and values which you have already formulated.

It is ideas and values then which provide the basis for differentiation between cultures. It is in this realm that we find the broadest uniformities in the cultures of groups of local communities and the sharpest differences between the cultures of different groups. And it is precisely because the sharpest differentiation between different sets of cultural regularities takes place at this level of social integration that we distinguish cultures as entities at this level.

Unfortunately, ideas and values are notoriously difficult to analyse or to describe precisely. A sort of popular Platonism, as we have already mentioned, often leads us to think of them as existing in a realm of their own, as floating somewhere over our heads or lying buried somewhere deep inside of us. In the last chapter, we agreed, however, in accordance with the empirical approach which we have adopted, to regard them, along with other dispositions and tendencies, simply as ways of thinking, feeling and acting. Some dispositions and tendencies, such as capabilities for instance, may be conceived of as existing only at the level of *observable* action. We may learn how to serve at tennis without ever distinguishing in consciousness the various muscular movements which we make. Ideas and values are best thought of, however, as modes of discrimination, inter-relating and evaluating our experience, whether this takes place inside, as processes of thinking, feeling—or, to use a more general term, perception—or outside, in overt behaviour. If you accompany someone to buy a pair of shoes, you can actually see him distinguishing between different kinds of shoes, and choosing the pair he likes best. You assume in addition that he discriminates in his mind between the different kinds of shoes and has positive or negative feelings about them, but it is the whole complex process of thought, feeling and action which we call 'choosing a pair of shoes' and on the basis of which you can say that he likes or 'values', for instance, long, narrow, black shoes. Indeed, every human action can be thought of as involving some discrimination and evaluation of the world about us, and most actions will involve some inter-relation of the parts already discriminated.

This use of the term 'values', it should be noted, differs considerably both from common usage and from the usage of philosophical ethics. In these latter a value is more often thought of as some common element in the objects of experience towards which the observer has a consistent affective or emotional reaction, which he 'evaluates' in some consistent fashion. For us, a value would be the common element in a series of acts of evaluation. Thus if someone prefers black shoes, the value in the common and philosophical sense would be 'black shoes', in our sense it would be 'preferring black shoes'.

It is important also to stress that ideas and values, as we are using the terms here, need not necessarily be formulated as verbal propositions by the person who holds them; they are not necessarily beliefs or norms. In the psychologists' terms, they may simply be cognitive and affective orientations which the man himself is unable to express in words. A woman may look through a rack of dresses and may distinguish the colours perfectly well without knowing the curious names which are often given to these colours; strawberry, burgundy, raffia or cerise. She will know which dress she likes and she may consistently choose bright colours with bold patterns without ever having said to herself: 'Bright colours with bold patterns are to be preferred.' In the same way in a given society distinctions of rank may play a large role without any one ever having said: 'Distinctions of rank are important' or 'All men are created unequal'.

Ideas and values thus may or may not be conscious. This is not to say, however, that for our purposes we need to think of them as unconscious, in the sense of existing in some subliminal realm. They may be simply unformulated. A large number of such unformulated ideas and values, besides of course many formulated ones, are to be found in every culture. Often, indeed, the ideals, standards, beliefs and norms which are formulated by the bearers of a culture differ strikingly from the ideas and values expressed in their actual behaviour. A good example of this is the class-structure which is emerging in Russia, an officially classless society.

Not every idea or value is useful for purposes of differentiation, but more particularly those which are to be found exemplified in many realms of behaviour, in many diverse culture-traits and complexes. Among such more general ideas and values will be broad notions about the character and inter-relationships of man, of nature and of the supernatural, notions about space, time and causality, general principles of conduct and morality, more especially as they regard the dealings of man with man, general aesthetic principles and the like. We might call these the *basic* or *funda-*

mental ideas and values of a culture, or if we prefer words which have fewer traditional associations, its basic *attitudes* or basic *orientations*.

In a sense, we might say that these are the most general aspects of behaviour, whether in an individual or in a culture, the elements or qualities which are common to the largest number of specific acts. The whole complex or configuration of the basic ideas and values of a culture I have already described as its *style*; another term for it which has won some acceptance in recent years is *ethos*, the Greek word for character. *Ethos*, however, has the misfortune of possessing an awkward, irregular plural, *ethea*, and had therefore best be used sparingly.

Traditionally, in the more developed societies, it has been the philosophers whose task it was to provide verbal formulation for the basic ideas and values. To analyse and describe the *ethos* of a culture not our own thus becomes a matter of stating the common assumptions—the basic metaphysical, ethical and aesthetic presuppositions—of the philosophers of that culture or of providing a philosophy for cultures where it does not exist. The task is made more difficult by the fact that the very words and structure of our own language are expressive of our own ideas and values. To express the different ideas and values of other peoples, we often have to borrow words from them, to invent new words, or to give old words new meanings. And in making clear to our readers the meanings of these words we will find ourselves describing much of the whole culture. Obviously this is far too difficult and complex a procedure if our only interest is to distinguish different cultures; though it is a necessary one, in the long run, if we are to understand a culture thoroughly. For purposes of differentiation in practice, then, we shall have to use the characteristic institutions in which the basic ideas and values are expressed. We must select a number of institutions of sufficient importance, scope and duration covering the major aspects of social life such as religion, art and political, economic and social organization. If these institutions usually appear together in a number of different local communities and especially if they are associated with a common language and a common political allegiance we can then use them to differentiate one culture from another and we can delimit our culture in space and time by observing whether the majority of these features appear in it or not.

I say 'majority of these features' and not 'all of these features' advisedly, for cultures are constantly changing, and we may easily find that we have been mistaken in regarding certain institutions or even certain ideas and values as basic. As long as the majority of the institutions we have chosen as basic do not change, however, we are safe in supposing that we are still dealing with the same culture. A change of a whole culture, though it may require several generations or even several centuries, involves a radical change of all the institutions, a reorientation of the whole style or ethos, a change of political allegiance and often even a change in the structure of the language. Such fundamental shifts are not difficult to recognize. The same is true when we come to consider the distribution of a culture in space. If we find some area where one or two of the institutions we have regarded as basic are missing, we shall conclude that we are still dealing with the same culture. If all or most are missing, we shall think that we are dealing with a new culture or some society in transition from one culture to another.

Obviously this heuristic procedure is not entirely a satisfactory one, but it is the best that we can devise in the absence of difficult and time-consuming analyses of ideas and values. In practice students of culture tend to differentiate cultures on the basis of a direct recognition of their styles and on the whole will agree about the names and identities of their different cultures and the main body of local communities and periods of time which they cover. It is only the transitional states which cause difficulties and these we can usually resolve by an appeal to a list of important institutions including language and political allegiance. Does Welsh culture, for instance, constitute a separate entity today? The answer would have to be no, because the inhabitants of Wales have adopted most of the principal English religious, political and social institutions and only a few traits, including in some areas language, of what was once a distinct culture still survive. We must therefore treat Welsh culture today as a regional variation of English (or, as it is now called, British) culture. It must be regarded as a separate culture, however, until at least as late as the sixteenth century.

There will be some periods, of course, when the culture of a particular group of communities is changing, which we shall have to treat as frankly transitional and which we can only describe by pointing out which features belong to the old culture and which to the new. The limits we give to such transitional periods will depend on the lists of characteristic institutions which we draw up and the weight which we give to each institution. Certainly, it would be unwise to ask for too much precision here. We can never say that a given culture began or ended on a certain day or even in a certain year, but only within a certain period, which will be long or short according to the closeness of our observations and the length of our lists of distinctive institutions.

Similar ambiguities are not unknown, however, in the worlds of physics and biology. We cannot indicate precisely the upper limits of the earth's atmosphere or describe precisely each stage of a chemical reaction. At what moment does a morsel of food become part of the human body? When it enters the mouth, the oesophagus or the stomach? When it is partially or fully digested? And at what moment is it fully digested? Indeed, all the entities of our experience have somewhat ambiguous boundaries in space and time, though it must be admitted that these boundaries can often be measured more precisely than those of cultures. Physical bodies are constantly exchanging molecules with their environments and gases are constantly mingling, just as different cultures are always influencing each other. We cannot in practice measure the movement of each molecule, any more than we can describe precisely the change of each culture-trait. It must suffice to define and delimit our entities as precisely as we can. No doubt, in time we shall be able to delimit cultures more and more precisely, as we study them more closely.

'A culture', then, can be defined as the aggregate of culture-traits and complexes present in a group of local communities. Which local communities to include will be decided in theory by their sharing a complex of ideas and values, but in practice either by a direct recognition of their style or by a listing of overt features including language, political allegiance and important and enduring institutions. In the light of this definition I can now go ahead to discuss and where necessary correct some of the common assumptions made about individual cultures.

One of the most common of these errors is to identify a culture with the society in which it is found and to talk about them both as if they were the same thing. No doubt it is perfectly possible to have a concept which includes both a group of people and their regularities of behaviour, but it must inevitably be confusing. Sociologists and social anthropologists do often use the word 'society' in this way, meaning not only an interacting group of people but also their interactions or rather the recurrent pattern of their interactions. I have tried, on the other hand, clearly to distinguish the people from their behaviour in order to be able to study their behaviour in isolation. The interacting human group after all may continue to exist in spite of a radical alteration in its culture; a classic example is that of Egypt where the culture of the Ancient Egyptians has entirely disappeared.

If we accept this distinction it is then, strictly speaking, illegitimate to speak of individuals as being 'members' of a particular culture; they can only be members of societies. Some anthropologists speak of 'culture-bearers'; we might also use the metaphors, 'carriers' or 'possessors' of culture. If we wish to be literal, we shall have to speak of people who behave—that is, who think, feel and act—in accordance with a certain culture. But this periphrasis is awkward; it is to be hoped that 'bearers' will come into more common use. There is no objection of course to our continuing to use the word 'members' as long as we realize that we are doing so in a sense somewhat different from the usual one. It should be noted that the members or bearers of a culture are not necessarily always identical with the members of the local communities whose cultural regularities constitute that culture. Tourists who travel abroad become temporary members of the communities in the countries they visit, yet they do not alter more than a few features of their behaviour; we might say that they 'take their culture with them'. If they are sufficiently numerous or influential we might have to treat them and their culture as a special feature of the communities they visit; when one country is conquered by the inhabitants of another we do have to treat the conquerors in this way. Here again we have ambiguities and transitional states which can only be resolved by a more exact description. In most instances, however, we can afford to overlook the migrations of individuals in stating the global facts about a culture.

Since a culture is not a society, it becomes inappropriate to compare it or to identify it with a biological organism, as many philosophers of history and most notably Spengler have done. No doubt sociologists and social anthropologists have found a number of useful analogies between the interactions of members of a society and the interactions of parts of an organism; but culture includes more than interactions; it covers all the regularities of behaviour and therefore perhaps can most usefully be compared with the personalities, that is, the regularities of behaviour of individual human beings. We may think of cultures as growing, developing, changing, as being more or less integrated, and so on, much as we think of personalities. Nevertheless even here the analogy is not perfect since the duration and scope of the personality are strictly limited by the life and activities of the person in whom it is found. Personalities never spread from one person to another, but cultures do spread from one society to another. Nor can we say, except by a gross exaggeration, that a person has acquired a new personality; groups of local communities can and do acquire new cultures. Cultures do not live or die, mature or decay, unless we assign new meanings to these words. They do not do anything; only people do things. We must think of cultures as *sui generis*, entities of a special and peculiar kind, whose properties can only be determined by examining them without reference to the properties of living organisms, or other phenomena. Organic analogies can at best do no more than suggest possible lines of research.

Another analogy, which is equally frequent and perhaps even

more misleading, is that by which we think of the changes in cultures as resembling the trajectories of physical bodies. Cultures are thought of as going up or down, as rising or falling, as following a linear or curved process of development. Philosophers of history have thought of the whole of human culture as developing in a linear or cyclical or even in a spiral fashion. Sorokin, who is fond of this sort of analogy, on one page commits the absurdity of depicting the development of culture by a spiral which at some points moves backwards in the time-dimension.[1] Doubtless, these geometrical or mechanical analogies would be useful if we were dealing with only one or two fairly easily measurable aspects of a culture, the number of its bearers, for instance, or the degree of urbanization. But cultures are extremely complex entities with numerous aspects and features, not all of which change co-ordinately and not all of which are measurable. We can scarcely reduce their changes to a single line. The writers who use these geometrical or mechanical analogies seem to have in mind the general goodness or badness of a culture or of the culture of mankind in general, and they appear to measure these moral qualities by a number of diverse and ill-defined criteria. In other words, under a show of mathematics they hide a moralizing and subjective attitude. It is for this reason that cyclical or organistic theories are thought to be vaguely wicked; they do not guarantee the ultimate triumph of the Good.

Cultures then are neither societies, nor organisms, nor moving bodies. Nor are they souls or spirits, in the sense of invisible agencies lying behind the regularities of behaviour and determining them. The word 'spirit' is, of course, sometimes used simply to refer to the basic ideas and values of a culture. This is presumably what Voltaire meant by '*esprit*' and what most writers mean by the spirit of an age or of a country. Thus, the spirit of the European eighteenth century would include the values order, reason and elegance, mechanical explanations of nature and so on. But in German usage, following Hegel, the word *Geist* is often thought of as referring to neither a mental nor a physical being, but to a 'spiri-

[1] Pitrim A. Sorokin, *Social and Cultural Dynamics*, New York, 1937–41, Vol. I, p. 184.

tual' entity or entities, a sum of possibilities or strivings which actualize themselves in visible human behaviour. Somewhat similar notions seem to be expressed in modern psychological theories of the 'group mind', in the 'collective consciousness' of Durkheim and his followers, and in the 'collective unconscious' of the Jungians.

Spengler, who prefers the word 'soul' (*Seele*), can provide us with an excellent example of this line of thought. He writes:

> A culture is born when a great soul awakens out of the proto-spirituality of ever-childish humanity, and detaches itself, a form from the formless, a bounded and mortal thing from the boundless and enduring. It blooms on the soil of an exactly-definable landscape, to which plant-wise it remains bound. It dies when this soul has actualized the full sum of its possibilities in the shape of peoples, languages, dogmas, arts, states, sciences, and reverts into the proto-soul.[1]

Intoxicating words! But do they mean anything specific to which we can point?

No doubt, we do all feel in situations where many men are acting together—a crowd, a dance, a political meeting or a primitive religious ceremony—some sort of mass emotion which seems to exist over and above the behaviour of the individuals and into which we feel sucked, as it were, against our will. We feel too, as has already been mentioned, that ideas and values are 'in the air' or 'above our heads', that they come to us by 'inspiration', that is, by 'breathing in', or that they 'rise up' from some dark realm below our conscious minds. It would be a fine thing if out of these and similar experiences we could construct a consistent theory which would order and explain the whole realm of group behaviour. Nor is there anything illegitimate or unscientific in postulating invisible entities, as long as they do actually help us to understand the phenomena. I have already spoken of the function of hypothetical constructs in the physical sciences, and in psychology the theory of the individual unconscious has come to play a useful, if not an indispensable, role.

[1] Oswald Spengler, *The Decline of the West*, tr. by C. F. Atkinson, New York, 1932, Vol. I, p. 106.

Collective minds might be thought of as analogous to the 'fields' of some varieties of modern atomic theory, in which the individual particles forming an atom and their inter-relationships are conceived as functions of an underlying but invisible entity, which cannot even be imagined in sensory terms.

Unfortunately no one has succeeded up to the present day in producing a clear and consistent theory of collective minds or souls. No one has been able to tell us just precisely how we can describe the properties of these hypothetical entities and how these properties would be made manifest in experience. Hegel is for the most part extremely vague and intuitive; his terms seem to have no fixed meanings. Few if any rules seem to guide the speculations of Spengler or the Jungians. Little progress indeed seems to have been made since Le Bon's studies of the psychology of crowds and of peoples at the end of the last century.[1] A psychiatrist, W. R. Bion, in a little-known series of articles has recently put forward some interesting suggestions about regular cycles of collective emotional complexes underlying the behaviour of small groups, which might well be transferred to the study of larger societies.[2] In addition, the French social anthropologist, Lévi-Strauss, has suggested certain basic structural factors in social relationships which can only be supposed to have their origin in the unconscious.[3] But all these formulations are still extremely tentative. For the present at least we must content ourselves with the study of observable phenomena. It is only by a close attention to the facts of experience that we can hope eventually to be able to formulate a consistent theoretical explanation. We must for the time being leave aside all notions of collective souls, minds, spirits and unconsciouses and use the word 'spirit' only to mean the basic ideas and values of different cultures, ideas and values which themselves are conceived empirically.

[1] Gustave Le Bon, *Les lois psychologiques de l'évolution des peuples*, Paris, 1894, and *La psychologie des foules*, Paris, 1895.

[2] W. R. Bion, 'Experiences in Groups', in *Human Relations*, Vol. I, pp. 314–20, 487–96; Vol. II, pp. 13–22, 295–304; Vol. III, pp. 3–14, 395–402; Vol. IV, pp. 221–8.

[3] Claude Lévi-Strauss, 'L'analyse structurale en linguistique et en anthropologie', in *Word*, Vol. I, No. 2 (1945), pp. 14–19.

If we must make analogies between cultures and something else, we had best look to the manner in which individuals acquire and develop techniques and skills. Cultures indeed in a sense are merely the techniques of large groups of people. They may be learned or invented; very likely they begin with feeble and uncertain gropings which later acquire greater definition and certainty; once developed, they may be polished and elaborated and even extended into new fields of behaviour. When the initial impetus is gone, they may settle into a routine with only occasional variations. And eventually perhaps they are abandoned for new types of behaviour. Throughout its history each culture is characterized by an individual style, that is, by a set of ideas and values, though the style may be in large part borrowed from a teacher, that is, imitated from some preceding culture. Some such analogies as these will doubtless prove very helpful in our attempts to understand the changes in culture, but it must be stressed that they are only analogies. What actually happens to cultures can only be determined by examining them.

It is worth observing before I close this chapter that the conception of basic ideas and values as we have described it seems to underlie not only the notions of style, *ethos* and spirit, but also the notion of cultural integration as it is used by many writers. By the integration of a culture they mean apparently that all or most of the various culture-traits and complexes of which it is composed exemplify certain very general ideas and values. For a culture to disintegrate is another way of saying that the people who bear it have adopted certain traits or complexes which do not exemplify the ideas and values which were formerly basic. Cultural integration must be clearly distinguished from the social integration which we mentioned above and the functional integration of which social anthropologists speak. By social integration we mean nothing more than the fact that there is a certain frequency and density of interaction among the members of a certain society. The notion of functional integration which has been borrowed from biology, and of which Radcliffe-Brown has been the chief exponent, implies that the patterns of interactions of which a social structure is composed all have effects, which may or may not be consciously intended, but which contribute to the stability and perpetuation of that structure.[1]

The notion of basic ideas and values also appears to be very close to what has traditionally been described as 'national character' and has more recently been formulated by the joint efforts of anthropologists and psychologists as 'basic personality structure'.[2] It has been observed that some of those regularities of individual behaviour which are called personality-traits may also be found recurring in the behaviour of fellow-bearers of the same culture. Out of these recurrent psychological traits we can form a picture of the typical personality of a bearer of that culture. Such a typical personality is in fact part of what we have defined as culture since it is composed of the regularities of behaviour of members of a society. But these recurrent personality-traits which go to form a 'national character' can almost always be formulated in terms of ideas and values. Thus aggressive behaviour can be described either as the personality-trait 'aggressiveness' or as 'valuing aggression', while peaceful behaviour can be conceptualized either as the personality-trait 'peacefulness' or as the value 'peace'. In other words, however people may behave, they may be presumed to value that behaviour and to distinguish it from other kinds of behaviour. We can thus translate descriptions of national character or of basic personality structure into lists of basic ideas and values, more particularly those ideas and values concerned with individual conduct. Basic ideas and values, however, is the more inclusive and therefore the more useful notion. The concept of basic personality structure has been developed chiefly in an attempt to explain certain broad regularities of behaviour found in particular cultures by the methods of child-rearing used in those cultures, an attempt which has not as yet proved entirely successful.[3]

[1] A. R. Radcliffe-Brown, *Structure and Function in Primitive Society*, London, 1952, p. 12.

[2] Abram Kardiner, *The Psychological Frontiers of Society*, New York, 1945 and Cora Du Bois, *The People of Alor*, Minneapolis, 1944.

[3] This subject, under the name 'personality and culture studies' has been much cultivated in America in the last two decades. A bibliography will be found in Margaret Mead, 'National Character', in *Anthropology Today*, ed. A. L. Kroeber, Chicago, 1953, pp. 662–7.

We have now defined an individual culture as the aggregate of cultural regularities found in a group of local communities, the size and boundaries of the group being determined in theory by the presence of a set of basic ideas and values, and in practice by the presence of a set of characteristic institutions. We have distinguished sub-cultures as the cultural regularities found in societies and segments of societies smaller than the group of local communities which defines a culture. And we have adopted the term super-culture for the level of integration more comprehensive than that of individual cultures. Cultures are not to be regarded as societies, organisms, moving bodies or invisible spirits; they are complex ways of life, styles of behaviour characteristic of large groups of human beings, which are integrated and differentiated by the fact that they exhibit in their various constituent elements different sets of basic ideas and values.

6

CULTURE AND ITS EXPLANATIONS

Now that we have defined 'culture' and 'a culture' we can begin to see how these concepts may be used to organize, clarify and make intelligible the whole field of historical events. In chapter 2, I roughly defined history as 'events involving or affecting large numbers of human beings', a definition which I based on the actual practice of historians through the centuries; roughly speaking, these are the things they have chosen to write about. This definition, however, is not entirely satisfactory from a scientific or logical point of view. It lacks homogeneity, since it includes events of two different kinds, not only those which involve large numbers of human beings, but also those which affect, or have been presumed to affect, them. Among these latter we might include geological and meteorological events, such as earthquakes and droughts, biographical events such as the deeds of kings and statesmen, and supernatural events such as the anger of the Almighty. Indeed, since every event in the universe may be presumed to affect, however slightly, every subsequent event, the historian who wished to push his inquiries far enough might include almost anything he chose, even the movements of the farthest stars. Our definition obviously covers a central core of events which we might call 'history proper', and an indefinite outer area of what we might call 'presumed causes of history'.

Let us leave aside all question of causation for the moment, and focus our attention on the essential core of history, the events which involve large numbers of people. It is these which give historical literature its interest and importance, for whatever involves large numbers of people might also involve us. Wars and revolutions, diplomacy and politics, the violent and the peaceful forms, that is, of the international and intra-national struggle for power, have provided the historians with their principal subject-matter ever since Herodotus. To these have been added more recently other aspects of the life of peoples: economics, religion, art and science, each of which has come to form an historical speciality. In each of these branches, it is the large-scale human event which is of major importance; it is what many people *do* that first of all concerns the historian.

Now we have defined culture as 'regularities in the behaviour of members of a society'. Putting this into non-technical language, we might say that culture is the *ways* in which large numbers of people do things. Since history proper is *what* large numbers of people do, we can see that culture is the patterned or repetitive element in history. Culture and history are not precisely the same thing, but rather culture is history's intelligible aspect.

This conclusion may seem surprising; it involves a sudden shift of focus from the unique individual events which fill the pages of most historians to the recurrent or patterned aspect of those events. The individual incidents are no longer thought of in and for themselves, but as parts of larger processes. We no longer look at the ripples on the surface of the wave, or even at the wave itself, but rather at the current of which it forms a part. And this current, this larger process, is itself a process of culture-change.

No doubt many historians in the last two hundred years since Voltaire have envisaged, dimly or clearly, the existence of processes of this kind. They have spoken of political and economic forces, of movements of opinion, currents of ideas and the like. The concept of culture enables us to embrace all these varying notions under the general heading of processes of culture-change and to deal with them all in a consistent and harmonious fashion. The rise of the bourgeoisie, the development of nationalism, the decline of religion and the family, the growth of science and individualism, all these are changes—and perhaps inter-related changes —in the various branches of Western-European culture in relatively modern times. If we see this fact clearly we shall no longer be tempted to treat them as independent and somewhat mysterious forces operating across the field of history, but rather as parts of the process of evolution of Western-European culture as a whole.

In the eighteenth and nineteenth centuries cultural or social history—*moeurs et esprit*—was thought of as excluding political and military history; it covered customs, family life, the arts and sciences, literature, economic life and perhaps also religion and philosophy, but *not* the arts of government and war. Thus Macaulay wrote in the Introduction to his History:

> I should very imperfectly execute the task which I have undertaken if I were merely to treat of battles and sieges, of the rise and fall of administrations, of intrigues in the palace and debates in the Parliament. It will be my endeavour to relate the history of the people as well as the history of the government, to trace the progress of useful and ornamental arts, to describe the rise of religious sects and the changes of literary taste, to portray the manners of successive generations and not to pass by with neglect even the revolutions which have taken place in dress, furniture, repasts and public amusements.[1]

He felt that he had accomplished this task when he stopped the course of his political and military narrative from time to time and gave his readers a broad picture of the life of the people at a given point in time. Only fairly recently, within the present century, have such authors as Trevelyan in England and Gaxotte in France attempted to treat political and military history as part of the total life of the people and to show this life as a whole gradually developing through the centuries. In this view of history as primarily a process of cultural (or, as they would call it, 'social') development, these historians approach fairly closely the point of view which we are advocating here. History is to be seen as the development of ways of life by particular peoples or societies, growing, changing, influencing each other, sometimes coming into conflict, or being abandoned for other ways of life. It is these large-scale developments which are of major importance and fortunately it is for them that we can most easily find the evidence that we need. They already represent a patterning, an appearance of regularities in the

[1] Macaulay, *History of England*, ed. C. H. Firth, London, 1913, Vol. I, p. 2.

lives of millions of people, and we may legitimately hope that their processes of change will also exhibit some intelligible regularity. If we are ever to understand the past activities of human groups, it is precisely at the broadest patterning of those activities that we must look.

A distinguished contemporary English historian, A. L. Rowse, expresses views very similar to these (though not without retaining his affection for the older kind of individualized history), when he writes:

> [History] is about human society, its story and how it has come to be what it is; knowing what societies have been like in the past and their evolution will give you the clue to the factors that operate in them, the currents and forces that move them, the motives and conflicts, both general and personal, that shape events.

And on the next page he adds:

> And though the individual is apt to be unpredictable (even he is not always), great social groupings, masses of men, classes, communities, nations tend to react in similar ways to similar situations. They give you the ground of history, so to say—the stuff upon which the more intricate and individual patterns have been worked. And so, though you may hardly say that there are historical laws of the regularity and exactness of the laws of the physical sciences, there are generalizations possible, of something like a statistical character.[1]

The historians, indeed, as we saw in the first chapter, have been evolving towards this more scientific point of view for generations, and it is for this very reason that we are now able to attempt to bring their subject-matter within the family of the sciences.

If the concepts of culture and culture-change then will serve to cover the intelligible or patterned aspect of history, what are we to do with the individual event? Are we to omit it from our considerations entirely? Not necessarily, but it will play in future a somewhat diminished role in our picture of what has happened. We will still wish to have accounts of revolutions and wars, but we shall look on them as parts of larger processes. In describing a

---

[1] A. L. Rowse, *The Uses of History*, London, 1946, pp. 16–17.

revolution, for instance, we shall be less interested in the deeds and the motives of the revolutionary leaders, less interested, too, in the day-to-day course of the struggle, and more interested in the cultural background, the growth of new classes and interests, the alterations of men's views how power and wealth should be distributed. It is these and similar factors which determine in the long run how the struggle will be resolved, and the incidental aspects of the struggle will be considered only as details in the process of cultural change, while the leaders will be looked upon, not as the originators, but as the instruments of that change.

Similarly in recounting the history of wars, we shall be less concerned with the tactics devised by generals, less with the details of battles or even of campaigns, and more with the resources, material, human and psychological, on either side and the effectiveness with which these resources are put into the field. A war may be looked on as a test of the strength of two or more ways of life, of the extent to which different cultures enable those who follow them to mobilize their resources and to impose their will on others. Even the resources themselves are largely cultural factors or the result of culture. This is obvious in the case of such psychological factors as morale, but the number of members of a society and the territory which it has at its disposal are also very largely the result of the actions of its members in the past. We shall not be wrong if we speak of a war as a conflict between two cultures, just as we speak of the pressure of a gas and the resistance of its container, without discussing the separate motions of the individual molecules.

It cannot be denied that the large-scale events which I have identified as the core of history may be decomposed into large numbers of individual actions. This is not the same thing, however, as saying that only individual actions are real and that the common or regular aspect of these actions is somehow tenuous, elusive, a construction of the human mind, and therefore unreal. No doubt, the individual and his actions are presented to us more forcibly and more distinctly in the course of our everyday observations, but, as we saw in chapter 3, they too are abstractions from the universal flux, the great sea of interconnected events which make up our experience. What I am proposing here is essentially that we should agree to consider these events on another, higher level of abstraction, that of the regularities in the behaviour of groups, and that we should do so not only occasionally, whenever it suits our convenience, as has been done in the past, but consistently and systematically. It is my hope that historical researchers will give up their futile attempts to establish the exact truth as to individual actions in the past, and seek more and more to investigate, as far as possible, every aspect of the culture of every period. Here, too, of course, the evidence is not always adequate, but it is always more ample than the evidence for individual actions; it is also more reliable since it is not spoiled by individual bias and the universal tendency to self-justification. It is no accident that the archaeologists, who must rely on relatively little evidence, have found the concept of culture a *sine qua non* for the understanding of their discoveries.

One of the difficulties of adopting this point of view is that the documentation for recent periods is almost too ample. And since it is for the most part cast in individual terms, the historian cannot see the wood for the trees. What I am proposing is that he should look only at the wood, for the time being, and neglect the trees; it would be a great thing if someone could invent a 'macroscope', an instrument which would ensure that the historian would see only the larger aspects of history and blind him to the individual details. It is only by remaining at this higher level of abstraction that we can hope to decipher the principal patterns of historical change, to identify the 'forces', whatever they are, which have made the world what it is today.

Even individual actions, it should be noted, are scarcely intelligible without reference to their cultural background. A man's most intimate desires and beliefs are very largely moulded by what he has been taught and what he has unconsciously absorbed from his fellows, while the situation with which he is confronted at any given time is also very largely the product of prior actions by members of the same or different societies. The very language which he speaks imposes on him certain well-defined modes of thinking about the situation. He cannot possibly escape from these influences since he is largely unaware of them. The most original of geniuses is invariably seen, after enough time has elapsed, to be very much a man of his period and country, to share more with his contemporaries than he or his contemporaries realized. When we discuss the behaviour of a member of our own society with our friends, we take this cultural background for granted, since it is the same for all; it is the man's personal idiosyncrasies which leap to the eye and call for explanation. But as we look back in time or out across national boundaries, individual differences sink into insignificance; it is the broad differences in behaviour between different times and places which must first be explained. Only when we know and understand this thoroughly shall we be able to isolate and identify what is peculiar to particular individuals.

Culture, then, is the intelligible aspect of history; it is the observable patterns in those large-scale events which have formed the core of the historian's interests. But what of those other events which I also included in my definition of history, the events which do not involve, but affect, large numbers of human beings? Must we not continue to include them in our subject-matter? Surely, it is legitimate for the student of culture to wish to be informed about any feature of the universe which might be related to the events in his chosen field, just as the biologist in order to understand the functioning of an animal or plant must see or imagine it in its native habitat, surrounded by its normal sources of nourishment, its enemies, parasites and friends. This is undoubtedly true, but the whole question is best treated as part of the somewhat larger question of the 'causes' of culture; that is: How can culture legitimately be understood and explained? In examining this problem, I shall automatically answer the question as to what non-cultural events may legitimately be studied by the culture-historian.

As we have already seen, causal explanation in its ordinary, narrow sense is only one example of explanation in general, although some writers use the term causality rather loosely to cover all kinds of explanation, or rather all the features of experience which may be used for explanation. From an empiricist point of view, all explanations of actual events or features of experience take the form of showing that what is to be explained is, in itself or with some of its attendant circumstances, an example of a regularly recurrent pattern of events or aspects of events. In the most common case of the ordinary explanation in terms of cause and effect, the event is shown to fit into a familiar pattern with one or more immediately preceding events. 'Why is there a red stain on your shirt collar, darling?' a wife might ask her husband. He would reply that he had cut himself when shaving. Cutting, it is well known, is often followed by a flow of blood and blood leaves red stains on cloth; in making this statement, the husband has attempted to show that the stain is part of a familiar pattern of events, although on closer inspection his wife may discover that this is not the particular kind of stain left by blood. Many natural laws are of this kind, notably chemical equations.

An explanation need not, however, be in terms of a recurrent pattern involving only a few prior events. It may equally well involve a large number of events both prior and posterior, which together form what is called a process. Thus we might explain the loss of milk-teeth in a child as caused by some immediately preceding glandular stimulation, but the occurrence of the glandular secretions themselves would have to be explained as part of the complex process of maturation or 'growing up', a sequence of events with which we are familiar from our observations of other children. Such explanations are, of course, commonplaces of biology, but they also occur frequently in some branches of physics such as mechanics, where we explain processes by showing them to be parts of more complex processes. We would not ordinarily say, however, that an earlier part of a process was 'the cause' or 'a cause' of a later part; the beginning of an arrow's flight does not cause its end, nor is the egg the cause of the chicken.

All the examples I have given so far are explanations in terms of patterns which have earlier and later parts, patterns which cover a period of time; these are often called diachronic explanations. It is also possible to have synchronic explanations, in which the pattern is composed only of simultaneous events. 'What is that bit of water over there?' we might say, looking down from a hill-top, and someone more familiar with the local geography might reply: 'That is a part of the river Thames.' Here what we see is explained as part of some larger object (or pattern of events) all of which exists in the present, but which we are familiar with from what we have heard about it or seen of it in the past. Such explanations rarely seem entirely satisfactory, perhaps because we do not often think of something as existing only for a moment in time; they tend to shade off into other kinds of explanations. We are apt, for instance, to think of a river as a continuous process rather than as some momentary pattern of contemporaneous events. Nevertheless, pure synchronic explanations do exist; the most famous is the law of gravity, where the force of attraction of one mass on another is supposed to act instantaneously.

Synchronic explanations are often confused with explanations by definition. The latter, even though they seem to be statements about the inter-relationships of events, are in fact statements about the meanings of words. 'Why does this animal have such a long nose?' some child might ask at the zoo, and his father might reply: 'Because it is an elephant. All elephants have long noses; they are called trunks.' In this example, the statement: 'All elephants have long noses', although it looks like a description of some recurrent pattern in the world of experience, is really simply an analysis of the meaning of the word 'elephant'. We define 'elephants' by a number of their characteristics, including the fact that they have trunks. In order to transform an explanation by definition into one which uses recurrent regularities, we require the additional assertion that the thing defined, 'elephants' for instance, exists and recurs in nature. But even if it occurred only once or not at all, an explanation of one of its features by its definition would still be valid. Thus I might explain that the archangel Raphael has wings because all angels have wings, even though Raphael and the other angels do not exist in any literal sense.

Returning to my example of the father and the child at the zoo, we can see that the father might have answered that the elephant had a long nose 'to pick things up with'. Here we have an instance of explanation by purpose, a variety of explanation which I have already described in chapter 3. Explanations by purpose are best understood as part of the larger category of psychological, as distinguished from physical, explanations. The regularities to which we point in these cases are to be found, partly or wholly, in that inner mental world of thoughts and feelings which we can observe in ourselves but must infer in others. Thus we might explain a man's eating by the fact that he was hungry, referring to the well-known regularity that the feeling of hunger leads to the act of eating. Here the feeling of hunger is a psychological event; it is inside, while the act of eating is an outside, physical event. Many psychological explanations involve, as this one does, a partial reference to physical events; our thoughts and feelings are usually stimulated by some outside event and often lead to external actions. But purely psychological regularities, involving only internal events, are perfectly possible; such are, for instance, the laws of association formulated by the nineteenth-century psychologists or the explanations of dreams given by the psycho-analysts.

Some philosophers have recently argued that when we discuss the behaviour of human beings, we often explain what they do, not so much by their purposes, as by the reasons or principles which they follow. Thus we may try to show that the tactics followed by Antony at Actium *were* the 'reasonable' or the 'right' thing to do, even though we have no evidence as to what calculations actually went on in his mind prior to the battle. Here it seems to me the difficulty is caused by the ambiguity of the word 'explanation'. Certainly in ordinary speech, we do use 'explanation' to cover argument in terms of reasons or principles. 'Explain yourself, young man', an employer might say to his tardy apprentice, meaning, 'Give your reasons for being late.' But for scientific purposes, it seems to me useful to limit the term 'explanation' to the elucidation of regularities and to call argument in terms of reasons or principles something else, perhaps 'justification'. Of course, when someone argues, not that a certain action *was* the right or reasonable thing to do, but that the actor *thought* it was tight or reasonable, we are dealing with a case of explanation in our limited, scientific sense.[1]

My example of explaining an elephant's trunk by its purpose is perhaps an unfortunate one, since it raises immediately the question: 'Whose purpose?' In what mind did the desire to enable elephants to pick things up once exist? If we try to answer this question, we find ourselves either bringing some metaphysical entity like God or Nature into the explanation, or postulating the existence of unconscious, but nevertheless effective, purposes in the ancestors of elephants. The biologists have tried to evade the question by substituting for the word 'purpose' the word 'function' which is thought not to have the same connotations. To explain an organ by its function is to explain it by the effects of its activity without introducing any psychological element. The adaptation of organs to their functions is itself explained by reference to the famous Law of Natural Selection, which describes a long semi-mechanical process held to be constantly recurring throughout the world of living things. It must be confessed that there is something tortured and forced about this procedure; nevertheless it cannot be abandoned without introducing some outside factor for which there is no direct evidence. As we shall see, somewhat similar problems arise in the study of culture, where the word 'function' has often been made to bear a similar burden.

Having explained some event or feature of an event as an instance of some recurrent regularity, it is always legitimate to go on and ask for an explanation of that regularity. Thus, having accepted the explanation that some smoke I see is due to burning leaves, I might go on to ask why it is that burning leaves smoke. The answer would involve the process of oxidization, the rising of hot gases, the suspension of particles in air and so on. If I pressed my interlocutor hard enough, and if he were well-enough informed, we might eventually arrive at some of the most fundamental laws of physics and chemistry. In all this he would be showing a particular regularity to be an instance of a more wide-

[1] W. H. Walsh, 'The Logic of Historical Explanation' (unpublished paper) and W. H. Dray, *Laws and Explanation in History*, Oxford, 1957, Chap. V.

spread regularity or regularities. This procedure may be applied even to the most general and well-accepted regularities. Einstein, for instance, showed that the Law of Gravity was a consequence of the structure of space as postulated by his theory of relativity.[1] All explanations of culture will, I need hardly say, be of this kind, since culture itself is already composed of regularities. In studying culture we shall want to look for regularities of regularities, broader patterns which include the particular patterns of which it is made up. There must nevertheless be a limit to this process of seeking ever broader explanations, a limit set either by our ignorance or by the arbitrary character of the patterns themselves. As we saw in chapter 3, neither the universe as a whole nor any subdivision of it can be fully ordered.

There is no need to give here an exhaustive account of the varieties of explanation or the various considerations which are raised by each type. The above sketch will serve us as a rough guide, as we turn now to consider the types of explanation which are useful and legitimate in the study of culture. First of all, clearly, we must look for regularities, for recurrent patterns within the realm of culture itself without considering anything outside that realm. These may be diachronic, as when we say that a decline in the birth-rate always follows industrialization, or they may be synchronic, as when we say that the birth-rate is lower among those strata of society which have greater wealth or education. In these examples, we have related the birth-rate to industrialization or wealth or education in patterns which we hold to be regularly recurrent. We might go on to ask for further explanations why these patterns exist and recur and then we might feel obliged to bring in matters extraneous to culture, such as the difficulties involved in raising large families in urban communities, or the psychological changes brought on in people by greater wealth or education. But we shall be perfectly justified in disregarding these non-cultural features at first and seeking merely for the patterns which happen to be exhibited by the culture, for the recurrent inter-relationships of various cultural traits and complexes.

[1] A. S. Eddington, *The Nature of the Physical World*, Cambridge, 1930, Chaps. VI and VII.

The two examples I have given involve relating one cultural feature to one or two others, but we may also look for complex recurrent processes involving many cultural traits. I used the word 'industrialization' above in the sense of 'possessing industries' rather than in the sense of 'acquiring industries'; industrialization in the second sense can be studied as a complex process involving many cultural traits which have recurred with greater or less regularity in many different societies. Among such traits would be the concentration of capital in a few hands, the greater use of machinery, working in the factory rather than at home, the growth of larger urban communities, the organization of larger markets and so on. We may even see one process as related to another in a common pattern, as when we say that the process of industrialization is always accompanied in its later stages by a decline in the death-rate.

So far I have chosen my examples from the domains of vital statistics and recent economic history, since it is in these realms that the greatest certainty about cultural regularities is most often to be found at the present time. The birth-rate and the death-rate clearly lend themselves to mathematical treatment, while recent economic history has received the attention of many scientifically-oriented scholars. Similar diachronic and synchronic patterning of culture may be found, however, in other fields, though rarely with equal certainty. Thus we may say that 'Every revolution is followed by a counter-revolution' or that 'Urbanization is accompanied by a decline in the closeness of family ties', propositions which we feel and believe to be true although they have never been fully demonstrated. The anthropologists have succeeded, however, in establishing a few propositions of universal validity which, if it were not for their lack of mathematical form, might very well be called laws. Among such are 'Every culture includes some form of religion' and 'Every culture includes prohibitions of some of the varieties of incest'. These statements may seem natural and even obvious; nevertheless they have both been questioned from time to time by experts and even contradicted by travellers' tales which later turned out to be inaccurate. The successful establishment of these universal regularities confirms our belief that the world of human affairs is not entirely disorderly.

Sociologists and social anthropologists, as I pointed out earlier, tend to study certain aspects of culture, more especially the regularities in the interaction of human beings, statically, that is, as they exist in the present. It might have been more exact, however, to say that these studies do not cover simply a moment of time, but rather short periods of time. Thus the explanations which they give, though they may loosely be called synchronic, are generally cast in the form of inter-relationships of short-term processes. The proposition which I stated in the preceding paragraph with regard to urbanization and the closeness of family ties is perhaps best thought of as a short-term diachronic regularity of this kind. Indeed, in a sense, since all behaviour is a kind of process, all explanations of culture are necessarily diachronic explanations; nevertheless it will be useful to maintain the distinction between 'diachronic' and 'synchronic', using the latter word to describe patterns involving contemporaneous processes so short-lived as to seem almost momentary.

One of the most frequent and most important forms of synchronic explanation is that which sees the form which some particular cultural activity takes as a manifestation of some idea or value widely current in a particular society at a particular time. Thus I might explain the use of the heroic couplet in eighteenth-century English poetry or some of the features of Mozart's music by referring to the values of order, elegance and balance which, it is well-known, were particularly favoured in Western Europe in the eighteenth century. Such explanations are most common in the arts, but may be used for any cultural trait. Thus it has often been pointed out that Darwin's Law of Natural Selection reflects the competitive values of the emergent industrial economy of the nineteenth century. Explanations of this kind may also serve to inter-relate processes; as many writers have pointed out, similar values seem to be expressed in the contemporaneous development of Protestantism, of science and of the bourgeoisie. I shall consider these explanations more fully in chapter 8.

A particular form of explanation by process is represented by the evolutionary theories which were current among anthropologists and philosophers of history in the last century. For instance, it was thought that the whole culture of every people necessarily passed through stages called 'savagery' and 'barbarism' on its way to 'civilization', each branch of culture being represented by a particular institution at each stage. Sometimes particular evolutionary theories were developed for particular institutions. For instance, it was thought that the patriarchal form of family organization, necessarily and in every case, evolved from a preceding matriarchy. The trouble with these theories was not that they were based on an illegitimate form of explanation, as has sometimes been suggested by the more enthusiastic social anthropologists, but that they were too schematic, too specific and based on too little evidence. The time is certainly now ripe for a re-examination of these theories in order to determine what portion of them can be validated. For instance, it cannot be doubted that the domestication of plants is a necessary pre-condition to the development of urban life in any society, and it may be legitimate partly to quantify this proposition, to ask whether a certain intensity of agriculture lasting a certain length of time was required before cities could arise. Some work on evolutionary regularities of this kind has been done by Professors Childe and White.[1]

So far I have only mentioned explanations, synchronic or diachronic, which are confined to revealing inter-relations of cultural traits and complexes within single cultures; we may also look for regularities in the relationships between different cultures. Historians have often been concerned to point out 'influences', the borrowing, that is, of particular traits and complexes by one culture from another. In the absence of any general theory as to how such borrowing takes place, however, their speculations are necessarily inconclusive and confined to the tracing of probable relationships. The anthropologists, on the other hand, have been working

[1] V. Gordon Childe, *What Happened in History*, Harmondsworth, Middlesex, 1942, and *The Dawn of European Civilization*, London, 1947; Leslie A. White, *The Science of Culture*, New York, 1949.

towards a general theory of the relationships between cultures, at first under the general heading of 'diffusion' and more recently, driven by the practical needs of colonial administrations, under the headings of 'culture-contact' or 'acculturation'.[1] The diffusionists have been more concerned with the transmission of particular traits and complexes from one culture to another, the acculturationists with the whole impact of one culture on another. Already it is possible to formulate certain hypotheses in this area, such as that technical devices are transmitted more easily than ideas and values, that the transmission of ideas and values is facilitated by superior political, military and economic power, that the reception of new ideas and values produces a crisis in the receiving culture, with the development of progressive and conservative factions, special hybrid forms of religion, and so on. Professor Toynbee, it must be added, has also devoted nearly a thousand pages to these questions; owing to his ignorance, however, of the work already done in this field, his formulations must appear to an anthropologist rather naïve.[2] Spengler, on the other hand, in his desire to emphasize the independent evolution of his cultures, tended to deny the possibility of one culture influencing another except by the diffusion of minor technological practices.[3]

In our search for explanations of particular features of culture, then, we may look for patterns, both synchronic and diachronic, within individual cultures as well as in the relationships between cultures. There is no reason, however, why we should limit ourselves to explanations of this kind. We are fully entitled to look for regularities which include non-cultural features of experience, for relationships between particular items of culture and other aspects of experience. There is one pitfall here, however, which is expressed, rather imprecisely, in the old rule that the cause must be adequate to the effect. In seeking to explain culture by its relationships with something else, we must be sure that that 'something else' is of such a nature as to affect all the members of a society in a

[1] A survey and bibliography will be found in Ralph Beals, 'Acculturation', in *Anthropology Today*, ed. A. L. Kroeber, Chicago, 1953, pp. 621–41.

[2] A. J. Toynbee, *A Study of History*, London, 1954, Vol. VIII, p. 88–Vol. IX, p. 166.

[3] Oswald Spengler, *The Decline of the West*, New York, 1926, Vol. II, pp. 55–60.

regular or a uniform way. In other words, we can only expect to find regularities which include entitites at the same level of abstraction as culture itself. This is not simply a question of relative size; it is quite possible, for instance, to think of a mouse as frightening an elephant. What we need to ensure is that the different parts of the pattern we perceive fit together because they are conceptualized in the same way.

The non-cultural features of experience which may help to explain culture may conveniently be divided into the human and the non-human. When I defined culture I deliberately omitted those regularities of behaviour which are considered to be hereditary; the time has now come for them to play their role; having been excluded from culture, they may now be used to explain it. First of all, in the human category, we may distinguish those universal characteristics of human beings, both physiological and psychological, which are held to be hereditary and which are assumed to be present in or to affect all human beings in a uniform or regular fashion. The most notable of these, of course, are the uniformities in the structure and functioning of the human body. We are so much accustomed to take these for granted that we rarely reflect that they are necessary for any full explanation of any overt human action. We cannot fully understand the acts of speaking, of eating, or of using tools, to choose only a few examples, without taking into account the structure and functions of the mouth and vocal chords, the digestive apparatus, and the hands. In addition, physiological explanations may relate cultural regularities not only to physiological uniformities, but also to universal physiological regularities such as the difference between the sexes and to universal physiological processes such as maturation and ageing. It should be pointed out that physiological explanations of this kind can never suffice to explain precisely what men do. A man must eat, but that does not tell us what he will eat. To use the older language of causality, physiological regularities are necessary but not sufficient causes of cultural regularities; we might also say that they are necessary 'conditions'. But they are never adequate in themselves; we shall always have to look for further explanations.

Besides the universal physiological uniformities and regularities which we observe in mankind, there are also presumed to be universal psychological traits, hereditary in origin, and present in every human being. These psychological uniformities and regularities form the domain of experience which is usually referred to as 'human nature'; it is the subject-matter of the nomothetic or generalizing branch of psychology. Clearly, human nature will have to be taken account of in explaining almost every feature of culture, not only the regularities of thought and feeling, but also the regularities of action. There are few human actions which we do not presume to have some inner, mental or psychological counterpart; the most notable exceptions are the physiological reflexes. Psychological explanations of this kind have been much favoured by some anthropologists; the best-known was Malinowski, who towards the end of his life attempted to formulate a general system of psychological explanation, based on the learning theory of the Yale psychologist, Hull.[1] The historians, too, as we have seen, often use this type of explanation, although they usually draw their assumptions from popular rather than from scientific psychology.

Unfortunately, although no one doubts that these universal psychological characteristics of mankind exist, we are very far as yet from having a clear conception of precisely what they are. The formulations of the psychologists are based on their observations of their neighbours, that is, on the behaviour of bearers of Western European culture, and undoubtedly are largely tinged by the peculiarities of that culture. There can be no assurance that these generalizations apply to all of mankind until all the immense variety of human behaviour has been studied; in other words, the study of culture must take place prior to the final establishment of the truths of nomothetic psychology. At the present time, only a few instincts, the psychological counterparts of biological necessities, such as hunger, sex and self-preservation, can be said with some certainty to exist in the whole of mankind. And even here

---

[1] Bronislaw Malinowski, *A Scientific Theory of Culture*, Chapel Hill, North Carolina, 1944, p. 75 seq.

we are not sure of their relative strength, of how one instinct may be transformed, sublimated or even completely frustrated when it comes into conflict with others. Psychological explanations must therefore for the present be treated with some diffidence; they remain, however, one of the permanent possibilities of explaining culture. In addition, like physiology, human nature can provide only partial explanations; it is a conditioning, rather than a fully determining factor.

Physiologists and psychologists have tended to study human beings as if they existed in isolation. It was Freud who first saw that the individual is best understood in his relationships with others. He tended, however, to emphasize the relationship between the individual and one other person; the method of psycho-analysis with its stress on the relation of patient to analyst is a re-flection of this. Individuals are also related in groups, however, and this aspect of human behaviour will obviously be of prime importance in the understanding and explanation of culture. In-deed, those uniformities which we may find in all the cultures of mankind will probably best be understood and explained as arising from universal human characteristics, both physiological and psychological, operating in a group-context. Such for instance is Durkheim's explanation of the presence of religion in all cultures; he saw it as a sort of self-worship of the community, a means of reassuring the individual as to his own survival through the force and virtue of the group.[1]

The sociologists and social anthropologists have tended to make great use of this sort of explanation, which we may therefore call 'sociological'. In trying to avoid the muddy waters of psychology, they have tended to stress the merely physical or mechanical prob-lems involved in the organization, defence and perpetuation of the community. It is here that the peculiar notion of 'sociological function' has arisen in imitation of the biological concept of func-tion; a particular cultural (or social) trait or complex is explained in the light of its effects as contributing ultimately to the survival of the particular community in which it occurs, without inquiring

[1] Emile Durkheim, *Les formes élémentaires de la vie religieuse*, Paris, 1912, pp. 593–600.

whether the members of the community consciously or unconsciously intended it to have these effects. It is difficult to avoid the conclusion, however, that the word 'function' is merely a euphemism for 'purpose' and that sooner or later it will be necessary to formulate some theory as to the psychological origin of sociological functions.[1] It may eventually be possible to show that the beneficial effects of features of culture can all be explained as the result of the purposes, conscious or unconscious, of the individual members. As we have seen, theories in which a 'group mind' or a 'collective unconscious' are postulated have not yet mustered enough evidence or been formulated sufficiently clearly to justify our accepting the existence of new invisible entities. For the present, we must accept the fact that this problem is unresolved and likely to remain so until societies and cultures have been more closely studied. Strictly speaking, the resolution of this problem would properly belong to specialists in the science of social psychology. Like the ordinary psychologists, however, the social psychologists have been too much concerned with the observation of groups within the framework of our own culture; they are not yet able to formulate propositions of universal validity.

Under the heading of sociological explanations we might also mention the economic or Marxist interpretation of history, which attempts to explain all the features of culture and all the particular incidents of history in terms of the conflicts of classes motivated by the common passion of 'greed', the desire to possess and control the means of production and thus of enjoyment. There is no doubt that these explanations are often illuminating; it is only the claim of the Marxists to have the one infallible means of explanation which must be severely questioned. Any unprejudiced observer can see that men have many motives besides purely economic ones. Religious and national loyalties often over-ride class interests. Indeed it is probably the desire to create and maintain a certain style of life which leads to the formation of classes in the

---

[1] The best discussion of this subject is by Robert K. Merton, *Social Theory and Social Structure*, Glencoe, Illinois, 1949, pp. 21–82. See also A. R. Radcliffe-Brown, 'On the Concept of Function in Social Science', in *American Anthropologist*, Vol. 37, 1935, pp. 395–6.

first place; the economic motive is only a secondary one, more a means than an end. We are certainly far from a full understanding of these phenomena, but we may be sure that there is no simple key for unlocking their secrets. Economic explanations must take their place along with the other possible modes of understanding.

Among the possible explanations of culture, we may agree, are the universal hereditary traits found in human beings. These may be either physiological or psychological, and may be looked on either as existing in separate individuals or as operating in a group context. We need not limit ourselves, however, only to the universal traits; hereditary traits may also be found in groups of human beings smaller than the whole of mankind and there is no reason why we should not use these also in explanations of culture as long as they are of such a nature as to affect the members of the society in which a particular culture is found in a uniform or regular fashion. These are the phenomena usually known as 'race'; like the universal hereditary traits they may also be divided into physiological and psychological categories.

There appears to be no doubt as to the existence of hereditary differences in the bodily structure of the different sections of mankind; aside, however, from a few traits found in large groups such as the colour of the skin and the shape of the hair, these differences do not appear to be very sharply defined; they take the form of predominant tendencies within a group rather than of sharp differences found in all the members of one group and in none of the members of another. It is questionable, indeed, whether we can legitimately distinguish the different entities called 'races', aside from a few very large groups such as the Negroes, the Mongoloids, and so on. It may perhaps be better to speak of the smaller groups which we wish to examine as 'breeding populations', leaving open the question of whether they differ consistently or not.[1] In addition, the bodily differences between different breeding populations are on the whole so slight that they can have had little effect on culture; no such group is physiologically incapable of engaging

[1] Stanley M. Garn and Carleton S. Coon, 'On the Number of Races of Mankind', in *American Anthropologist*, Vol. 57, 1955, pp. 996–1001.

in any of the major varieties of human activity. Nevertheless, we may suppose that some of these differences do have a slight effect: the small stature of pygmies, for instance, very likely leads them to build smaller shelters than larger men might find necessary. Differences in bodily appearance have undoubtedly affected the aesthetic ideals of different peoples. It is possible also that there exist hereditary differences in physiological functioning, as distinguished from structure, which are as yet undiscovered by science and which may lead a people to prefer one kind of cultural activity to another. Thus an immunity to mosquito-borne diseases might enable one people to settle in swamps and practice agriculture by irrigation where another people would find this impossible. Mr. Haimendorf has suggested that among the Apa Tani whom he studied in Northern Assam it may be a fact, as they themselves believe, that young girls are incapable of bearing children during the first few years after puberty.[1] If this is true (and there does seem to be good evidence of low fertility, at least, among adolescents in many countries[2]), it would enable this people and others like them to permit a large amount of sexual experimentation by adolescents and to avoid the sexual repression which has had such widespread consequences within our own culture. Here again, it should be noted, I have used the word 'enable' rather than 'cause' or 'determine'; differences in the physiology of races can only be necessary or limiting conditions, they cannot be fully determining causes.

We know that different breeding populations do differ in their physiological heredity; the question of how far they may also differ in their psychological heredity has unfortunately been confused by the introduction of extraneous political considerations. Exaggerated racial theories were used by the National Socialists in Germany to justify some of their most hideous crimes and, by a natural reaction, this has led many anti-Nazi writers to deny the existence of hereditary psychological differences altogether. There is no doubt that much of what is commonly regarded as evidence

[1] Christoph von Fürer-Haimendorf, *Himalayan Barbary*, London, 1955, pp. 67–8.
[2] Frank Lorimer, *Culture and Human Fertility*, Paris (UNESCO), 1954, pp. 46–9.

of racial differences, the varying characters of different nations, for instance, is in fact culture. Such psychological differences have been shown to be, for the most part, not inherited but acquired in early childhood.

Nevertheless, there is good reason to believe that some psychological differences may be hereditary. In the analogous case of domestic animals, the different breeds of dogs, for instance, can be clearly distinguished as to their intelligence, loyalty, courage and so on. Galton amassed a large amount of evidence on the inheritance of intelligence from the study of family-trees.[1] Yet, though we may believe that individuals inherit some of their psychological traits and that therefore large groups of mankind very likely also do so, it is for all practical purposes impossible to demonstrate this in any single instance. An individual is subjected to cultural influences from the moment of his birth; any particular action of his is probably the result of both hereditary and cultural influences and it is impossible in practice to distinguish the two. No one has been able to devise a psychological test which will reveal only the inherited aspects of personality.

Perhaps eventually some dictator of the future will arrange for several large groups of children from different parts of the world to be brought up together in precisely the same fashion. But until that has been done, the extent of the psychological differences of race must remain a mystery. It seems probable, in any case, that the different strains of mankind are very much less pure than the different strains of dogs, and that at most their psychological differences amount to slight tendencies for the members of one population to behave differently from the members of another. Such tendencies might serve to explain differences in the general orientation of whole cultures; they might have given the original impetus for a culture to develop in one direction rather than another. We may imagine, for instance, though we cannot prove, that the Chinese have inherited a tendency towards a calm and placid disposition and this might help to explain the relatively high value placed on passivity, harmony and repose in their culture. But these

[1] Francis Galton, *Hereditary Genius*, London, 1883.

must remain speculations for the present and for the foreseeable future.

This completes our account of the non-cultural aspects of human life which may be used to explain culture. We may think of them as falling under the two categories of 'human nature' and 'race', that is, universal and localized hereditary traits, each of which may further be divided into physiological and psychological sub-categories. When we turn to the *non-human* phenomena which may be used to explain culture, what is generally called the 'environment', we find that this too can be divided into the two categories of universal and local phenomena. The universal phenomena include all the more general facts about nature, the laws of physics and chemistry, the cycle of the day and of the year and so on. Like the universal features of structure and function in the human body, these are usually taken for granted. We would not bother to mention the law of gravity in explaining the fact that human beings walk upright; nevertheless it should be included in any full explanation. Similarly fully to understand human speech we would need to consider the physical properties of sound-waves and how they are formed and propagated. The movements of the human larynx, mouth and tongue and the consequent vibrations of molecules of air, will then be seen as particular instances of these more general phenomena.

The environment may also be considered in its local aspects, the different local environments in which different human groups find themselves. Here we would want to consider the resources, mineral, vegetable and animal of a particular area, the configurations of land and sea, the properties of the soil and so on. This approach has been ably developed by the human geographers, especially in France and England,[1] and undoubtedly contains many still unexplored possibilities. There are several observations, however, which we must make about this type of explanation. First of all, it is important to note that to explain culture, the environment must be conceptualized in such a way as to fit into general pro-

[1] Jean Brunhes, *La Géographie humaine*, Paris, 1934; C. D. Forde, *Habitat, Economy and Society*, London, 1948.

positions along with features of culture. We may use only those aspects of the environment which are sufficiently broad to affect the bearers of a culture in a uniform or regular fashion. The environment must be seen, so to speak, as itself behaving in a uniform or regular way towards a group of human beings.

Secondly, the environment like the other types of causes we have mentioned, can only be a necessary or limiting condition; it cannot be a fully determining factor as some authors, notably Montesquieu[1] and Buckle,[2] have supposed. After all, nature simply lies there, passively. It is up to the human beings to decide whether, and in what way, they are going to use it. We shall always need at least both a physiological and a psychological explanation to supplement an environmental one. Once this is said, we must recognize that the limitations set by the environment are often very severe ones. You cannot develop a complex civilization in the desert or on the polar ice-caps. Italy's ambitions to be a great power in the modern world are made futile by her lack of the necessary mineral resources. These limitations, of course, diminish in some respects with the progress of technology but they are always there. No one has yet developed techniques for moving mountains or drying up seas.

Finally, although environmental explanations clearly must play a greater role in explaining the economic and technical sides of a culture, their role need not be limited to those sides. Economic and technical considerations obviously enter into all the aspects of culture. The organizations of classes is clearly dependent to some extent on the economic resources available; the differentiation of national cultures and regional sub-cultures is undoubtedly related to geographical considerations. Britain could not have built up her empire if she had had only the sea-coasts of Bohemia. Even religion is influenced by the cycle of the seasons and metaphysics by the actual constitution of the universe. We might say that the effect of the environment diminishes in those areas of culture where men deal less with things and more with other men or with the super-

---

[1] Montesquieu, *L'Esprit des Lois*, Book XIV, Chaps. 1 and 2.
[2] Henry Thomas Buckle, *History of Civilization in England*, London, 1857.

natural. So far, however, no one has satisfactorily demonstrated an effect of the environment in the realm of general ideas and values. Such suggestions as have been made, as, for instance, that the vague yearnings of the Russian soul derive from the boundless-ness of the Russian plain, or that the simplified character of Islamic monotheism derives from the simplicities and aridities of life in the Arabian desert, do not appear to be valid cross-culturally. The plainsman of the American West is not given to vague yearningss and the nomads of the Gobi desert do not practice a simple mono-theism. Environmental influences of this kind may exist; they have yet to be proved.

This completes our list of the non-cultural elements of experi-ence which may be used in explanations of culture. Human nature, race, and environment appear to exhaust the possibilities. If we wish we may divide the environment into two categories, universal and local. Let us call them 'nature in general' and 'local environment'. Then we shall have four categories which fall into two different sets of pairs. The human will contrast with the non-human pair: 'human nature' and 'race' with 'nature in general' and 'local environment', while the universal will contrast with the local pair: 'human nature' and 'nature in general' with 'race' and 'local environment'. In addition the human pair may be sub-divided into psychological and physiological sub-categories. These are the sorts of formal inter-relationships of concepts which delight system-builders and are often taken as a sort of aesthetic proof of the truth of a theory.

There are two other categories of entities which have often been used in explanations by historians and philosophers of history and which we should consider before closing this chapter. These are, first, invisible entities such as deities and impersonal forces held to lie behind the phenomena; and, secondly, the actions of indi-viduals.

The invisible entities like the human and non-human factors may be divided into universal and local categories. We have already had occasion to speak of such localized invisible entities as 'group minds' or 'the souls of nations' and in this category may also be included the localized deities of polytheism. As I pointed out in the last chapter, these entities are not excluded from the explanation of culture *a priori*; they may be regarded as similar to the hypothetical constructs of the natural sciences. But no one has yet shown that they are necessary nor constructed any consistent theories how they might work. No one has yet clearly described the operation of a group mind; while local deities, like the Yahweh of the Old Testament, are generally held to act in a highly arbitrary manner, by fits of anger and love. It may be, however, that in the future the existence of some of the more impersonal of these entities may be justified by our studies; it hardly seems likely that this will ever prove to be the case with the more personal ones. Their virtue seems to lie more in their ability to satisfy emotional needs, to give objective form to our wishes and fears, than in any strictly explanatory function. All explanation is, of course, in some sense a defence against the unknown, nor should we blame anyone for devising imaginary or unverifiable explanations to conjure away pressing terrors, but in the long run the utility of any explanation and its general acceptability must depend on its conformity with the facts of experience.

Similar objections hold with regard to the universal categories of invisible entities, whether these are regarded as personal beings such as the God of Christianity and Islam or as more impersonal entities, such as the 'life-force', the '*élan vital*', the 'World-Spirit' or the Brahman of the Hindus. Terms like 'man', 'mind' and even 'history' are also often used as if they referred to some sort of entity standing behind the phenomena, not simply the phenomena themselves. While these latter entities are not thought of as operating within the whole universe of experience, they may be called 'universal' in the sense that their scope covers the universe of our present discourse, that is, the world of human affairs. Theories of this kind have not only failed up to the present to exhibit any necessity or consistency, but they are also open to the objection that, while they might be useful to explain everything in general, they cannot help to explain anything in particular. No doubt, they have their place in theological and metaphysical speculation, but they are of no great help in the understanding of history. One may well believe in the existence of God and hold that He is the underlying cause of all phenomena; nevertheless one still needs to know how He works in particular instances and this can only be discovered by empirical examination.

The explanation of culture by the actions of individuals is of quite a different nature. These explanations are excluded, not by the fact that they are not sufficiently well-formulated, but by the nature of our theory, by the way in which we conceptualize the data. We must remember that what we are talking about are regularities in the behaviour of groups of human beings, ways of doing things. For us, an individual action is only relevant in so far as it is an instance of some cultural regularity; we cannot think of an instance as causing the regularity of which it is an instance, the particular as causing the general. Individuals and their actions are abstractions on a different level from that on which we propose to conduct our investigations.

No doubt individual actions may properly be looked on as the causes, or rather the partial causes, of other individual actions and these of still others. But if we wish to conduct our inquiry at this level we must then examine the flow of events in great detail; we must consider all of the individual interactions in which the individual was involved. We need to consider not only what the general said to his officers in giving the orders for battle, but also all the prior conversations which led to the formulation of those orders and how each officer individually reacted. We simply do not have sufficient evidence to establish the sequence of events at this level and, even if we had, we should not have the time to study it in all the necessary detail. As I have already suggested, this is probably the major reason why history has proved unintelligible up to date. Our inveterate and natural habit of conceiving human events at an individual level has led us to persist in a hopeless undertaking.

This argument may seem excessively theoretical to the reader and yet it is, I believe, the only correct way of judging the matter. We are engaged in theory-construction and the consistency of our theory is a primary consideration. Nevertheless, if we look at the actual structure of events, we shall see that it is very difficult to conceive of the action of a single individual as affecting, not the actions of other individuals, but the way in which they do things. A Prime Minister or a President may address millions of his fellow-citizens over the radio, and his speech may be read by other millions the next day. They may react to it in their conversations, their private thoughts or even in their actions. They may decide to take, for instance, private economic precautions against the outbreak of war or continued inflation. Nevertheless, the *way* in which they react will be determined by their own habits, beliefs, characters and so on. In addition, of course, every statesman's speech is very carefully formulated in advance by him and his advisers in order to meet the expectations and preconceptions of the people in general; it is a response to pressures brought on him by the representatives of foreign countries and domestic factions. He himself has been chosen for his high office because he represents some prevailing political trend. It is possible, of course, that some fortuitous idiosyncratic element will creep into his speech, but this, it seems likely, will be disregarded by his hearers. In any case, how can it affect the *way* in which they react?

It has sometimes been suggested that we should look on the role of the individual as similar to that of the spark which causes an explosion. The spark is here the immediate efficient cause, but its role is a small one compared to the nature and condition of the material which explodes. The analogy is not an exact one, however, for in history it is the explosive material itself which produces the spark, groups of human beings who produce their leaders; we are dealing with spontaneous combustion. Moreover, at the level at which we propose to study history, it is not the explosion itself which is our primary datum, but the way in which the explosion takes place and this can only be explained by the nature and conditions of the chemical elements present, and other general factors of this kind, such as the laws of chemistry and physics. Sparks may help to cause explosions, but they do not cause the laws of chemistry or physics or the reactive properties of chemicals.

The most common instances in which individuals are held to have caused cultural phenomena are those of invention and discovery. Here, if we examine what actually happens, particularly in recent centuries, where we have plenty of evidence, we find in most cases that a number of different people have been working on the same problem. Quite often several of them reach the same solution very nearly at the same moment; the list of simultaneous inventions is astonishingly long.[1] Sometimes one of them reaches the solution first, but whether his solution or certain parts of it are generally accepted by the society in which he lives depends not on him but on the other members of the society. Occasionally a man makes a discovery long before society is ready to accept it; his invention is premature. A familiar example which combines both the features of prematurity and of simultaneity is that of the Mendelian laws of heredity. They were discovered by Mendel in 1866 but his writings were disregarded until nearly fifty years later in 1900 when the same principles were rediscovered by three different biologists within a few weeks of each other and then revealed to a waiting world.[2] It is difficult to think of a single instance where a new idea or invention was immediately accepted without any premonitory developments. Even the most famous example of individual influence, involving one who is often regarded as the greatest of all men, that of the teachings of Jesus, can be looked on as forming part of a more widespread religious development in the Near East at about the same time. This point of view has recently been strengthened by the discovery of somewhat similar teachings, ascribed to a different teacher, in the Dead Sea scrolls.[3]

Theories such as Carlyle's which give a prominent role to great men appear to be based on presuppositions which derive from our day-dreams rather than from our knowledge of how people actually behave. We like to think of ourselves as kings or artists or

[1] See Wm. F. Ogburn and Wm. I. Thomas, 'Are Inventions Inevitable?', in *Political Science Quarterly*, Vol. 37, 1922, pp. 83–98.

[2] The evidence for regarding invention as a cultural process is well marshalled by A. L. Kroeber, *Anthropology*, New York, 1948, pp. 352–74.

[3] Millar Burrows, *The Dead Sea Scrolls*, New York, 1955, pp. 326–45.

inventors, entirely free, somewhat larger than life, and command-
ing the obedience or admiration of passive herds of subjects or
followers. Here we are assuming that a few men are entirely self-
determined, while the remainder of mankind are mere passive
instruments. In fact, all men are more or less active and constantly
interacting and influencing each other. Even kings have their
advisers and their subordinates who are by no means mere tools.

No doubt, when we are dealing with a small society, a football-
team, a club or an office with at most a few dozen members, the
actions of a single individual may be of considerable importance in
our explanations. But the events of history involve thousands or
even millions of individuals; evidently we cannot study all of their
interactions and so we must confine ourselves, if we wish to understand them, to the more general features which they exhibit.

An amusing example of how a tenacious belief in the role of
great men can lead historians to distort the facts has been brought
to light by Professor White. The Pharaoh Ikhnaton has been presented to the world as the inventor of monotheism and the ori-
ginator of the abortive religious revolution which took place
during his reign. In doing so, the Egyptologists were simply echo-
ing the official eulogies contained in contemporary inscriptions.
This theory suffered a grievous blow, however, when a mummy
believed to be that of Ikhnaton was discovered and turned out to
be that of a young man, so young that he must have been only a
boy during the first years of his reign when the revolution took
place. Rather than abandon the great-man theory, however, the
Egyptologists succeeded in persuading an eminent physiologist to
discover that Ikhnaton had suffered from a little-known disease
which made his bones appear much younger than they really
were.[1] Even the later discovery of temples to Aton built during
the previous reign has not sufficed to destroy the Ikhnaton myth.

Numerous examples of this kind could be quoted. Richelieu's
testament has been declared a forgery by most historians because it
is incompatible with their picture of him as an evil genius, sowing

---

[1] Leslie A. White, 'Ikhnaton: The Great Man vs. The Culture Process', in *The Journal of
The American Oriental Society*, Vol. 68, Pt. 2, 1948.

hatred and dissension throughout Europe. The evidence as to Tiberius' tyranny and dissipation during his last years has been rejected because other evidence shows that the Roman Empire was rather well run during his reign; a successful emperor, it is argued, cannot have been tyrannical or dissipated. For his admirers Roosevelt was responsible for the winning of the war and the revival of American prosperity; for his enemies he was responsible for the Russian conquest of Eastern Europe and the Communist successes in China. Indeed, the more we consider particular cases and the rival claims of various great men, the more clearly we see how fruitless it is—how much a source of endless and futile argument—to assume that they had any substantial effect on the general course of events.

Discussion of this problem of the role of individuals commonly takes the form of speculations as to what would have happened, let us say, if Newton had never lived or if President Truman had not decided to drop the atomic bomb on Hiroshima. These speculations are always inconclusive and necessarily so, for they are based on the assumption that we already know how such events work out in practice. Propositions of the form, 'If this happened, then that would have happened,' are only valid if they are particular instances of general propositions which it will be the task of our science to discover. If our science, however, is to be a reliable one it must be internally consistent; it must deal with a homogeneous set of features abstracted from the flux of experience.

The instance of President Truman and the atomic bomb is the one that I have run across most frequently in conversation and argument with historians and philosophers on this subject. Recently, when it was proposed at Oxford to give an honorary degree to President Truman, a lady don of idealist principles raised some objection on the ground that his decision to drop the bomb was immoral. Oddly enough, at the meeting of Convocation which had to pass on the proposal, it fell to a distinguished historian and firm believer in the role of the individual, Mr. Alan Bullock, to argue that Truman was not really responsible. And of course it is quite true that he was not responsible, in spite of his own boasts.

His decision was dictated by his view of the situation, by the advice of his counsellors and by the popular temper in the United States at the time. The historians cannot have it both ways as they like to do; they cannot make their heroes responsible only for good deeds and their villains only for bad.

The same considerations as to the unimportance of the individual apply to our present undertaking. If the approach to history advocated in these pages is destined to win a general or even a wide acceptance, it will be because it is a natural outgrowth, a development inherent in the development of ideas about history in Western-European culture in recent centuries. I have no doubt that at this very moment, in Germany or in America, other students are attempting to formulate very similar theories. It will be for the public to decide, in Wittgenstein's famous phrase, which of these theories to adopt, or whether to adopt any of them at all. And this decision will be based on the preconceptions and values of the public, not on the character of the individual advocate of a particular theory.

The fact that one cannot claim credit even for what appear to be one's own ideas was brought home to me very forcibly in the course of writing this book. I give, in chapter 5, a rather sketchy account of how societies and cultures have come to be integrated and differentiated. The theory of different levels of social and cultural integration was based on my rather imperfect acquaintance with the anthropological literature, but I did feel that it represented a novel and valuable insight. Some months after writing this passage, when the manuscript had already been typed, I came across Professor Steward's *Theory of Culture Change* and found that he had put forward, in much greater detail and with much better documentation, an almost identical theory. He even uses the expression 'levels of socio-cultural integration' where I speak of separate 'levels of social integration' and 'levels of cultural integration'. Although his treatment is considerably better than mine, I have allowed my original version to stand as a shining example of how new ideas are produced by the culture and not by individuals.

Having put forward all these arguments, we must recognize

that they are not likely to convince very many of our readers. Nothing arouses more passion among professional historians or even among laymen interested in history than an attempt to deny the role of the individual in historical explanation. Judging from the intense heat usually generated by discussions of this subject, it is not difficult to surmise that there is some psychological necessity behind it; something makes most men cling to a belief in the importance of the individual. It is of course easier for most people and more in accordance with their ordinary habits to think in individual terms, but this in itself is scarcely a sufficient explanation of the tenacity of the prejudice. More likely it is related in some way to our self-picture; we *have* to believe that individuals can influence history or else give up our belief in our own importance.

For those who are not convinced by these arguments, then, it is essential to point out that our main thesis does not depend on them. It is perfectly possible to admit that occasionally individuals do affect culture and still to maintain that the elucidation of cultural processes and the broader features of experience which affect them is the most promising method of making historical events intelligible. From this point of view, the part played by individuals will be seen as a random or inexplicable element within our field of study as we have mapped it out. As we have already argued, some random elements very probably do exist in every such field. It is the features of order, however, that we shall be looking for, even though we cannot hope to find our field of study fully ordered.

Let me now attempt to summarize the position which we have reached. History, we have suggested, is most likely to become intelligible if individual historical events are seen as instances of cultural regularities and our inquiries are pursued on the level of culture. In explaining culture, we shall want to look for broader cultural regularities in which individual culture-traits find their places as parts of a pattern, as well as for regularities in the relationships between culture and other similarly conceived regularities of experience: 'human nature' and 'race', 'nature in general' and 'local environment'. We shall exclude explanations in terms of individual actions and those in terms of invisible entities, either personal or impersonal, though for different reasons in the two cases. Individual actions are excluded *a priori*; invisible entities because they have not, up to the present, been shown to be either necessary or useful.

It is perhaps not inconceivable that all cultural regularities may ultimately be explicable in terms of the four non-cultural categories we have mentioned. Universal features of culture may be explicable in terms of 'human nature' and 'nature in general', while the particular features of particular cultures may be explicable in terms of 'race' and 'local environment'. Such 'reductions' as they have been called, have had some success in the physical sciences, but it should be noted that this success has not up to the present been unqualified. No one has yet succeeded in deriving all the chemical properties of the different chemical elements from their physical properties, nor in bringing the physical laws which govern large-scale phenomena in accord with those which govern small-scale phenomena, in producing, that is, a unified field theory. It is quite possible then that culture may have irreducible regularities of its own, that it may form an 'emergent' level of organization in the universal evolutionary process. In the present state of our knowledge, we cannot hope to resolve this question, though a rough survey of the varieties of culture does appear to indicate that they are much greater than the variations in race and environment would lead us to expect.

In any case, it is clear that there is little hope for progress in reductionism at the present time. Every full non-cultural explanation of culture must contain a psychological element as one of its terms. Yet we are only beginning to know something about the psychological side of 'human nature', the psychological regularities present in all mankind. And we are barred by our respect for the individual from experimenting in order to determine the existence and scope of the more restricted psychological regularities, those found in races and breeding populations. We seem limited for the present to explanations in terms of 'nature in general', 'local environment' and the physiological side of 'human nature' and 'race'.

These, as we have already pointed out, can only provide partial explanations in the absence of a well-established universal and racial psychology.

Evidently, our best hope for the present and our first task must be to seek to establish those broader regularities in culture itself which may serve to explain individual culture-elements, leaving non-cultural explanations for later consideration. Moreover, within this restricted field, it is the very broadest regularities for which we should first search, since these are likely to be necessary for the explanation of any smaller phenomena. It is no accident that the mechanical branch of physics made its first leap forward with the formulation of the law of gravity. Any experiments with moving bodies were inevitably inconclusive until the effect of gravity could be identified and discounted. For this reason, our new science must begin by searching for regularities in the development of whole cultures, since these are the largest comparable phenomena found in our field of inquiry. The cultural development of mankind as a whole, we have already had occasion to point out, is not itself susceptible of comparative study. Vico then was right in devoting his *Scienza Nuova* mainly to comparing whole cultures. Some of his conclusions may well turn out to be valid, when we come to examine them. Unfortunately, he himself could not establish them firmly, partly for the lack of a clear definition of the concepts 'culture' and 'a culture' and partly because the evidence was not yet available. Before exploring this question further, however, we need to equip ourselves with one more definition, that of 'civilization'.

7

CIVILIZATIONS

I HAVE already made clear that I intend to use the term 'civilization' to distinguish the larger, more complex cultures, which embrace the fields of events usually studied by historians, from the smaller, simpler ones which have traditionally been the exclusive preserve of the anthropologists. The distinction between 'civilized' and 'primitive' men is one which is often made in common speech, though no doubt the ordinary person would be hard put to it to state precisely on what criterion it is based. It is this common-sense distinction which we propose to clarify and to adopt for our own purposes.

As we saw in chapter 4, the word 'civilization' has had a history rather similar to that of 'culture'. In technical usage in the nineteenth century, especially in France and England, it came to mean precisely or almost precisely the same thing as 'culture'. Tylor consciously uses the words as identical,[1] and many authors have spoken of 'primitive civilizations', showing clearly that they did not differentiate between 'primitive' and 'civilized'. 'Culture', however, has now won the day and become the standard term; 'civilization' is free for such other uses as we may care to give it.

Some German sociologists at the turn of the century attempted to distinguish 'civilization' and 'culture' as two different aspects of what I have here called 'culture'; they were imitated by a number of American sociologists, though not by anthropologists. Thus Barth wished to limit 'culture' to its technological aspects, the 'sway of man over nature', and use 'civilization' to refer to the modification of human instincts by society, 'man's sway over

---

[1] E. B. Tylor, *Primitive Culture*, London, 1871, p. 1.

himself'; he was followed in this by the Americans, Lester Ward and Albion Small. Almost precisely the opposite distinction was made by the Germans, Tönnies and Alfred Weber, followed by the Americans, MacIver and Merton. For them, 'civilization' would be defined as 'a body of practical and intellectual knowledge and a collection of technical means for controlling nature', while 'culture' would be limited to 'configuration of values, of normative principles and ideals'.[1] This use of the two words appears in a work of Merton's as late as 1949.[2]

It is not at all clear why this distinction should have been thought necessary.[3] We do need to have one word to cover all of the manifestations of collective human behaviour in order to see their essential homogeneity; if we wish to make distinctions within culture, we have such well-established terms as 'technology', 'ideas and values' and so on. In addition, the distinction made by the sociologists does not appear to be exhaustive; it is not clear whether such important features of collective behaviour as politics, religion or philosophy would be 'civilization' or 'culture' in their terms. This line of thought indeed seems to reflect the standard German dichotomy between *Geist* and *Natur*, 'spirit' and 'nature'; it is not appropriate for a science which purports to study 'spirit' naturalistically.

Spengler also uses the term 'civilization' in a special sense; he means by it the late, decadent uncreative stage which terminates the development of his 'great Cultures'.[4] This distinction reflects his peculiar metaphysics. 'Civilization', for him, stands to 'Culture' as being to becoming, as intellect to soul; it is something final, dead. His 'decline' of the West is not a decline in the ordinary sense; it is the fact that the West has attained 'civilization'. Obviously his usage involves a number of special assumptions which we can hardly share; they seem to give the word much of the

[1] The history of these distinctions is discussed by A. L. Kroeber and Clyde Kluckhohn in *Culture*, Cambridge, Mass., 1952, pp. 15–18.

[2] Robert K. Merton, *Social Theory and Social Structure*, Glencoe, Ill., 1949, p. 254.

[3] But see A. L. Kroeber, *The Nature of Culture*, Chicago, 1952, pp. 152–66.

[4] Oswald Spengler, *The Decline of the West*, tr. by Chas. Francis Atkinson, New York, 1932, Vol. I, pp. 31–4.

flavour of 'overcivilized' in ordinary speech; it has become a term of condemnation.

We may safely disregard then these previous attempts to give a technical meaning to 'civilization' and consider ourselves free to use it for our own purposes. Let us agree then to use 'civilizations' to refer to the larger, more complex cultures and 'civilization' for the kind or kinds of culture found in them. We need to be somewhat more precise than this, however. Without further definition we shall be unable to decide in many cases whether a culture should be classed as a civilization or not.

The mere size of a culture, that is, the number of people who 'bear' it, whose way of life it is, does not of itself appear to be a significant feature; though of course the political and economic organization of large areas involves somewhat different problems from those of small areas. But having regard to size alone, we should not know where to draw the line between 'civilizations' and 'primitive cultures'. Would it be at the hundred thousand mark? Or must we have a million people sharing a culture for it to be called a civilization? Or five million? Any decision here seems purely arbitrary.

Somewhat similar problems are involved if we try to use complexity as the distinguishing criterion. Complexity in itself is difficult to define; it appears to mean something like 'the number of different specialized activities engaged in by particular groups and not by all the bearers of the culture'. But here again it would seem to be a purely arbitrary decision what number of specialized activities would characterize a civilization and difficult also to say what constitutes a specialized activity as a distinct numerable entity. Clearly we need some other criterion.

In recent decades, American anthropologists, in their anxiety to avoid the value-connotations of the terms 'civilized' and 'primitive', have taken to speaking of 'literate' and 'non-literate' cultures; they wished to imply that each type of culture was valuable in its own way. This usage, which appears to be something of a euphemism, had its greatest vogue just after the recent war; its popularity is now declining. Certainly the use of writing seems to be charac-

teristic of most of the cultures which we would like to call civilized; it is not found, however, in all. The Peruvian culture, for
instance, before the arrival of the Spaniards, seems to resemble
closely in its general character that found in Mexico and Central
America or, indeed, the culture of the Ancient Egyptians. But the
Egyptians and the Aztecs were literate and the Peruvians were not.
India developed an elaborate culture with what can only be called
an extensive oral literature well before the adoption of writing.
On the other hand, there are a number of tribes in the Philippines
and Indonesia, for instance, the Tagbanua of Palawan and the
Mangyan of Mindoro, whom we should call primitive in every
other respect, and who nevertheless possess alphabets of their own.
Literacy therefore cannot serve as the distinguishing criterion of
civilization.[1]

Perhaps we had best turn to the etymological derivation of
'civilization' and to what still seems to be one of its major connotations; civilization, let us say, is the kind of culture found in
cities. Civilizations then would be those cultures which include
among their features the building and inhabiting of cities. But how
are we to define a city? Here again mere size or density of population could only be arbitrary criteria. Do you need 5000 or 10,000
souls to make a city? And how many of them must be packed into
a square mile?

There is one feature of cities, however, which does appear to be
significant and on which many of the characteristics which we
usually associate with civilization appear to depend. This is the fact
that many or most of the inhabitants of a city are not engaged in
agriculture. Or perhaps, since we shall wish also to exclude hunting
and fishing villages, let us say that city-dwellers are not, for the
most part, engaged in producing food. It is this freedom from the
need of directly producing their own food which presumably enables the inhabitants of cities to devote all their time to specializa-
tion and so to complicate their culture; the same freedom also
enables them to travel, to trade, and to exert military power over
large areas and thus to extend the area of their culture. Literacy,

[1] Isaac Taylor, *The Alphabet*, London, 1883, pp. 285–361.

though it may occur outside cities, must have been developed and cultivated by specialists who did not have to devote their energies to subsistence. We may even surmise that some of the systematic, 'rational' qualities which seem to distinguish the culture of cities derive from the fact that men are no longer immediately dependent on the vagaries of nature.

Specialists, to be sure, do occur in what are usually regarded as primitive communities, but they are relatively rare and few of them can devote all their time to their specialty. Agricultural communities, on the other hand, are a necessary part of every civilization, but their character is substantially altered by the fact that they have become culturally dependent on cities. This whole question of rural–urban differentiation has been extensively explored by the Chicago anthropologist, Robert Redfield and his associates[1] and there is no need to reproduce their findings here; but it seems clear that the mere fact of living together in cities away from the land and its daily pressures has been a major factor in the development of the larger, more complex cultures and in the determination of their peculiar features.

Civilization, let us agree then, is the culture of cities and cities we shall define as agglomerations of dwellings many (or to be more precise, a majority) of whose inhabitants are not engaged in producing food. A civilization will be a culture in which cities are found. In order to preserve the unity of our entities we shall continue to call a particular culture a civilization even though in its earlier stages of development no cities may be present. I am not sure that this contingency will ever in fact arise. Where our evidence is adequate, it would appear that the emergence of cities is coincident with the appearance of new values and new institutions, i.e. a new culture, but it would be impossible to prove that this is the case for civilizations whose past has not been thoroughly explored by archaeologists, India and China for instance. For the time being then, we must make the reservation that a civilization

[1] Robert Redfield, *The Folk Culture of Yucatan*, Chicago, 1941 and *The Primitive World and its Transformations*, Ithaca, N.Y., 1953. See also C. M. Foster, 'What is Folk Culture?', in *American Anthropologist*, Vol. 55, 1953, pp. 159–73, and Sidney W. Mintz, 'On Redfield and Foster' in *American Anthropologist*, Vol. 56, 1954, pp. 87–92.

may have its beginnings before the appearance of cities; cities must appear in its later stages, however, or we shall not call it a civilization.

The desirability of distinguishing civilizations from primitive cultures in this way is an excellent example of how qualitative rather than quantitative considerations play a primary role in our new science. We are more concerned with drawing significant distinctions than with counting or measuring the phenomena. Our methods may be compared with those of biology; animals and plants are not classified by their size, but rather by significant features of structure, significant in the sense of being accompanied by a large number of concomitant similarities and differences. Thus bats were formerly classified as birds because they had wings and flew, while whales were classified as fish because they had fins and swam. But in the course of time it has become clear that these features are not so significant as the fact that both bats and whales are viviparous and nurse their young. They are now classified as mammals and many features of their structure have now become intelligible as variations on the basic mammalian pattern. It may be that in the future some other criterion for classifying cultures may come to seem more useful, but for the moment the presence or absence of communities not primarily engaged in producing food seems to be highly significant and neatly serves our purpose of distinguishing the domain of the science of history from that of anthropology in general.

It will be recalled that I distinguished cultures from sub-cultures and super-cultures as the primary distinctive level of cultural integration, the level of nations and tribes, for instance. It does not appear desirable, however, to follow this procedure in defining civilizations. The reason for this is the fact that, as we shall see in the last chapter, many of what were once civilized super-cultures embracing a number of distinctive national cultures have in the course of time become integrated into single cultures. We shall therefore use the term 'civilization' simply to mean the largest distinctive entities which we happen to find in our survey of the field. Thus the Chinese culture, though now that of a single politically-integrated unit, will be called Chinese civilization, because there is no larger entity in which it can be included. Similarly the Western European super-culture will be called a civilization, but its component parts, British and French cultures, will be technically called sub-civilizations. Of course, there can be no objection to the loose literary usage of referring to British and French civilizations, as long as we are clear that it is not to these units that we refer when we speak of a civilization or civilizations in general.

Having defined 'civilization' and 'a civilization', we are now in a position to identify the major units which we find in the field of history. We must recall that cultures, and therefore civilizations, are differentiated and integrated by the presence of a set of basic ideas and values, but that in practice their boundaries in space and time are to be determined by the presence or absence of a set of characteristic institutions. These criteria are, of course, only an attempt to give precision to what both scholars and laymen feel as differences and similarities in style or general character between the cultures of various states and peoples at various periods. It is therefore not surprising that when we apply our criteria—we only need to do so roughly at first—we find that our major units of civilization are very much the same as those which have long been recognized.

Eight of these are fairly clearly defined and generally accepted. They are the Egyptian, the Babylonian, the Chinese, the Indian, the Classical, the Peruvian, the Middle-American and the Western-European. Most of these are familiar to any well-read layman, but perhaps a few remarks will make clearer the scope of some of the names.

By Egyptian I mean the civilization prevailing in Egypt from Early Dynastic times (about 2700 B.C.) until its extinction in the first centuries of the Christian era. Babylonian includes the sub-civilizations of Sumer and Akkad prior to the rise of Babylon and the sub-civilizations of the Babylonian, Kassite, Assyrian, Neo-Babylonian and Achaemenian Empires which are generally recognized by archaeologists as closely inter-related. It endured from about 3000 B.C. until some time after the conquests of Alexander;

cuneiform tablets are found as late as the first century B.C. Mesopotamian might have been a better term than Babylonian and is in fact used by Frankfort,[1] but Babylonian has the sanction of long usage; for some reason the specialists in this field call themselves Assyriologists. The Chinese and Indian civilizations are familiar to everyone. We do not have sufficient evidence to give a date for their beginnings; perhaps 1500 B.C. would be a good guess in both cases. They have endured until the present and still exist, though with a veneer of Western-European culture among the upper classes.

Classical includes the Greek and Roman civilizations. These may be recognized as separate sub-civilizations, but obviously together form a larger unit. It began sometime after 1200 B.C.—we cannot fix a more precise date for lack of evidence—and lasted until about the fourth century A.D. The Peruvian civilization has often been called Incan, or Andean, though specialists now prefer the term Peruvian; it includes not only the culture of the Incan Empire, but also the various other local cultures in Western South America which the Incas superseded. Middle-American is also a specialists' term which covers the Aztec, Toltec and Mayan (both Old Kingdom and New Empire) sub-civilizations as well as the other local sub-civilizations which once flourished in the region of modern Mexico and Guatemala. Both the Peruvian and Middle-American civilizations appear to have lasted from about the beginning of the Christian era until shortly after the Spanish conquests in the early sixteenth century. The Western-European civilization is, of course, our own; its distinctive forms appear to have emerged in the tenth and eleventh centuries.

The more precise delimitation of these civilizations in time and space would require intensive study and examination and the careful application of the criteria which we have already set up; it must form part and parcel of the study of the civilizations themselves. But there is another major unit of civilization which is not so easy orecognize and its disentanglement will provide an opportunity to show how these criteria might be applied.

[1] Henri Frankfort, *The Birth of Civilization in the Near East*, London, 1951.

This ninth civilization is best called by a geographical term, the Near-Eastern. The difficulty in recognizing it is due to the fact that, unlike our other civilizations, it emerged in an area already for the most part occupied by a previous civilization, the Classical. For several centuries at the beginning of the Christian era there took place a gradual transition from the cultural forms of one civilization to those of the next. If however we take a period when the Near-Eastern civilization was flourishing independently, say the ninth century A.D., we can see that the various peoples of the Near East at that time shared a large number of culture-complexes and so possessed a common super-culture, i.e. a common civilization. Among these culture-complexes were: a religion with a single all-powerful God revealed by a prophet in sacred books, the endogamous and residentially-separate religious community as the primary level of social, political and legal organization, sacred (but not deified) rulers at the head of both Church and State, non-representational or semi-representational art-forms emphasizing the immanence of the divine in man and nature, the dome in architecture, and even such minor factors as the steam-bath and common styles of dressing and preparing food. This common super-culture is found not only among the Byzantine Greeks, the Muslims, and the Armenians but also among the Jews, Copts, Maronites, Parsis, Nestorians and other religious groups which did not possess states of their own. It was imitated, though not fully adopted, by the backward peoples of both Eastern and Western Europe, Central Asia and the horn of East Africa at that time.

Taking the ninth century then as our base-line, we can trace this civilization both forward and backward in time by determining the persistence of this basic list of culture-complexes or institutions. To do this in detail would require many careful studies. We can see roughly, however, that while some of the institutions can be traced back to about the eighth century B.C. among the Jews and the Persians, they began to emerge *as a group* in about the first century A.D. both in the eastern half of the Roman Empire and in Parthia. Classical cultural forms were quickly eliminated in Parthia, but within the Roman Empire, Near-Eastern civilization only became dominant in the fourth century about the time of the reign of Constantine; the last traces of Classical culture lingered on considerably longer.

At the present time, most of the area of this civilization falls within the territory of Muslim states. It was no accident that the Byzantines preferred being conquered by the Turks who shared the same civilization to being rescued by the alien Western Christians. More recently, in the last century or so, the Greeks, the Jews and the peoples of the Balkans have more or less successfully converted themselves into nations of the modern Western-European type. On the level of popular culture, however, many Near-Eastern traits still survive in these countries; Greek and Armenian cooking still tastes remarkably like Turkish or Syrian. But on the whole there would be no objection to calling the Near-Eastern civilization as it stands today Islamic civilization, as long as it is clear that this may include the cultures of the followers of other religions besides Islam in the same area.

There has long been a common-sense recognition of this cultural entity. The inhabitants of countries bordering on the Eastern Mediterranean, whether Muslims, Greeks, Jews or Copts, have been popularly classed together as Levantines. The foreign offices of Great Britain and the United States still count Greece as part of the Near or Middle East, not of Europe.

Spengler, however, was the first writer clearly to distinguish this civilization as a separate entity; unfortunately he gave it the misleading name 'Magian'.[1] His list of civilizations is in fact almost identical with ours and this suggests that he must have used, unconsciously or intuitively, criteria very similar to our own. Perhaps the principal difference between his approach and the anthropological one is that he believed that ideas and values exist in some spiritual realm and are known by direct intuition or 'historical tact', as he called it, while we hold that they are a part of nature—mental or psychological facts which can be studied empirically.

We might note in passing the curious fact that six of our nine civilizations fall into three pairs which are neighbours in space and

---

[1] Spengler, op. cit., Vol. II, p. 189 et seq.

roughly contemporaneous in time. These pairs are the Egyptian and Babylonian, the Chinese and Indian, and the Peruvian and Middle-American civilizations; their relationships are shown in the adjoining chart. In addition, we seem to discern between the members of each pair similarities, not so much of culture as of general character or level of development. This feature of order, which might be called the 'twinning' of civilizations, has not, so far as I know, been noted by any of the philosophers of history. Certainly none of them has attempted to explain it and we do not at the present time even have any idea as to how it might be explained. It is a question which we can only hope that future scientific students of civilization will be able to resolve. The other three civilizations, the Classical, Near-Eastern, and Western-European seem to form a temporal sequence following on the first of our pairs, the contemporaneous Egyptian and Babylonian civilizations. Counting this pair as the first member of our sequence we appear to have a regular alternation between East and West, another feature of order which we must reserve for future study. It is clear, however, that some order does prevail even in these vast congeries of phenomena.

Besides our nine major civilizations, there have existed a considerable number of what might be called peripheral or secondary civilizations. These are cultures (containing cities) which, while they have borrowed a number of the features of some nearby major civilization, especially art-styles and technology, have not adopted the whole list of basic institutions and so cannot be classed as a part of that major civilization. Many of their features are indigenous and some may even be borrowed by the neighbouring major civilization. Among these secondary civilizations we might mention, in the Egypto-Babylonian area, the Hittite, Mitannian, Syro-Phoenician and Aegean (Creto-Mycenaean) civilizations, and to the east of Babylonia, the Indus Valley civilization. In the area between India and China we find Burmese, Ceylonese, Siamese, Khmer, Cambodian, Malayo-Indonesian, Annamite and Tibetan civilizations. The Nepalese appears to be dependent on the Indian civilization alone, while similarly Korea and Japan have

THE NINE MAJOR CIVILIZATIONS

(showing distribution, but not extent, in space and duration in time)

civilizations peripheral to that of China. Similar phenomena, as far as I know, are not to be found in America prior to the Spanish conquest although the Chibcha culture in what is now Colombia had borrowed a good deal from the neighbouring civilizations and might eventually have developed cities.[1]

The Egyptian and Babylonian civilizations became peripheral to the Classical before they disappeared, and perhaps we can distinguish separate Etruscan, Iberian and Celtic secondary civilizations before they too were absorbed by the Classical. Greco-Bactrian is clearly peripheral and so are the Arabian and Ethiopian civilizations at the beginning of our era. Secondary civilizations surrounding the Near-Eastern include those of the Teutonic Kingdoms in Western Europe in the first millenium, the Ethiopian again and, in the present millenium, the Russian and the Indo-Muslim.

All the surviving civilizations, whether major or secondary, have become peripheral to the Western-European within the last two hundred years. This is a restatement in our more precise terms of a fact which is usually phrased more loosely as: 'Western-European civilization has spread over the whole earth' or even, 'Western-European civilization now embraces all mankind.' It is true that it would be difficult to find a people which has not adopted some Western-European culture-traits; perhaps a few remote tribes in New Guinea, the Eastern Himalayas or the Amazon basin are still practically unaffected. But even in countries like India where the borrowing has been quite extensive, the daily life of the mass of the population still follows on the whole the old traditional patterns. We cannot call them members or bearers of Western-European civilization, nor can we take their civilizations as wholes and call them parts of Western-European civilization, if we wish to use the term 'a civilization' with any clarity.

This list of secondary civilizations is almost certainly not exhaustive. Very likely I should add a Kushite or Nubian dependent on the Egyptian, an Elamite on the Babylonian, and a Turco-Tatar on the Near Eastern. In West Africa there appear to have

[1] Kroeber, *op. cit.*, pp. 283–8.

been cities before the arrival of the Europeans and perhaps I should speak of a West African civilization peripheral first to the Near East and now to Western Europe. There are almost sure to be other cases which we have overlooked. It is quite possible, too, that this list is not entirely accurate; some of these secondary civilizations may have to be divided in two or merged with others. All I am really seeking to do here is to set up a category of secondary civilizations into which some of our phenomena can be classed; the identity and precise extent in space and time of the members of the category must be determined by detailed studies. The category is made necessary, however, by the fact that I have defined our entities 'a culture' and 'a civilization' more precisely than other writers; most of the philosophers of history have been content either to disregard the secondary civilizations or to count them as parts of the major civilizations on the basis of a superficial resemblance. Archaeologists and historians, however, have generally found it useful to distinguish them.

On a purely speculative basis it might be supposed that there is something artificial about this category, that on the periphery of a major civilization we are likely to find a continuous spectrum of cultures in all stages of assimilation, from those which have borrowed a few technological devices to those which have adopted nearly, but not quite all, the basic institutions, and the basic ideas and values of the major civilization. The acculturation studies made by the anthropologists, however, have shown, I believe, that a fairly sharp line can be drawn between those cultures, on the one hand, whose bearers are seeking to retain their traditional ideas and values in spite of borrowing many culture-traits from their more powerful neighbours and those cultures, on the other hand, whose bearers are in process of abandoning their traditional ideas and values, on which their basic institutions rest. There are of course transitional periods, but they are clearly transitional and describable as such.

As far as we can judge by a rough survey, these secondary civilizations are on the whole much shorter in duration than the major ones. They do not appear to go through any development of their basic institutions which does not reflect the development with a major civilization. In addition, they seem on the whole to lack originality or at least we may say that those features of their culture which are original are rarely borrowed by other civilizations. None of the great art-styles and systems of thought which have had so much influence throughout the world can be ascribed to a secondary civilization, though Celtic art did influence the Teutonic kingdoms of the first millenium and through them the beginnings of our own civilization.

The great religions may appear to be exceptions to this generalization. While Christianity, Hinduism and Buddhism all originated within a major civilization, the Jews did invent ethical monotheism about the eighth century B.C. and the Persians ethical dualism about the same time. Yet these may be looked on as premonitory developments prior to the rise of the Near-Eastern civilization, while the Arabians had already absorbed that civilization at the time of the invention of Islam.

Indeed, in this respect, the record of the uncivilized peoples is rather better than that of the secondary civilizations. The Scythian animal-style appears to have had some influence both on China and the Near East, while it seems to have been the Chalybes, a primitive people in Southern Armenia who invented iron-working, well after the rise of Babylonia and Egypt. The only important invention made by a secondary civilization that occurs to me is the invention of the alphabet by the Phoenicians.

A possible exception to these generalizations is the case of Japan. Japanese civilization is clearly not a part of Chinese civilization since many of the basic Chinese institutions have been lacking there, for instance, the mandarinate, ancestor-worship and Confucian ethics. It is clearly peripheral to Chinese since it has borrowed from China its style of writing, many of its art-styles and the Chinese form of the Buddhist religion. In the last century there has also been extensive borrowing from Western Europe. Nevertheless, in some respects Japanese civilization appears to resemble the major rather than the secondary civilizations. Its social institutions, for instance, seem to have undergone independently a development involving first feudalism and then the rise of a merchant class, a development which is also found in some of the major civilizations, but in China only at a much earlier date.[1] It is possible therefore that we should class Japanese civilization as a major civilization in spite of its borrowings from China. This question cannot, however, be settled until we know a good deal more about the processes of development of the major civilizations. Similar considerations may also apply to Russian civilization which appears to have been peripheral first to Near-Eastern and then to Western-European, but also in the last century or two to exhibit some of the earmarks of a major civilization in its early stages. These are questions which the practitioners of our new science must decide. It seems evident, however, that with the world as crowded with civilizations as it has now become, it would be impossible for a major civilization to grow up nowadays without coming first of all under the influence of one of its neighbours.

My definition of 'a civilization' has now enabled me to set up two categories, one of major civilizations with nine (or possibly eleven) members, and one of secondary civilizations with an as yet undetermined number of members. I have also provided the criteria for determining the identity and the extension in space and time of the members of these two categories.

I am also able now to criticize in terms of my definition two conceptions which have had a wide currency. The first is that of 'Christian civilization', an entity which is suppose to include the cultures of all Christian peoples. It seems to be a general, or at least widespread, phenomenon for the bearers of a culture to feel that their basic ideas and values have supernatural sanction; their religion often, therefore, seems to them somehow the heart or centre of their culture. If we were to identify religion with basic ideas and values this would, in a sense, be true, but then we should need another term to describe the beliefs and practices connected with the supernatural which constitute religion in the usual narrow sense. The basic ideas and values of a culture are manifest not only

[1] C. B. Sansom, *Japan, A Short Cultural History*, New York, 1943.

in its religion, but in all the other aspects or departments of culture. Men deal not only with the supernatural, but also with nature and with each other. Religion is therefore only one aspect of culture and cannot give its name to the whole; we are no more and no less entitled to speak of 'Christian civilization' than of 'Democratic' or 'Monarchical civilization' or, for that matter, of 'Tea-drinking civilization'. These terms do not cover empirically-discoverable entities; they are rather classes into which we put various cultures because they share a single culture-trait or complex. The possible number of such classes, as we have already seen, is infinite, or at least indeterminately large.

If in fact we examine the history of Christianity we see that its rise, spread and development during the first millenium after Christ was part of the rise, spread and development of the Near-Eastern civilization as a whole. It was adopted by the Teutonic kingdoms of Western Europe along with a number of other features of Near-Eastern civilization. When these kingdoms began to develop a distinct major civilization of their own around the beginning of the second millenium, they retained Christianity but modified it profoundly in accordance with their new ideas and values. This is how we can explain in our terms the Great Schism between East and West and the theological activity in Western Europe in the early Middle Ages. In accordance with the development of Western Europe, Western-European Christianity has been even further modified and has now taken on a secular and rationalist cast in accordance with the character of the present age. Though many of the forms of belief and practice, especially among Catholics, are similar to those of Oriental Christians, the spirit— the basic ideas and values—is quite different. Both of the two great families of Christians feel that the other has perverted the true nature of Christianity; though to an outsider it must be evident that Christ and his disciples were Near-Easterners, not Western-Europeans, and that they shared ideas and values which still persist in the various Oriental churches, and for that matter in Islam. 'Take no thought for the morrow', for instance, is a conception much closer to Islamic fatalism and immediate dependence on

God than to Western Christian activism. On the other hand, there can be no objection to thinking of Christianity as an independent phenomenon or factor in the course of history, to tracing its rise and development and inquiring into the influence which it may have had on the other aspects of the civilizations in which it has flourished. We are even entitled to feel, as Christians do, that it is the most important factor in history, though it is doubtful that this could be proved by purely empirical means. Our objection is rather to speaking of 'Christian civilization' as a separate entity, a procedure which makes the rational classification and comparison of civilizations difficult, if not impossible.

'Christian civilization', then, while it will undoubtedly continue to be an encouraging conception for Christians, appears to be of little use from the point of view of our proposed science. Another entity which our definitions force us to dispense with is that of 'Western' or 'European civilization', taken as including both the Classical and Western-European civilizations which we have already distinguished. This appears really to be a counter-conception to 'Christian civilization', an idea developed by the humanists who wished to counter the influence of the Near East, including of course Christianity, on our own culture. There can be no doubt that the Classical civilization and our own resemble each other in certain respects more closely than they do the Near-Eastern. Both are this-worldly rather than other-worldly in their general orientation; both have strongly representational art forms, elective governments and irreligious types of science and philosophy among their cultural features. In the Renaissance, and even before that, in the Middle Ages, Western-Europeans who were seeking new forms to express their new ideas and values turned to the remains of Classical civilization for models. But what was borrowed was misunderstood and distorted at the time of borrowing and in the following centuries has been even more profoundly modified. One only needs to compare a Palladian villa with a Greek temple, a statue by Bernini with a statue by Phidias, modern representative government with Greek municipal democracy, to see how profoundly different the modern forms are. An archaeologist of the future who digs up a Western-European city and compares it with a Greek one will not hesitate a moment in classifying them as belonging to two different civilizations; he will find that only a few Classical forms had been revived and then as decorative rather than structural elements. Nevertheless we may if we wish treat 'humanism', like Christianity, as an independent factor in the historical process.

Many of the propositions in the last three paragraphs, like others in this chapter, require more detailed proof than I can give them here. Yet I am convinced that any one who investigates these matters carefully, and who uses the word 'civilization' in the precise sense which I have given it will come to the same conclusion. In terms of our conceptual framework, it would certainly be correct to say that Western-European civilization had been more or less profoundly influenced by both the Near-Eastern and the Classical civilizations, but it would not be correct to see it as a prolongation of one or the other, or for that matter as simply a synthesis of the two traditions. It contains basic ideas and values and basic institutions of its own. In future, I shall use the terms 'Western', 'European', 'Western-European' and 'Occidental' as equivalent names for our own civilization as I have delimited it.

As we have seen, Spengler's list of 'Great Cultures' is almost precisely similar to our list of major civilizations. Toynbee's list, on the other hand, is a peculiar jumble of incompatible and incomparable entities which it might be instructive to examine. In the first place we must observe that his definition of a civilization as an 'intelligible field of historical study' offers no clear means of identifying or delimiting these entities. He does not tell us whether these fields consists of events, persons or societies. From his discussion it seems clear that he conceives of civilizations as groups of nations (that is, in our terms, groups of politically-integrated societies) which interact with each other. Yet since all societies interact with and influence their neighbours, it would follow, if we take his argument literally, that there is only one civilization, that of mankind as a whole. He does at one point say something about these nations undergoing similar developments and possibly here we have the germ of a conception similar to our concepts 'a culture' and 'a civilization'. It is never made specific, however.

If we examine the way in which he actually goes about drawing up his list of civilizations in the first chapters,[1] we see that one of the major criteria, in fact though not in theory, is whether the civilization can be made to fit into his scheme of apparentation-and-affiliation. For Toynbee, it is necessary that a civilization should end in a 'Universal State' followed by the rise of a new religion (here called a 'Universal Church') which itself 'gives birth, to a new civilization or civilizations. The first civilization is said to be 'apparented'; the later ones are 'affiliated'. Using this scheme, he then goes hunting through space and time for entities which will fit it, likely candidates for the roles of parent and daughter. It is not surprising that he comes up with a curious variety of civilizations, many of which have been distinguished by no other writer. Indeed in the eighth volume he confesses that his units of classification are 'relative to the objects of his study'.[2]

Four of his civilizations seem to be identical with members of our own list of major civilizations. These are his Egyptiac, Andean, Hellenic and Western which we may take as equivalent to our Egyptian, Peruvian, Classical and Western. Two more, his Japanese and Russian, we have also identified, without being sure whether they can be classed as major or as secondary civilizations. Another two of Toynbee's, the Minoan and the Hittite civilizations, are clearly secondary in our terms, the Minoan being the same as our Aegean. Three more of our major civilizations have each been divided by Toynbee into two in order to provide him with an instance of apparentation-and-affiliation: Chinese becomes Sinic and Far Eastern; Babylonian becomes Sumeric and Babylonic; while Indian becomes Indic and Hindu. The Middle American civilization is divided into three for no apparent reason: Mayan, Yucatec and Mexic. His four remaining civilizations, the Syriac, Iranic, Arabic and Orthodox, all apparently form part of what we have called the Near-Eastern, although Syriac seems to include as well what we have called the Syro-Phoenician secondary civilization and part of the end of the Babylonian civilization, i.e. the Achaemenian Empire; the civilizations of the Parthian and Sassanid Empires seem to be left out of his considerations entirely.

This completes his basic list of twenty-one civilizations. In the later volumes, he introduces a twenty-second, the 'Medieval Western City-State cosmos', which he regards as part of, and yet still somehow distinct from, the Western civilization.[1] The purpose of distinguishing it seems to be to provide another example of 'moral breakdown'. These twenty-one or twenty-two civilizations are, in our scheme, reduced to nine major civilizations, two possibly major, and two secondary. Most of our other secondary civilizations he simply does not mention at all, although it is not clear whether he was ignorant of their existence or included them as parts of the civilizations already mentioned; he does speak of the Indus Valley civilization as the 'Indus Culture' and toys with the idea of setting it up as a separate civilization on its own. He seems to prefer, however, to treat it as a part of the Sumeric civilization, even though his Sumeric civilization seems to have ended before his Indus culture began.[2]

Besides the basic list Toynbee also describes three 'abortive' and five 'arrested' civilizations.[3] Of the first three, his Far-Eastern Christian civilization is simply the Nestorians; their civilization would clearly form part of our Near-Eastern. Why one sect of Oriental Christians should be given a civilization of their own and not the other sects, such as the Copts, the Armenians, and the Maronites is not at all clear; perhaps it is because Toynbee enjoys speculating on what might have happened if the Mongols had been converted to Nestorian Christianity.

His other 'abortive' civilizations, the Far-Western Christian (i.e. the Irish in the first millenium A.D.) and the Scandinavian, are probably best classified as uncivilized cultures or super-cultures which had borrowed extensively from the neighbouring civiliza-

---

[1] *Ibid.*, Vol. VII, p. 277.
[2] *Ibid.*, Vol. VII, p. 410.
[3] *Ibid.*, Vol. II, pp. 322–85; Vol. III, pp. 1–79.

tion. We have already mentioned an example of this class, the Chibcha culture in Southern America and no doubt numerous other examples can be found. Offhand one can think of the cultures of the Mongols and the Manchus in the Far East and of the Huns and Avars in the West in the first millenium.

The names which Toynbee gives to his five 'arrested' civilizations clearly indicate that he does not distinguish between a people and the culture or civilization of that people. These names are the Eskimos, the Polynesians, the Nomads, the Osmanlis and the Spartans. In our terms, we would prefer to think of the Eskimos and the Polynesians as possessing cultures (or more technically, super-cultures) of an uncivilized or primitive type. Why among the many thousands of primitive cultures, these two should be thought of as potential but 'arrested' civilizations is by no means clear; perhaps it is simply because they can thus serve to illustrate the 'law of challenge-and-response'. The Nomads, of course, are not a single people with a single culture; the term is customarily used to describe a number of tribes in various parts of the world who share one feature of culture, the fact that they migrate in search of grazing for their animals, on whom they are largely dependent for their food. Thus Toynbee's Nomad 'arrested' civilization is really a class of primitive cultures. His last two arrested civilizations, the Osmanlis and the Spartans, are, from our point of view, participants in the Near-Eastern and the Classical civilizations respectively. Toynbee too recognizes implicitly that they shared in larger civilizations; he even has the Osmanlis providing the 'Universal State' of his Orthodox civilization; but he finds it convenient also to distinguish them as separate entities, because it makes it possible for him to make certain moral observations about the effect of militarism on character.

In one of the most recent of Toynbee's volumes the number of 'abortive' civilizations has mysteriously risen from three to five, while the number of 'arrested' civilizations has dropped from five to four. In spite of consulting the index with great care, I have been unable to discover the names of the two new 'abortive' civilizations, or which 'arrested' civilization no longer qualifies for the list.

The inconsistency and confusion in Toynbee's list should provide us with a salutary lesson in the necessity of having clear criteria. Before we can compare civilizations, as Toynbee purports to do, we must distinguish them. And to distinguish them we must choose criteria which are likely to be significant and then apply these criteria systematically. We cannot rely on our whims of the moment or devise entities to fit into preconceived schemata formulated largely in crypto-moral terms, such as 'apparentation-affiliation' or the 'law of challenge-and-response'. Toynbee has done a great disservice to the comparative study of civilizations and tended to bring discredit on the whole enterprise by undertaking his investigations in so ill-conceived and unscientific a manner. He represents, even in comparison with Spengler, a step backwards towards the pre-scientific moralizing philosophy of history; as the apocalyptic visions in the later volumes show, he is primarily a prophet—a prophet disguised as a 'modern Western student of history'. Spengler, on the other hand, in spite of his wild exaggerations and his reliance on intuition, did have a concept of culture which approaches the anthropological one and used it far more systematically and with far more respect for the evidence than his successor. It seems quite likely that future empirical studies, such as we are trying to provide a basis for, will validate some, though of course certainly not all, of his conclusions.

In contrast with Toynbee I have here sought to provide criteria which will prove to be significant, which will enable us to distinguish entities which are genuinely comparable. Such are my definition of a culture in terms of shared ideas and values and of a civilization in terms of the presence of cities. I must admit that we are not yet able to delimit these entities with absolute precision, but at least we can identify them and give their approximate boundaries with a certain assurance, which is a good deal more than previous writers in this field have been able to do. How useful our criteria will prove can only be finally known when we have examined and compared the entities which they give us. We may derive some encouragement, however, from the fact that the entities thus distinguished correspond, on the whole, with those which both specialists and laymen have been accustomed to distinguish in the past. Presumably my definitions are merely refinements of the intuitions of common-sense.

If I have criticized Professor Toynbee's work somewhat harshly in the last few pages, it is only because it seems desirable, indeed necessary, to give an outstanding example of the difficulties and confusion into which a lack of clear definitions can lead us. It would be foolish to question his intellect, his erudition or his earnest desire to understand. We can only think it unfortunate that his education, like that of so many historians, was exclusively humanistic; he has been deprived of the tools he needed for his self-appointed task.

8

THE COMPARATIVE STUDY OF
CIVILIZATIONS

HAVING now defined 'a civilization' and provided a tentative list of actual civilizations, I shall go on to consider just what the comparative study of civilizations entails. In this I shall be guided by the discussion in chapter 6 of the various types of explanation. As we saw, it is a basic empiricist assumption that explanation invariably involves a reference to recurrent patterns of events or aspects of events. It is precisely these recurring configurations which we should look for in our comparisons.

The fact that civilizations appear to fall into two categories, major and peripheral (or secondary), suggests that comparative study will be most fruitful when it is confined to one or the other of the two categories. No doubt some similarities, some recurrent patterns, will be found running through both categories, but a greater number is likely to be found among the members of a single category. Since the major civilizations are so much larger, since they occupy so much more of the field of history, it will be well to begin with them and to leave the secondary civilizations for later examination.

Within the major civilizations, there will be various kinds of regularities that we can look for. First of all, we must distinguish between those regularities which are found in all civilizations and those which are found in only one or a few of them. In other words, comparative study involves observing not only similarities, but also consistent differences. These differences also constitute a kind of regularity, which must ultimately form part of our total picture.

An example will perhaps help to make this point clearer. As I observed earlier it is not true that all the nine major civilizations were literate, i.e. that they included among their features the art of writing throughout their long history. It would be true, however, to say that all nine included some device for preserving accurate texts or records. The Indians, before they adopted writing, had devised a mnemonic technique, involving constant repetition, for preserving their sacred texts. The Peruvians on the other hand had invented a system for keeping records by means of knotted cords, the so-called *quipu*. Thus we are able to make a broad generalization about all the major civilizations, a generalization which suggests, without proving it, the further conclusion that some means of preserving continuity, of counteracting the unreliability of the average memory, is needed before civilization can become really complex. On the other hand, the differences in the techniques used by the Indians and the Peruvians can be seen as consistent with other features of those two civilizations, the Indian emphasis on religion and neglect of history, the Peruvian development of a highly centralized governmental administration. Thus the differences in these techniques will help us to characterize these two civilizations; eventually we may hope to be able to give some psychological or environmental explanation of these general differences in character.

Four of our remaining civilizations used an ideographic rather than an alphabetic (or phonetic) form of writing. These are the Egyptian, the Babylonian, the Chinese and the Middle-American. It is instructive to observe that the first three of these retained their ideographs long after they had become acquainted with the alphabetic forms of writing used by other peoples; the fourth vanished before this possibility could arise. From these facts, along with others, it might be possible to argue that there is some sort of inherent conservatism connected with a traditional style of writing, even though these facts are only true of three or four of our civilizations.

An analogous situation may be found in biology, where the consistent differences between species and genera are in their way as interesting as their similarities. Similarly, in psychology we may study recurrent regularities in the behaviour of one person or one type of person as well as regularities valid for all men. Indeed our most profound understanding of human nature in general has been derived from the study of 'sick', that is, unusual cases.

Comparative study, then, involves an examination of consistent differences as well as of consistent similarities. Another way in which we may divide regularities, as we have already seen, is into diachronic and synchronic, those whose parts are distributed in time and those whose parts are co-existent in time. Thus in examining our nine major civilizations we shall want to see whether certain combinations of culture-traits and complexes are found regularly co-existing in time and also whether other combinations are found regularly succeeding each other in time. And here again we shall be interested both in similarities and in differences, both in cultural configurations found in all our civilizations and those found only in one or in a group.

The sociologists, as I have already pointed out, have largely concerned themselves with a minute analysis of one variety of these configurations, the synchronic regularities in the relationships between individuals (the so-called social structure) as it is found in our own civilization. Max Weber, indeed, saw the necessity of comparing the social structure of our own with those of the other civilizations, if we are to be able to make generalizations valid for all mankind, but his initial studies have never been followed up by the sociologists.[1] It is the social anthropologists who have begun to examine Chinese and Indian social structure in the last decade or two. In addition they have made many synchronic studies of this kind among individual primitive peoples; large-scale comparison of these results, however, remains more of an intention than a fact, though some first essays in this direction have been made.[2]

But social structure is only one possible kind of synchronic

---

[1] Max Weber, *Essays in Sociology*, tr. by H. H. Gerth and C. W. Mills, London, 1947, pp. 267–301 and 396–44.

[2] For instance, C. P. Murdock, *Social Structure*, New York, 1949.

regularity. Perhaps the most important kind for our purposes will be those regularities to be found in the articulation of whole civilizations. By this I mean the extent to which the major divisions of culture, such as politics, economics, religion, science, etc., are to be found in each civilization, the emphasis placed on some of these divisions rather than others, their elaboration, their inter-relationships and so on. An example of the sort of generalization which can be made in this field is the common observation that in most primitive cultures kinship ties, whether through descent or marriage, play a primary role in welding together the community, while in the more complex cultures the political and class-order has taken over some of the functions of kinship. For this reason kinship ties and the obligations associated with them are often given a precision and elaboration in primitive cultures which is very much greater than in our own civilization and somewhat greater than in Chinese or Indian civilization.

Unfortunately, no one has yet succeeded in devising a list of these divisions of culture which is logically coherent, systematic and exhaustive. The terms which we are accustomed to use, such as politics, economics, religion, art, law and so on, unquestionably have a certain rough utility and have served us well so far, but they are difficult to define precisely and they do not form a coherent system among themselves. Nor can we be sure that any list of them will cover all the possible varieties of culture-traits and complexes. Malinowski did attempt to draw up such a list on the basis of a psychological classification of human instincts or motives,[1] and more recently a much more elaborate attempt has been made by two linguists, Hall and Trager, in connection with the Human Relations Area Files.[2] Neither of these attempts has won general acceptance, however, possibly because the categories on which they are based do not themselves appear to be logically coherent or exhaustive.

[1] Bronislaw Malinowski, *A Scientific Theory of Culture*, Chapel Hill, North Carolina, 1944, pp. 91–136.
[2] Edward T. Hall, Jr. and George L. Trager, *The Analysis of Culture*, Washington, 1953; Hall, Trager and Donald H. Hunt, *Technical Aspects of the Theory of the Analysis of Culture*, mimeographed, Washington, 1954.

Certainly such a logical classification of the varieties or divisions of culture is an urgent desideratum and the progress of our science will necessarily be limited until it is achieved. Very likely such a classification would depend on the interplay of a number of different kinds of criteria: the parts of the body used, the motives involved, whether (and if so what kinds of) other persons and objects are implicated, and so on. The problem does not appear to be irresolvable by its nature, but at the moment no one seems to know how to resolve it. For the present we must content ourselves with the well-worn and fairly reliable terms which have served us so long.

Another type of synchronic regularity of great importance is what I have already referred to as ideas and values, the broadly defined ways of thinking and feeling which are found manifested in many different divisions or aspects of a culture within a given period. These are regularities of regularities, broad uniformities among the various traits and complexes of which a culture or a civilization is composed. Some historians, especially those who are generally thought to be the greatest or most profound, have shown great skill, though usually of an intuitive and artistic kind, in making clear to their readers the ideas and values of another age or country. It is these broad uniformities of thinking and feeling which, as we have seen, serve to integrate a culture or a civilization and thus to give it its identity.

Some anthropologists have held that any culture is necessarily integrated in all its parts; in other words, that the basic ideas and values are expressed in every one of its culture-traits and complexes. Spengler appears to have held a similar view; his cultures are spiritual in nature (that is, in our terms, consist of ideas and values) and form entirely independent entities, self-determined and unaffected by the environment or by their contacts with each other. It seems likely, however, that these points of view are too radical and not in accord with the facts; very probably a culture may be more or less integrated at different times and under different circumstances as well as in its different divisions. At times it may even disintegrate. Presumably the role of ideas and values is less in such fields as technology where the nature, qualities and availability of material objects are important factors and greater in such fields as religion and art where the individual is free to express himself with little reference to physical reality. These are empirical questions which the comparative student of civilizations must certainly investigate. He will wish to inquire to what degree a civilization must be integrated both as a whole and in its various parts, how this integration varies under differing circumstances, what relationships prevailing ideas and values may have among themselves at any given time, and so on. He will also wish to see how the ideas and values of one civilization compare with those of other civilizations and with those of the same civilization at different times.

If I have stressed here the importance of looking for synchronic regularities in two broad areas, that of the inter-relationships of the major divisions of a civilization and that of the ideas and values which serve to integrate a civilization, it is because it seems likely that it is in these areas that we shall be able to make generalizations of a scope and universality analogous to the laws of physics. We must attempt first of all to deal with the largest scale phenomena in our chosen field, those which embrace, or perhaps better, are abstracted from the largest number of smaller phenomena. We are not likely to be able to understand the inter-relationships of particular traits and complexes until we understand some of the more general phenomena which they in part exemplify. The movements of bodies in and near the earth's surface could not be understood until one component of this movement had been abstracted and assimilated to the movements of the planets; only then could the other components of their movement be rationally analyzed and a science of mechanics become possible. In the same way comparisons, let us say, of the structure of the family in China and in Western Europe are likely to be fruitless unless we can see to what extent the similarities and differences are due to similarities and differences in the ideas and values of the two civilizations and in their total articulation. The traditional emphasis on direct personal relationships in Chinese ethics and Chinese thought together with the relative weakness of the State and of other organized institutions, may go a long way towards explaining the relatively greater strength of family ties in China.

Similar considerations apply when we come to investigate the diachronic regularities in civilizations. We may of course choose to investigate the development of a particular culture-trait or complex and then to compare its development with that of another trait or complex within the same civilization or a similar trait or complex in some other civilization in the hope of finding regularities. We may apply this method also to larger configurations of cultural phenomena, institutions, states, churches, styles of art and schools of philosophy, to choose a few out of a vast number of possibilities. We may also study the relationships between the development of different traits or complexes or even larger configurations, as Weber and Tawney, for instance, studied the relationship between the Protestant religion and the rise of capitalism[1] and Merton the relationship between the same religion and the rise of science in Western Europe.[2] And by comparing what has happened in one civilization with what has happened in the others we may seek for regularities applicable to all.

Yet here too it is unlikely that these relatively minor phenomena will yield to our analysis, will become intelligible, until we have sought and found whatever regularities may apply on a larger scale. The development of Protestantism, of capitalism and of science in Western Europe must be seen partly as an example of the articulation of whole civilizations, an articulation which undoubtedly varies in time and probably has its own diachronic regularities. And these same developments must also partly be understood as examples of the development of the basic ideas and values of Western European civilization, of such phenomena, for instance, as individualism and rationalism, for which we may also hope to find parallels in other civilizations.

The problems of the contacts between civilizations, the influ-

---

[1] Max Weber, *The Protestant Ethic and The Spirit of Capitalism*, tr. by Talcott Parsons, London, 1948; R. H. Tawney, *Religion and The Rise of Capitalism*, London, 1926.

[2] Robert K. Merton, *Social Theory and Social Structure*, Glencoe, Ill., 1949, pp. 329–46.

ences which they have on one another, are probably best considered as a variety of process in which we must look for diachronic regularities. Here too we may study and compare the diffusion of individual traits, complexes and larger configurations, but the most important regularities are likely to be found in the processes of transmission of whole areas of culture, such as religions or modes of political organization and the even larger though rarer phenomena of the diffusion of ideas and values.

All this leads us inevitably to the conclusion that the most important task of the scientific student of history will be the comparative study of the development of whole civilizations. And this from two points of view, that of articulation (that is, the character and inter-relationships of their major cultural divisions) and that of basic ideas and values. Indeed, it is not at all unlikely that the articulation of civilizations may eventually be seen, in so far as it is stable and uniform, as the effect of certain permanent psychological and sociological necessities and in so far as it is variable, as the expression of prevailing ideas and values. The search for regularities, then, in the development of the basic ideas and values of a civilization will become the key to the understanding of the development of civilizations and of history viewed as a whole.

I must confess that it is with some reluctance that I have come to this conclusion. Ideas and values, even as conventionally conceived, are notoriously difficult to analyse or describe with any accuracy. As we are using the words here, ideas and values include not only beliefs and judgments which the agent consciously formulates, but also unconscious or non-conscious ways of thinking and feeling, ways of categorizing, inter-relating and evaluating experience. These unconscious ideas and values must be all the more difficult to describe and to analyse. Within the limits of our own civilization, we do have a certain rough agreement about the terms in which we can describe them; even though the denotations of these terms often cannot be defined, their connotations are roughly the same for every one. But when we come to describe the ideas and values of other civilizations, our difficulties are multiplied. Not only is our vocabulary inherently defective, since it has been developed to meet the needs of our own culture, but also the very structure of our language, its grammar and syntax, as the new school of linguists has clearly shown, is itself dependent on unconscious presuppositions regarding the way in which experience should be divided into categories and these categories related to one another.[1] Our own ideas and values are embedded in our language, and yet our language is the only tool we have with which to describe alien ideas and values.

Nevertheless the proposition that the comparative study of the development of ideas and values is the key to the understanding of history seems to be an inescapable deduction from the very nature of our subject-matter. Once we have seen clearly that ideas and values are the largest, the most inclusive of cultural phenomena, that they embrace aspects of the largest number of individual culture-traits and that it is these same ideas and values which serve to integrate and differentiate our civilizations, we cannot avoid making their description and explanation the central objective of the scientific study of history. Although we are likely to find some regularities in the development and inter-relationships of lesser cultural phenomena, these cannot be fully intelligible until we see what regularities may be found in the development of ideas and values. Indeed, it seems probable that the difficulties which have been encountered so far by sociologists and anthropologists in formulating generalizations of universal validity are due in large measure to the fact that they have been looking for them on the wrong level; they have concentrated on the lesser cultural phenomena and neglected the greater. They have sought to correlate particular features of culture: traits, complexes or elements of social structure, without taking into account the framework of ideas and values in which they are embedded. No doubt, the objective study of ideas and values is fraught with much greater

[1] Benjamin Lee Whorf, *Four Articles on Metalinguistics*, Washington, 1950; *Language in Culture*, ed. Harry Hoijer, American Anthropological Association Memoir No. 79, Vol. 56, No. 6, Part 2, 1954.

difficulties than that of particular items of culture, but the rewards of such a study are likely to be equally great.

There seems to be no reason to suppose that an objective analysis of ideas and values is inherently impossible. After all, as long as we define them empirically, we are dealing with facts of experience which presumably have at least some elements which remain the same for all observers. If they did not we should not be able to talk about them at all. The difficulty in defining them precisely is due, I believe, to the fact that each individual's ideas and values, his ways of thinking and feeling, vary to some extent from those of his neighbour. My idea of freedom is not the same as Sir Isaiah Berlin's and his not quite the same as Karl Popper's. Historians of ideas like other historians have tended to carry on their studies on the individual rather than the cultural level, and in order to avoid making endless distinctions between individuals they have tended to use the same words to describe the *common* elements in the ideas and values of many individuals as well as the same ideas and values in all their *fluctuations* from individual to individual. Thus ideas and values have appeared to lack precise boundaries, to be indefinitely variable. But for our purposes ideas and values must be conceived culturally; we are only concerned with what is common to all the members of a group and this can be defined with somewhat greater ease and precision.

The actual technique of describing cultural ideas and values is a fairly simple one. It consists of listing all or, at least, a number of the forms of cultural behaviour, the speech, and actions in which they are expressed, and the artifacts which result from this behaviour. It is left to the reader to perceive for himself how he would have thought and felt if he had engaged in the same behaviour. How effective this technique can be has been clearly demonstrated in recent years in the well-known works of Ruth Benedict.[1] When we come to define a cultural idea or a cultural value, we only need to say that it is the common element in thought or feeling underlying such and such cultural behaviour.

[1] Ruth Benedict, *Patterns of Culture*, New York, 1934; *The Chrysanthemum and the Sword*, Cambridge, Mass., 1947.

We do lack, it is true, a coherent logical framework in terms of which we can classify all ideas and values. The situation is similar to that which we found in the case of the articulation of cultures; there is no lack of terms but the terms are not logically related to one another. Various interesting attempts have recently been made to fill this gap. Professor Parsons has been working for a number of years with several different associates in an effort to develop a set of logically inter-related categories to cover what might be called general types of orientation; his name for them is 'pattern-variables'. The particular ideas and values of particular cultures would be seen as examples of these types of orientation. I must refer readers to his publications for further details of his scheme;[1] it cannot really be judged until further attempts have been made to use it in the actual description of cultures.

Dr. Florence Kluckhohn has been working on rather different lines and has elaborated a typology of alternative preferences for certain large categories of behaviour and experience.[2] Her scheme is reproduced on an adjoining page. It must be admitted that it is quite possible that her categories are derived from discriminations which, though they are important in Western-European civilization, may not be quite so important in other civilizations and cultures. There is something too neat in the way the last of each of her sets of three categories fits the prevailing modern European, and more particularly American, ideas and values. If we examine her three possible preferences in the time-dimension, we see that they do not appear to fit Indian civilization at all; the Indians prefer to look away from time altogether to what is unchanging and eternal. It is probably inevitable, however, that the first formulations of schemes of this kind should be more or less culture-bound, and this need not prevent them from being useful in a preliminary clarification of the phenomena. The utility of this scheme must be judged in its application and it will be interesting

[1] Talcott Parsons and Edward A. Shils, *Toward a General Theory of Action*, Cambridge, Mass., 1951; Parsons, *The Social System*, Glencoe, Ill., 1951; Parsons, Shils and Robert F. Bales, *Working Papers in the Theory of Action*, Glencoe, Ill., 1953.

[2] Florence Kluckhohn, 'Dominant and Substitute Profiles of Cultural Orientations', in *Social Forces*, Vol. 28, 1950, pp. 276–93.

to see the results which Dr. Kluckhohn has obtained from her attempts to apply it to five different cultures, results which are due to appear in a forthcoming publication.[1]

Another as yet unexplored possibility which might enable us to formulate an objective classification, at least of ideas, arises from the linguistic difficulties which I have already mentioned. As I pointed out a few pages back, the linguists have clearly demonstrated that the differing grammatical structures of different languages reflect different ideas, that is, different ways of categorizing and inter-relating experiences. The grammatical structure of English may very well prevent us from giving clear expression to the

ALTERNATIVE CULTURAL VALUE ORIENTATIONS
(after F. Kluckhohn)

Innate Predispositions of Man	Evil (mutable or immutable)	Neither good nor bad (mutable or immutable)	Good (mutable or immutable)
Man's Relation to Nature:	Man subjugated to nature	Man in nature	Man over nature
Time Dimension:	Past	Present	Future
Valued Personality Type:	Being	Being-in-Becoming	Doing
Modality of Relationship:	Lineal	Collateral	Individualistic

ideas of other peoples. It is well known that other similar difficulties are encountered by translators due to the incommensurability of the vocabularies of different languages, but the grammatical difficulties are probably more serious because we are less conscious of them; the grammar of our own language seems to us necessary and inevitable. It may be, however, that we can turn this defect of language into a virtue by using the differences of grammatical structure to define the differences in the basic ideas of different cultures. A general typology of grammatical constructions might also serve as a general typology of ideas, not of all ideas, indeed, but of the broader ways of looking at experience. In much the same way, the psychologists have used a formal analysis

[1] Personal communication from C. Kluckhohn.

of the reactions to the Rorschach test to provide a classification of the more general types of individual psychological orientation. Unfortunately, no satisfactory classificatory scheme for grammar as yet exists; the older division of languages into 'isolating', 'agglutinative' and 'inflectional' is far too simple, while the more detailed schemes developed by Sapir and Jespersen are only tentative steps in the right direction.[1]

Comparative grammar then may be able to help us to classify the broader kinds of ideas; it may also help us with values. At this level of generality, indeed, it is doubtful whether ideas can be clearly distinguished from values; cognitive and affective orientations, to use the technical language of psychology, appear to be fused. People tend at the same time to think that something is so and to feel that it ought to be so. Let us take an example which is fairly obvious though not quite so general as the sort of orientations that grammatical structures express. The proposition 'Man is the master of the universe' is on the face of it a statement of fact, that is, in our terms, an idea expressed in words. Yet intimately tied up with this idea is the feeling that man ought to make every effort to extend and exploit his mastery, that 'Man *should be* master of the universe'. We can make a verbal distinction here between statements of fact and statements of value, but in the individual certainly thought and feeling are inextricably commingled. It is not then inconceivable that our typology of grammatical constructions may also serve to analyse the most general kinds of values. Since it is precisely these most general ideas and values which are both of the greatest interest to us for understanding civilizations and also at the same time the most difficult to define, the further development of scientific comparative grammar may well provide us with the key to many of our difficulties. Traditional humanistic grammar will be of little use to us, since it has been chiefly concerned in attempting to define what is correct, rather than actual, speech in accordance with Greek or Latin models.

[1] Edward Sapir, *Language*, New York, 1939, pp. 59–156; Otto Jespersen, *Analytic Syntax*, Copenhagen, 1937.

In classifying and describing ideas and values we may seek for help not only from the linguists, but also from the psychologists. As we saw in chapter 6, the more general, less conscious kinds of ideas and values can also often be described in the language of personality traits. There is very little difference between saying that a man *is* aggressive and that he *values* aggression, if we take a value, as we do here, to be a pattern of thought and feeling for which both what a man says and what he does are evidence. Aggression as a value corresponds to aggressiveness as a personality trait. We usually formulate ideas and values as propositions which people are thought of as holding or believing, consciously or unconsciously. This procedure is convenient in some circumstances, but in others we may find it more convenient to formulate them as qualities of behaviour and to borrow the language of the psychologists. Studies of 'national character' seem to be nothing more than studies of the cultural ideas and values, conscious and unconscious, prevailing in particular nations.

It follows then that the progress of psychology in describing and classifying the more general kinds of psychological orientation will also be of use to students of civilization who wish to describe and compare the more general kinds of cultural orientation. So far, the most systematic and rational methods of describing personality have grown up around the projective tests, particularly the Rorschach and the Thematic Apperception Test,[1] though it must be admitted that their rationality still leaves something to be desired. Graphology has also developed its own system of describing personalities.[2] The student of civilizations will do well to keep abreast of progress in these branches of science.

As far as the development of ideas and values is concerned, there has also been no lack of suggestions as to how these might be analysed. We have the famous Hegelian dialectic, the sequence of thesis, antithesis and synthesis, which it appears should really be

[1] H. Rorschach, *Psychodiagnostics*, tr. by P. Lemkau and B. Kronenberg, New York, 1942; Bruno Klopfer and Douglas M. Kelley, *The Rorschach Technique*, Yonkers-on-Hudson, N.Y., 1946; H. A. Murray, *Explorations in Personality*, New York, 1938; Murray et al., *The Assessment of Man*, New York, 1948.
[2] Klara G. Roman, *Handwriting*, New York, 1954.

ascribed to Fichte. It is probable that this should be looked on as a special case, that of binary differentiation, of a more general process of differentiation and integration.[1] We may also find it useful to borrow certain terms, such as 'definition', 'elaboration' and 'exhaustion' from the analyses of stylistic development made by the art historians.[2]

All is not without hope, then. For the present, indeed, we must be content to explore the domain of cultural ideas and values with such conceptual tools as are ready to hand, but we may confidently expect that eventually, with the help of the linguists, the psychologists and others, we shall be able to render even this elusive and recondite field amenable to rational analysis. After all, we have all the vast resources of humanistic learning at our command. Even now it should be possible to get the experts in some field, the classicists, for instance, to agree on a fairly long list of ideas and values in which the Classical civilization differed from our own. We may be confident that here, as in other fields, a rational approach will eventually emerge as a refinement of preliminary intuitions.

While the comparative study of the development of the basic ideas and values of civilizations will provide, I believe, the most widespread and therefore the most important regularities, there is no reason why we should confine our studies to these matters alone. We shall want to look at the development of civilizations from every point of view that might be fruitful. Certain aspects of their development may even be measurable: the changes, for instance, in the number of bearers of a civilization, in the geographical area it covers or in the degree of its urbanization. There are many vast fields of research open here which can engage the efforts of many scholars for many generations.

One difficulty will doubtless have occurred to many readers. Civilizations are entities of vast complexity, they are abstractions from innumerable particular events each of which is in some

[1] See also Murphy's use of Spencer's developmental scheme: Gardner Murphy, *Personality, a Biosocial Approach*, New York, 1947, p. 66 *et sqq.*

[2] Meyer Schapiro, 'Style', in *Anthropology Today*, ed. A. L. Kroeber, Chicago, 1953, pp. 87–312.

respects different from the next. How can we ever hope to make valid general statements about civilizations as wholes? We cannot hope to examine every event, every scrap of evidence which survives from the past. And there are many events, perhaps the majority, for which we have no evidence. Yet if we do not consider all the evidence, how can we be sure that any general statements we make will not be overthrown at a later date by additional evidence?

To overcome this difficulty we must rely, first of all, on the procedure known as 'sampling'. This has been developed into a highly sophisticated technique by the statistical sociologists; how successful it can be is shown by the successes of the psephologists in predicting the results of elections, successes which far outnumber their occasional well-publicized failures. In essence, sampling amounts to choosing a number of instances sufficiently numerous and sufficiently varied in their character and attendant circumstances to give us a fair representation of the total number of instances in all their intrinsic variability. We may then examine our limited number of instances in respect to the particular feature in which we are interested, and our results are likely to be valid for the total number of instances, as experience shows, within certain limits of accuracy.

Sampling will work well enough when we are investigating recent periods of history for which we have adequate surviving evidence, so that we can pick and choose to build up our sample. But if we turn to more distant periods for which only a little evidence survives, are we entitled to treat this evidence as an adequate sample? Certainly not, according to the rules of sampling drawn up by the statisticians. We may be able to guard against the bias in our sample caused by the circumstances of preservation, the fact that, for instance, our knowledge of Ancient Egypt is almost entirely based on what was buried in tombs. And to some extent we may be able to see that the surviving evidence is adequately varied, for instance, in geographical distribution. But in many instances we cannot be sure that it is sufficiently varied in every respect likely to be significant.

And yet archaeologists do often make inferences from a small amount of evidence which turn out to be valid when more evidence is dug up. The same is often true of historians, and it is astonishing how much information about a culture an anthropologist can learn from a single informant. The truth seems to be that culture is much more uniform or regular than the layman might suppose. We are misled by the fact that we are acutely conscious of individual variations within our own culture and often do not even see the regularities. We are aware of the differences in the colour of men's neckties and we take for granted the fact that, at least on certain occasions, almost all men in our culture will wear neckties. But when we come to look at another culture or our own culture in the past, it is the consistent differences between one culture and another rather than the differences between individuals which leap to the eye. All Chinese look alike to Europeans and all Europeans look alike to Chinese. It seems likely too that students of culture develop intuitive criteria for judging in what respects a culture is likely to be uniform and in what respects individual behaviour is likely to vary. The cut and colour of a garment may vary, we feel, but not its general shape and purpose. It would certainly be extremely helpful if we could formulate these criteria explicitly and rigidly and to do so must be one of the early tasks of our science; we shall then be able to make inferences from a few instances with much greater assurance.

A somewhat similar problem arises from the fact that our civilizations are rather limited in number. Can we make valid generalizations from only nine major civilizations? Would it be safe to predict that any regularities found in the development of all nine of these would also be found in a tenth? And if we cannot predict, can we call our study a science?

The fact is that the generalizations we obtain in the sciences, even the 'laws' of the physical sciences, cannot claim to be absolute truth; they only represent more or less close approaches to the truth and predictions based on them are only valid with varying degrees of probability. For the physical sciences, this probability is very high; for our science, it will be relatively low, but by no means negligible. An induction based on nine out of nine instances is not to be despised. Indeed, most of the 'laws' of the physical sciences were originally established by a single or a few crucial experiments. It is only much later (and by no means for all 'laws') that the evidence of hundreds or thousands of instances has been added. Here again it seems to be the isolation of factors likely to give variable results which is all-important. In an experiment these other factors are held constant; in sampling they are deliberately varied; where our sample is given and not constructed we must do what we can to discount their effect. But if we find regularity in our nine instances we may safely suppose that the relevant factors have been constant, and if we find regularity in only seven or eight, this will spur us to look for the factors which have varied.

An example from biology may make this problem somewhat clearer. It is quite possible for a biologist to make an inference about a species from a single specimen, and the palaeontologists in fact often do so. But their ability to do so rests on the fact that they know fairly clearly in what respects the bodily structure of a species is likely to be uniform and in what respects it is likely to vary. Similarly the isolation of variable factors in human behaviour and more especially in culture should enable us to strengthen the validity of the generalizations and the inferences we may make about history.

Empirical generalizations have usually been considered as statements about how events actually occur. Another view of them, however, has lately become fashionable and has proved especially useful in economics; it may well therefore also be of some use in studying other aspects of culture. According to this view, the facts themselves are often (or, some would say, always) too varied to be accurately and simply described. In order to understand them, what we must do is to set up '*models*', theoretical formulations which describe no actual state of affairs, but rather an ideal state of affairs, with which the actual events tend to conform, although they never do so absolutely. The great advantage of models is that they enable us to make a more simple and more rigid formulation than the evidence or the state of our knowledge fully justifies. Professor Lévi-Strauss is at the present time the chief exponent of this approach in social anthropology.[1] We may well find that it will turn out to be useful also in the study of civilizations, where for instance it might be possible to set up a model for the development of a major civilization which would help us to order more of the facts than a simple description of the regularities we actually find in their development, even though no single civilization actually conforms to the model.

Advantageous as such an approach may be, it seems to me best to look on models as a heuristic device rather than as the goal of our studies. In so far as the models appear to be valid, we might look on them not indeed as a description of the events, but as a description of the inter-relationships of certain factors present in the events. A full understanding of the events would involve the elucidation of all the other factors present, factors which we may not yet be able to identify. In this way, our view of empirical generalizations as essentially descriptive can be preserved.

When all is said and done, of course, the generalizations formulated by the science of history are unlikely ever to become as precise or as highly probable as those of the physical sciences. But this is no reason to give up the search for them. We must make them as clear and as valid as the nature of the subject-matter and the limitations of our knowledge and understanding permit. Even if their validity is relatively low, if they apply at best to most cases and not to all, nevertheless we shall have made a considerable step forward in man's understanding of himself. Our undertaking is in its way at least as important as the attempt to extend man's control of nature; it may in the end be even more conducive to human happiness. We must therefore be gratified with every increase in the rationality and precision of our science and not waste ourselves in vain regrets. On the other hand we must constantly avoid the common pitfall of claiming a greater certainty than we have in fact been able to achieve.

With these remarks I may conclude our present inquiry. I have now defined 'culture' and 'a culture' and examined the various

[1] Claude Lévi-Strauss, 'Social Structure', in *Anthropology Today*, ed. A. L. Kroeber, Chicago, 1953, pp. 524-53.

means of explaining culture. I have shown that it is through the empirical analysis of cultural regularities that we are most likely to make intelligible the events which the historians have described. I have gone on to define 'civilization' and 'a civilization' and to show that civilizations are the major phenomena within the field of history. From these definitions it follows that the most important cultural regularities, those which will help to explain the largest numbers of particular events, will be those which appear in the development of civilizations as wholes. And among these the most significant are likely to be those regularities found in the development of basic ideas and values.

What I have set forth in the preceding chapters is not in itself an answer to the manifold problems of the 'meaning' of history. It is merely a programme, a conceptual framework in terms of which we hope to be able to reformulate and so to render more amenable some of the difficulties hitherto encountered in understanding and explaining historical events. Undoubtedly, this framework is susceptible of further improvement and refinement; the attempt to put it into use will surely lead to modifications of it. It is even quite possible that some quite different scheme may in the end prove more successful. The proof of the pudding will lie in the eating of it; we shall only be able to judge our scheme when we have applied it to the actual facts of history and seen what results it gives us.

In the last chapter, I shall consider some examples of regularities which appear to emerge from even a very rough survey of the development of the major civilizations. These may be taken only as probable indications of the utility of the concepts and methods we have proposed; their value cannot be fully demonstrated without much more detailed study. We may also be able to obtain some confirmation of my belief that our approach is the correct one—or something very near the correct one—from another point of view. This is the fact that our scheme is not really a very novel one; as I have already observed, it seems to be a natural outgrowth of developments in a number of fields within our own civilization over the last two centuries. Our main concepts are all to be found in embryo as far back as Vico; he sought to uncover the different principles of thought underlying the various forms of the activity of nations at different stages in their development. Here 'principles of thought' corresponds to our 'basic ideas and values', 'activity' to our 'culture' and 'nations' to our 'civilizations'. While the anthropologists and sociologists have been rationalizing and systematizing the study of culture, the historians have been turning more and more to culture history; they have been accumulating the data for our new science. At the same time, the philosophers of history have been exploring the 'spirits' of civilizations; they have sought to define and compare ideas and values, even if they conceived of them as 'spiritual' rather than empirical facts. My only contribution here has been a matter of synthesis and refinement; I have attempted to bring together and to give a somewhat sharper edge to tools already invented. In a sense our scheme is designed to reconcile the idealist and positivist approaches to history; it places ideas and values in a central position, but it defines them empirically. The sciences of man would indeed be barren if everything mental or 'spiritual' were eliminated from them. We must recognize the overwhelming importance of 'spirit', but we must think of that 'spirit' as composed of ways of thinking and feeling, forms of human behaviour which are empirical facts and like other empirical facts are susceptible of rational analysis.

9

SOME EXAMPLES

IN this chapter I shall examine a few examples of similarities in the development of civilizations. A word of warning to the reader, however, is necessary before we begin. In setting forth these examples, it is not my intention to provide models or paradigms for future students of civilizations, but rather indications that, in certain fields at least, their studies are likely to be crowned with success. I am trying to show that the theoretical approach outlined in the preceding chapters provides a useful perspective on our subject-matter; that it is likely to produce valuable results.

In order to have any scientific value, comparative studies of civilizations, and more particularly of their development, will of course have to be conducted much more thoroughly than I have been able to do here. Not that the statements made below are untrue, or cannot be justified by reference to standard authorities; they are based on generally-accepted historical knowledge or on the writings of well-known specialists in particular historical fields. But in order to be 'scientific', in order to compel the acceptance of the sceptic and to be useful for prediction, these statements would have to be based on a much more detailed presentation of the evidence. I should have to take into account differences as well as similarities and, above all, I should want to define my terms precisely rather than make use of the loose vocabulary of literature and of ordinary speech. Yet precise and useful definitions of basic terms can only be formulated after, not before, the facts have been carefully examined. I have already made fairly detailed studies of a number of the points put forward below, but the evidence is too bulky to be presented here and must be reserved for future publications.

With these reservations in mind, then, let us turn to the first of
our examples. I shall begin by examining and comparing the development of only two out of our list of nine major civilizations.
These are the Classical (or Greco-Roman) and our own, the
Western-European (or Western, for short). They are most suitable for a preliminary comparison, partly because more is known
about them than about any of the others, and partly because the
resemblances between them are so very striking. It is on the comparison of these two that most of Spengler's and Toynbee's conclusions are based.

From the very beginning the resemblances are remarkable. We
can trace each civilization back to its dim origin in the invasion by
barbarian tribes of territory dominated by an older but declining
civilization. In the West, it was Teutonic tribes which overran and
settled in the western half of the Roman Empire, while in Greece
it was Hellenic tribes (Ionian and Achaean) which settled on the
Greek mainland, the coasts of Asia Minor and the adjacent islands,
which were then under the domination of Crete. In both cases, the
invaders adopted in large measure the older civilization they found
there, which nevertheless continued to decline. After some centuries, they each set up a loosely organized central monarchy of
their own, the Carolingian Empire in the West from A.D. 800 and
the Mycenean kingdom in Greece from about 1400 B.C. But these
early monarchies and the older civilizations were both submerged
after a century or so by new waves of barbarians, the Vikings in
Western Europe and the Dorians in Greece.

These barbarian invasions and the early centralized monarchies
they produced are merely the preliminary setting of the stage.
While at this period a few culture-traits may be found which persist in later centuries, on the whole the emergence of the new ways
of life which constitute the new civilization comes only towards
the end of the second set of invasions. From about A.D. 1000 in
Western Europe urban life begins to revive. In every section of
the culture new forms appear. Society is reorganized on a basis of
feudalism. The Latin Church breaks away from the Greek and
develops rituals, dogmas, an organization and a theology of its

own. New forms of art and architecture, the Romanesque and Gothic styles, are developed, and we can see the first feeble beginnings of science and technology. This is the period known as the later or High Middle Ages; it lasts about five hundred years. We may conceive of its culture as essentially an attempt to organize life around personal emotions, faith and loyalty, assisted but not controlled by reason. It reaches its highest point of integration and creativity in northern France in the thirteenth century and thereafter becomes over-elaborate and torn by internal dissensions.

The evidence for the corresponding period in Greece is scanty. Its history has come to us in half-legendary form and most of the works of art and architecture have perished. Nevertheless we can discern in its broad outlines a development similar to the Middle Ages in Western Europe. We cannot fix the dates precisely, but the pottery in the Geometric style which has survived shows a long-term evolution running from about the twelfth to the seventh century B.C. with its climax about the ninth century in Athens. Homer, writing in the later part of this age, described a society of warrior-lords ruling over serfs which distinctly resembles feudal society. Homer's poems themselves are a polished form of epic such as we find in the later European Middle Ages. It is in this age too that the Greek religion with its pantheon of anthropomorphic gods must have been invented and elaborated. We are justified then in saying that both in Greece and in Western Europe the growing civilizations passed through an Age of Faith and Feudalism lasting about five hundred years.

Meanwhile in both civilizations the towns had continued to grow and their progress was more rapid in areas bordering on more ancient civilizations, Italy in one case and Ionia in the other. It is in these that we see, well before the end of the Age of Faith, the beginnings of a freer, more rational way of life. Feudalism has disappeared and we have a society of free peasants and artisans confronting wealthy land-owners and merchants. The first experiments in urban democracy lead to the establishment of tyrannies. Art in this new period begins by imitating older alien forms, Oriental in Greece and Classical in Western Europe, but soon succeeds in establishing new, indigenous styles of its own. In succeeding centuries the movement spreads to other areas. New, more personal forms of religion appear, Protestantism and the Mystery Cults.

Essentially this movement is one of growing rationalism and individualism. It reaches its creative peak in the seventeenth century in France (the Age of Louis XIV) and the fifth century in Athens (the Age of Pericles). This is the period when faith and reason are perfectly balanced, the period of the great triumphs of art and thought when the basic forms of the civilization are laid down once for all. In the succeeding century reason already begins to dominate and art becomes more refined and more elaborate.

The growth of rationalism had all along been accompanied by a territorial expansion of the culture. The Greeks had sent out colonies all over the Mediterranean world, and especially to Southern Italy and Sicily, while the Europeans had conquered the Americas and set up outposts elsewhere. But from about A.D. 1800 in Europe and 335 B.C. in Greece there begins a century of rapid expansion. Greek culture spreads all over the known world, and European culture all over the planet. Countries which are not conquered adopt the new civilization voluntarily. In each case the century begins with a short-lived attempt at political unification of the whole culture area, attempts which we associate with the names of Napoleon and Alexander. Thereafter, wealth, science and technology increase by leaps and bounds. Great new states grow up on the periphery. The arts become at first sentimental and then more and more experimental, complicated and sensational. Belief in religion shows a marked decline and philosophy turns towards a radical scepticism.

Our comparison has brought us up very nearly to modern times in Western Europe. The Age of Faith has been followed by an Age of Reason and a Century of Expansion; and now we enter what Toynbee calls the 'time of troubles' and Spengler the era of 'contending states'.[1] In the Classical civilization the great new peri-

---

[1] Arnold Toynbee, *A Study of History*, London, 1934–54, pp. 51–128 *passim* and Oswald Spengler, *The Decline of the West*, New York, 1932, Part II, pp. 416–31.

pheral states begin to fight among themselves for world domination. Very soon one of these states emerges as stronger than any of the rest. By 197 B.C., about a century and a half after the beginning of the Century of Expansion, Rome had conquered Carthage and liberated Greece from the Macedonians. Only Syria remained to challenge Roman supremacy.

The resemblance to what has just happened in the modern world is indeed astonishing. Carthage, like Japan, was a naval power, which had recently adopted the new Greek civilization, though it had an older civilization of its own. Macedonia, like Germany, was a land power, close to the older centre of Greek civilization, which it had for a time brought under its sway. Syria, like Russia, was a Hellenized Oriental monarchy. The masses in the Greek cities mistakenly thought that its despotic ruler would bring them the benefits of Stoic Communism. And Rome, like America, was a republic whose practical and efficient citizens had developed a simplified and technically more advanced form of Greek civilization. Like the Americans, the Romans at this period did not seek to conquer the world; they wanted only an end of aggression and the peaceful self-determination of all states. And like the Americans, they were torn between isolationist and internationalist factions, the parties of Cato and the Scipios. We can even find movements which correspond to New Dealism and McCarthyism.

We have now seen that our two civilizations follow closely similar courses of development and this for more than a thousand years, if we count the preliminary stages. I have mentioned only the similarities; there are also many differences, of course. For one thing Western civilization throughout its history has been considerably larger in scale. In its later stages, it has been technically and scientifically much more advanced. Its religion is a monotheism while the Greeks and Romans were polytheists. Large territorial states appeared earlier in the West; the Greeks preferred the small city-state and they established democratic governments much earlier. But nevertheless the similarity in the main course of development is clear, and many of the differences can be explained by the difference in character of the two sets of peoples, the Greek preference for what was small, near and corporeal and the Western liking for energy and the organization of infinite abstract spaces.[1]

If we try to reduce the whole process of development as it is exhibited by the two civilizations to its simplest terms so that we may understand it more clearly, we seem to perceive that what has taken place is a gradual process of 'rationalization'. The forms of the culture have become more explicit, more conscious, more formal; a smaller and smaller role is played by unconscious, intuitive and emotional elements. Indeed, once it is clearly envisaged, this progressive 'rationalization' seems to have almost an inherent necessity of its own, a sort of 'internal logic', as it might be called, though it should be noted that the 'logic' here is dialectical or psychological rather than formal. No doubt, we have this feeling about this process because a somewhat similar process is exhibited in the maturation of individual human beings and more especially in the formation of their personalities; they grow more rational as they grow up.

At the same time that the two civilizations were growing more rational they were also growing in size (that is, in the number of their bearers), in the area occupied and in the complexity or variety of their forms. So too human beings grow in size, in strength and in the variety of their skills and knowledge.

The analogy of human development would lead us to suppose that the development of our two civilizations was more unilinear, more continuous than it is in fact. Far from being a steady development, it seems to come in two pulses or phases, two ages, one of Faith and one of Reason, each of which seems to exhibit the sequence of 'definition', 'elaboration' and 'exhaustion' which we have mentioned as being characteristic of the development of an art-style. In Western Europe we have the High Middle Ages followed by the so-called 'Modern' Age which begins with the Renaissance. In Greece we have the Geometric or Homeric Age

[1] This summary account of the two civilizations is based on general reading. It may be verified, however, by reference to any recent and fairly complete historical accounts, for instance, for the Classical civilization, *The Cambridge Ancient History*, Cambridge, 1923–39, Vols. IV–XII; or Methuen's series on the *History of Greek and Roman World*, London, 1932–?; and, for Western Europe, H. A. L. Fisher, *History of Europe*, 2nd ed., London, 1938.

followed by the 'classic' (in the more general sense) age of the Greek city-states. Why there should be these two phases is by no means clear; perhaps it has something to do with conflicting tendencies towards integration and differentiation or with the predominance of the countryside in the earlier phase and of the towns in the later. Certainly such markedly distinct phases are not to be found in the development of human beings; we might perhaps force an analogy with the period of childhood prior to puberty and the period of adolescence and early maturity up to the age of about thirty, but in human beings the continuity of development is much more marked.

Are we justified on the basis of this rough sketch in predicting that our own civilization will in the coming centuries follow the course of the Classical civilization after 200 B.C.? Is the whole Western world destined to become part of an American empire similar to the Roman empire? Will the next centuries in America be disfigured by the civil wars which raged in the last years of the Roman republic? Will there be an American emperor?

The difficulty in making predictions of this kind is not simply due to the fact that two civilizations form a rather small sample out of the total field of nine. The validity of inductive inferences depends not only on the size of the sample, but also on the complexity of the pattern observed, the number of detailed similarities. After all, we can identify a man by comparing a single fingerprint with one other on file at police headquarters, or a rare fossil by a fragment of a jawbone. And in this case, our two civilizations do exhibit a large number of similarities, many more than I have been able to put forward here. It is therefore likely that they will continue to resemble each other fairly closely. The trouble is rather that predictions of the kind suggested in the paragraph above are too specific; we have not yet learned to isolate the relevant factors in the common process we have observed, to say which features of the process are likely to be repeated and which not. We shall be on much safer ground if, for the time being at least, we confine ourselves to predictions of much greater generality. We can find confirmation in our observations, for instance, for a number of beliefs about the future of our civilization which are already widely held, but which have been based, not on comparative studies, but on the supposition that certain very general trends already visible in our own times are likely to be continued. We may say for instance that it is probable that the nations whose culture is primarily Western European will eventually achieve some form of political unity, as the Classical world did under the Roman Empire, though what form this political unity will take we cannot at present specify. Again we might say that a simplified form of the common culture suitable for mass-consumption (such as we now identify as American) is likely to become predominant in our civilization as it did in the Classical civilization under the Roman Empire. Or again we may think it likely that the development of rationalism in our civilization has on the whole run its course and that we can look forward to a partial return to religion, a search for a stable balance between faith and reason in the next centuries, something similar to the revival of religion in the ancient world under the Caesars.

It must be stressed that these predictions are only statements of probabilities—fairly low probabilities—as long as our comparative studies have not been carried out in greater detail and with greater precision. They are put forward here only as examples of the sort of results that we may legitimately hope to establish with a fair degree of certainty when civilizations are studied in a thorough-going and scientific manner. It should be noted also that these tentative predictions are all phrased in very general terms; they are attempts to say something about whole civilizations or to characterize all the ideas and values underlying the various aspects of the civilization at different periods. It is on this level, as I have already pointed out, that we are most likely to obtain fairly secure results in our initial investigations.

Even from this rough comparison, however, we may come to one fairly definite negative conclusion. There is nothing to indicate that the disappearance of Western-European civilization is imminent, as Toynbee seems to think.[1] Classical civilization continued

---

[1] Toynbee, *op. cit.*, Vol. VI, pp. 312–21, esp. p. 320, but later in Vol. IX, pp. 406–644, he withdraws this prediction.

for at least five centuries after 200 B.C., that is, after the point in its development which seems most closely to parallel the present stage in Western Europe. And Classical civilization had one of the shortest spans of existence of our nine civilizations. Only the Middle-American and the Peruvian were shorter and both of them were, as we know, destroyed by the Spanish, that is, by an external agency, not by their own internal developments.

Spengler's thought on this point, by the way, has usually been misinterpreted or misunderstood; the title of his work, *The Decline of the West*, is certainly rather misleading. He uses the terms 'decline' and 'death' to mean not the end of a civilization, but the end of its youthful, creative phase. Thus for him the 'death' of Chinese civilization took place about 200 B.C. and that of Indian civilization about a hundred years earlier.[1] The changes and developments which have taken place in these two civilizations in the following two thousand years are for him simply 'meaningless'. We may say with a good deal of conviction, then, that prophecies of imminent doom for our civilization are not justified by the facts; *pace* Professor Toynbee, there is no reason to despair. It does seem likely, on the other hand, that Western Europe itself, the birthplace of our civilization, will play a much smaller role in its future development, much as Greece lost its importance in the Late Hellenistic and Roman periods.

Let us now see if some of the features of the process of development which we have found to be characteristic of two civilizations can also be found in the other seven major civilizations. Obviously, the most interesting feature to study will be the most general one, the process of rationalization which took place in two phases, an Age of Faith and an Age of Reason. To these two we may add a third phase for which we only have evidence from one of our civilizations (the Classical), the other civilization (the Western) having not yet lasted long enough; this is a period of standardized mass-culture with a partial revival of faith, the condition of Classical civilization under the Roman Empire.

The evidence that such a development took place in China is

[1] Spengler, *op. cit.*, Part II, pp. 48–51.

quite strong. Under the Shang dynasty and in the first centuries of the Chou dynasty we see a society with a social and political organization resembling that of Europe in the Middle Ages. Chinese feudalism indeed is closer to Western-European feudalism than either to the social order of Greece in the Homeric Age. In this period too we find an elaborate development of religion and the beginnings of distinctively Chinese art. Later, but still under the Chou dynasty, from about 800 B.C. or perhaps earlier, we find the growth of towns and of a merchant-class, the rise of national states with standing armies, the spread of the civilization over a much larger area, the development of philosophy, sometimes of a rather sceptical and irreligious cast, and the writing of systematic treatises on a great variety of subjects. Under the Han dynasty (202 B.C.– A.D. 220) we find a standardization of the culture and the disappearance of local variations. There is also in Han times a revival of religion in the forms of popular Taoism and official Confucianism. Buddhism too won its first converts in China in this period.[1]

When we turn to Indian civilization, we are faced by a singular dearth of historical and archaeological evidence for its early periods. Nevertheless, we do have a large number of religious, philosophical and other texts surviving from these early times. On the basis of these texts and by the use of a number of ingenious arguments, the Indologists have been able to reconstruct a sequence of cultural developments for which no exact dates can be fixed but whose order seems highly probable. It must be admitted that in making this reconstruction the scholars concerned were using, among other arguments, several more or less unformulated assumptions as to the course which the development of a civilization would normally take. The fact that the sequence which they have established fits quite neatly into the pattern which we have found in three other civilizations, will help, of course, to confirm both the validity of their reconstruction and the validity of our more general pattern, but it does not provide as strong confirma-

[1] Kenneth S. Latourette, *The Chinese, Their History and Culture*, New York, 1934, pp. 32–90.

tion as more direct chronological and archaeological evidence might do, if it were available.

In India, then, it is believed that a number of wandering Indo-Aryan tribes settled in the upper plains of the Indus and the Ganges around 1500 B.C. There their culture at first had a distinct religious flavour. From the earliest times we have the Vedic hymns followed by an elaborate development of sacrificial ritual in the ensuing centuries. In the later texts known as Brahmanas we see a definite over-elaboration with fantastic complications of the ritual, collections of riddles and passages of excessive obscurity. (It should be noted that this feature of over-elaboration at the end of the Age of Faith is more marked in the Indian and Western civilizations than in the Classical or the Chinese.) The Indian epics, the Mahabharata and the Ramayana, reflect an order of society resembling feudalism which presumably prevailed about the same time.

We may place the end of this period somewhere between 1000 and 800 B.C. It is followed by a growth of rationalism. This is clearly exhibited in the Upanishads, whose authors were seeking a more rational and individual form of religion. Later we have the atheistic religions, Buddhism and Jainism; and still later comes the development of the six classical systems of philosophy. Although all of these still retained salvation as their goal, they were highly systematized. We also know that about this time there flourished highly sceptical schools of philosophy, some of which went so far as to deny the existence of the soul. The first systematic studies of various subjects, grammar, law and music, for instance, also belong to this period.

It is under the Maurya Empire from about 300 B.C. that we find a standardization of the culture and a return of faith. Buddhism becomes less sceptical and begins to develop the more popular theistic form known as Mahayana, while the native polytheism revives and begins to take on the shape which we now know as Hinduism.[1]

The early stages of Chinese and Indian civilizations, then, do

[1] *The Cambridge History of India*, ed. E. J. Rapson, Cambridge, 1935, Vol. I, Chaps. III-XX.

appear to conform fairly well to our pattern of 'rationalization' in
three phases. What of the Near-Eastern civilization? The picture
here is confused by the absence of any break between the rise of the
Near-Eastern and the decline of the Classical civilization. There
was no interruption of the continuity of urban life such as took
place before the rise of Western-European civilization. Yet we
may certainly detect an Age of Faith in the Near East in the first
five centuries or so after Christ. The rise of numerous new religions, the elaboration of theological and ethical systems (not only
by the Greek fathers of the Christian Church, but by the Neo-
Platonists and the authors of the Talmud and the Zend), the revival
of magic and popular superstitions, the disappearance of science,
all these are signs of a predominance of faith. At the same time we
may observe a distinctly feudal social order in the Arsacid and
Sassanid Empires[1] and under the Ghassanids and Lakhmids to the
north of Arabia,[2] while independent land-owners with vast estates
and private armies are also to be found even in the Byzantine
Empire.[3]

The rise of Islam in the Near East was, like Protestantism, a
movement for the simplification and individualization of religion,
and after the Arab conquests we do find something like an Age of
Reason: a revival of Greek philosophy and science followed by
intensive native developments. This is the great classical period of
Islam, when medicine, astronomy, history, geography and law all
flourished and there even appeared sceptical philosophers. After
the eleventh and twelfth centuries, however, we have the con-
solidation and standardization of Arabic culture; philosophy and
science no longer develop, orthodoxy and popular superstitions
revive.[4]

That there is some resemblance in the development of these five
civilizations seems quite certain. To state precisely what this resemblance is, I should have to define much more precisely what we

[1] Arthur Christensen, *L'Iran sous les Sassanides*, Copenhagen, 1944, pp. 16 sqq., 101 sqq.
[2] Philip K. Hitti, *History of Syria*, London, 1951, pp. 375-409.
[3] Louis Brehier, *La Civilisation Byzantine*, Paris, 1950, pp. 149-70.
[4] G. E. von Grunebaum, *Islam*, Chicago, 1955 (also as Memoir No. 81 of The American
Anthropological Association, Vol. 57, No. 2, Part 2, 1955), pp. 1-57.

mean by 'faith' and 'reason' and point out what we consider to be indices of their presence in all the various aspects of cultural life. But we may be satisfied for the present with the assurance that this resemblance exists. To have established it even for five of our nine civilizations is already a great step forward, a promise that our method is likely to give us results of the greatest importance.

When we come to examine the other four major civilizations, the Babylonian, Egyptian, Peruvian and Middle-American, our problem becomes more difficult. The evidence for their development is largely archaeological; documents are scarce and for some periods entirely lacking. In addition, careful studies of the changes in these civilizations from century to century are only beginning to be made. In the excitement of uncovering them, the archaeologists have for the most part been content to classify the 'material culture', that is, the artifacts, and to leave the inferences to be drawn from them for later study. Often they have treated vast stretches of time, half a millennium or even a millennium, as a single period in which few or no changes were thought to have taken place. To make matters still more difficult, none of these civilizations ever developed abstract thought, philosophy and science. They seem in this respect at least to form a class apart from the other five civilizations. We might speak if we wish of 'more advanced' and 'less advanced' civilizations, taking abstract thought as the differentiating criterion. Yet the presence of abstract thought, of philosophy and science is what we have been using as our principal index of an Age of Reason.

In spite of these difficulties, however, we may dimly perceive in the development of these four civilizations something resembling our process of 'rationalization'. In the first millennium or so of their existence, the forms grow more definite and more complex, the artists grow more skilled and the territory occupied by their members increases. Moreover, surprisingly enough, in each case their histories fall quite naturally into three distinct phases which later examination may show to correspond to the three phases which we have found in the 'more advanced' civilizations. For Babylonia it is perhaps best to classify the periods on the basis of the art-forms, which gives us an Early Dynastic Period (about 3000–2350 B.C.), an Akkadian and post-Akkadian Period to the rise of Babylon (about 2350–1800 B.C.), and a Babylonian Period (1800–1600 B.C.). I should include with the latter the period of Kassite rule (1600–1100 B.C.) which did not differ greatly in its art-forms.[1]

For Egypt the division into Old Kingdom (2700–2050), Middle Kingdom (2050–1550) and New Empire (1550–1090) has long been recognized by Egyptologists.[2] (In giving the dates I have included the intermediate periods with the preceding period in each case). For Peru we have the Early Classic Period (covering the Mochica and Nazca art-styles, about A.D. 0–1000), the Postclassic Period (covering the Tiahuanaco art-style, about A.D. 1000–1400) and the Inca Period (A.D. 1400–1532). In Middle America it was formerly customary to distinguish the Mayan Old Kingdom (A.D. 0–600 or A.D. 300–900), the Mayan New Empire (A.D. 600 or 900–1400) and the period of Aztec predominance which was just beginning when the Spanish arrived. Perhaps a more satisfactory modern classification is based on art-forms; it divides Middle-American history into a Classic Horizon, a Toltec Horizon and an Historical Horizon covering roughly the same stretches of time.[3] For all four of these civilizations there was of course a long formative period prior to the dates we have given for their beginnings, but these formative periods were not civilized in our sense.

Only further study can decide whether we shall be able to formulate a single pattern for all nine of our major civilizations. Certainly, if we did so, it would have to be cast in terms more general than those we have used in describing the five 'more advanced' civilizations. It may well turn out to be more convenient to formulate two patterns, one for the 'more advanced' and one for the 'less advanced' civilizations, while recognizing that there is a vague

[1] Henri Frankfort, *The Art and Architecture of the Ancient Orient*, Harmondsworth, Middlesex, 1954, pp. 18–64.

[2] John A. Wilson, *The Burden of Egypt*, Chicago, 1951, pp. vii–viii.

[3] For both Peru and Middle America see Gordon R. Willey, 'The Prehistoric Civilizations of Nuclear America' in *American Anthropologist*, Vol. 57, 1955, pp. 571–93. For Middle America see also Alfonso Caso, 'Middle America', in *Anthropology Today*, ed. A. L. Kroeber, Chicago, 1953, pp. 226–37.

resemblance between the two. It is clear, in any case, that this will be a fruitful area of research.

Finally, let us consider one more example of how the nine major civilizations might be compared. Here we shall be examining, not the civilizations as wholes, but rather one of their cultural aspects, the political, and for that matter only one aspect of politics, that of political differentiation and integration. As we have already seen, the development of the Classical civilization took place in a group of more or less independent states bound together by their common culture. Only after a millennium or so was the whole area covered by the civilization united in a single political unit, the Roman Empire. Western-European civilization has similarly developed in a number of separate states. (To speak more accurately, we should say that in its political aspect, the civilization has taken the form of separate states, since the mode of political organization is itself a culture-trait.) And within our civilization we can easily observe at the present time a tendency towards political integration, notably in the appearance of the United Nations with its many subsidiary international organizations, and in the rise of the United States to a position of predominating power.

It is this development which Toynbee refers to as the rise of Universal States. Unfortunately, although much of the evidence he presents is relevant, his treatment is confused by the fact that not all of his civilizations are really comparable entities, that he insists on seeing this development even when it did not take place, and that he regards it as somehow wicked and immoral, the last brutal gesture of a dominant minority.[1] Spengler, perhaps more sensibly, treats the rise of Universal States as part of the development of a general political attitude which he calls Caesarism.[2] To examine the evidence for the existence of this attitude would, however, take us too far afield. Let us see whether in fact our other civilizations, like the Classical and the Western, have also grown up in a number of independent states, and, like the Classical, have at length found unity in a single political entity.

---

[1] Toynbee, *op. cit.*, Vol. I, pp. 51–128 *passim*; Vol. VII, pp. 1–6.
[2] Spengler, *op. cit.*, Part II, pp. 431–5.

Certainly there is good evidence that something similar took place in five of our major civilizations. The Babylonian civilization grew up among the independent states of lower Mesopotamia. There was a short-lived unification under Sargon of Akkad, but the definitive unification only took place under the Babylonian Empire about 1800 B.C. Chinese history begins with dynasties of emperors, the Shang and the Chou, but it seems likely that they exercised little more than a loose hegemony similar to that of the Holy Roman Emperor in Western Europe. Certainly in later Chou times when our historical picture becomes clear, the separate states were fully independent; the final unification took place under Ch'in Shih Huang Ti (214 B.C.). In India the various states were unified under the Maurya dynasty (322 B.C.), while in Peru it was the Incas who played the same role; the unification was here completed about A.D. 1400. In Middle America the Aztecs had already achieved predominant power before the arrival of the Spanish; most authorities agree that it seems quite likely that they would have conquered the whole area if they had not themselves been destroyed by an external force. It is interesting and important to note that in each of these cases the political unification coincides with the third of the cultural phases, the age of the standardized mass-culture for the 'more advanced' civilizations and the as yet nameless third age of the 'less advanced' civilizations.

For the remaining two major civilizations, however, the Egyptian and the Near-Eastern, the evidence flatly contradicts the pattern which we have outlined. Egypt was politically unified from the earliest times that we know anything of. It is true that separatist tendencies are to be found at various early periods and that at one point the rulers of some of the nomes achieved effective independence. But these phenomena were relatively short-lived and cannot justify us in counting Egyptian civilization as an example of our pattern. In the Near East, on the other hand, political unity was never achieved. Under the Omayyads, Byzantium was still independent; much later, at the apogee of the Turkish Empire in the seventeenth century, Persia retained its freedom. And, surprisingly enough, at the moment when we should expect the appearance of a 'Universal State', in the eleventh and twelfth centuries at the beginning of the third phase, divisive political tendencies seem to have been at their height.[1]

We cannot then count these two civilizations as examples of our pattern of political differentiation and unification. Yet that a similar pattern should have been found in seven out of our nine major civilizations is already sufficiently striking a fact to warrant further investigation. It may be that we have failed to cover all nine cases because our pattern is formulated in terms which are too specific. Perhaps we shall be more successful if we find terms of greater generality, perhaps descriptions of general political attitudes, such as Spengler's Caesarism, or even perhaps terms designating features of the development of whole systems of ideas and values. It is not inconceivable that after further investigation we shall find that these trends towards political differentiation and integration are only one aspect of a general process of differentiation followed by integration in the whole culture and more especially in its idea-and-value system. The merely political phenomenon of separate states followed by political unification will then be seen as the *normal* shape which the political aspect of this development takes. Then we might be able to explain the deviations from this normal pattern by special circumstances in each case. In Egypt the explanation for the absence of separate states might be the small area occupied by the civilization, the lack of opportunity for expansion in the surrounding desert, or the necessity of a single authority to control the distribution of the waters of the Nile. We might even perhaps find a sounder, though apparently vaguer, explanation in that pervasive element of style which many students have found in the arts as well as in the political history of Egypt and which they describe as its 'monolithic' quality. Presumably this refers to some broad and enduring value underlying many aspects of Egyptian culture which, if we could define it more precisely, would be a useful tool of explanation. As for the Near-Eastern civilization the predominance of divisive political tendencies there may be related to the most exceptional aspect of its circumstances, the fact

[1] These political developments may be verified in the various works cited above.

that it arose in territory partly occupied already by the bearers of another civilization and on which two more civilizations had only recently become extinct.

If this hypothesis of a general process of differentiation and integration in the whole culture should prove to be true on further investigation, it would support my contention that it is the most general features of cultural development which should be investigated first. Certainly, as we have seen, to attempt to treat the political aspect of civilizations, or rather one feature of it, separately leaves us with exceptions which are unexplained and perhaps inexplicable on that level of generality.

In giving these examples, I have made no attempt to compare the various time-spans involved in the various developments. I have deliberately avoided this issue, partly because the dates involved are often uncertain, especially towards the beginnings of the various civilizations, and partly because their establishment often involves obscure technical points which would be out of place in a rough presentation of this kind. Nevertheless, we may say, with a fair degree of certainty, that the whole process of development from the beginnings of a civilization to the formation of a 'Universal State' (or, where this is absent, to the full development of the third phase) takes between a thousand and fifteen hundred years. It is not inconceivable that, after detailed investigations, we may be able to narrow the margin of variation in this time span, and to say for instance that it lasts between 1100 and 1300 years. It would probably be unreasonable to expect anything more precise than this.

These few examples of comparisons between civilizations, though still only roughly formulated, will suffice, I hope, to achieve the purpose for which they are intended. That there is something here worth investigating is certain. Large-scale recurrent patterns embracing vast numbers of historical events and covering many centuries do indeed exist, even although we are only able to perceive them dimly at present. The 'philosophy of history' is no idle dream, as many sceptics have supposed; it is not to be explained away as simply the fantasies of arm-chair system-builders. A whole vast new world lies before us waiting to be explored by the methods of rational inquiry. To map it thoroughly will be the task of generations of future scholars. Here I have only attempted to provide a sketch of that dark continent, based on the unsystematic accounts of early travellers, and to suggest the most profitable lines of approach, the compass-bearings most likely to bring future explorers into fair and well-watered havens.

BIBLIOGRAPHY

THE following list of publications contains all the works referred to in the footnotes and most of those referred to in the text. It is by no means exhaustive—the literature on these subjects, even if we limit ourselves to English, is enormous—but it does contain the more influential works which have been written or translated into English.

A few remarks will perhaps be helpful to those readers who wish to pursue these matters further. The best account of the methods and purposes of historians is probably still to be found in Teggart's *Prolegomena to History* and in his *Theory of History*, although copies of both of these works are now hard to find. More recently Rowse has written a semi-popular work on the same subject; Renier and Bloch are also worth consulting. The rather special question of the methods of historical explanation has been treated at length by Gardiner, while Walsh, in his book, discusses the problems of historical knowledge. For all these subjects, Croce and Collingwood are indispensable because of the wealth of their insights, though few historians or philosophers nowadays would accept their exaggerated form of idealism.

There is, as far as I know, no thorough account in English of the history of the philosophy of history, that is, of what men have believed about the meaning and pattern of historical events, whether they were philosophers who treated it as a separate subject, or historians who expressed their beliefs in their historical works. Shotwell deals only with classical historiography; Flint was unable to complete his great project; while Füter has never been translated into English. A French version of Füter does, however, exist. Walsh gives a brief sketch in his book of the principal philosophers of history, while Croce has provided a short and schematic account in his *Teoria e Storia* of the philosophic presuppositions underlying historiography at different periods. Thierry is also worth reading for his description of French historiography up to his own time.

Of the philosophers of history themselves, perhaps the idealists, as represented by Vico, Herder, Hegel and Spengler, have contributed most to the views expressed here, in spite of the fact that our approach has been empirical. The more rationalist or positivist writers of this kind, among whom we might mention Kant, Condorcet, Comte, Herbert Spencer and Marx, generally tend to stress the material or technical side of human life and to believe in the inevitability of human progress. This emphasis and this faith are probably still predominant in the thinking of both historians and laymen; perhaps the best modern expression of them is to be found in H. G. Wells. The contemporary philosophers of history: Toynbee, Sorokin and Northrop, raise many interesting points and problems, but their views have had little effect on the concepts and methods worked out in this book.

Undoubtedly the best introduction to cultural anthropology is Kroeber's *Anthropology*. His other works also contain many suggestions as to how the methods of anthropology might be applied to history. A monumental survey of developments in cultural anthropology was published under the auspices of the Viking Foundation in 1953. This is *Anthropology Today* which Kroeber also edited; its extensive bibliographies will enable the student to pursue the ramifications of any branch of the subject as far as he cares to go. The very latest developments will be found in the various journals, notably the *American Anthropologist* and the *Southwestern Journal of Anthropology*. For the history of anthropology, Lowie is the only source; a more detailed study is certainly much to be desired.

ANTHROPOLOGY TODAY. See A. L. Kroeber, Ed.

ARISTOTLE. 'Poetics', tr. by I. Bywater, in *Works*, Oxford, 1908–27.

ARNOLD, MATTHEW. *Culture and Anarchy*, London, 1869.

AUGUSTINE, ST. *The City of God*, tr. by F. R. M. Hitchcock, London, 1922.

BAGBY, P. H. 'Culture and the Causes of Culture', in *American Anthropologist*, Vol. 55, 1953, pp. 535–54.

BARTH, P. *Die Philosophie der Geschichte als Soziologie*, Leipzig, 1897.

BEALS, RALPH. 'Acculturation', in *Anthropology Today*, ed. A. L. Kroeber, Chicago, 1953.

BENEDICT, RUTH. *Patterns of Culture*, New York, 1934.
      The Chrysanthemum and the Sword, Cambridge, Mass. 1947.

BERLIN, ISAIAH. *Historical Inevitability*, London, 1954.

BION, W. R. 'Experiences in Groups', in *Human Relations*, Vol. I, 1948, pp. 314–20, 487–96; Vol. II, 1949, pp. 13–22, 295–304; Vol. III, 1950, pp. 3–14, 395–402; Vol. IV, 1951, pp. 221–8.

BLOCH, MARC. *Métier d'historien*, Paris, 1949; tr. by Peter Putnam, New York, 1953.

BOSSUET, JACQUES BÉNIGNE, Bishop of Meaux. *Discours sur l'histoire universelle*, Paris, 1681; tr. by J. Elphinstone, London, no date (about 1925).

BRÉHIER, LOUIS. *La Civilisation Byzantine*, Paris, 1950.

BRUNHES, JEAN. *La géographie humaine*, Paris, 1934.

BUCKLE, HENRY THOMAS. *History of Civilization in England*, London, 1857–61.

BURCKHARDT, JACOB. *Cultur der Renaissance in Italien*, Basel, 1860; tr. by S. G. C. Middlemore, London, 1898.

BURROWS, MILLAR. *The Dead Sea Scrolls*, New York, 1955.

BURY, JOHN BAGNELL. *An Inaugural Lecture*, Cambridge, 1903.

BUTTERFIELD, HERBERT. *The Whig Interpretation of History*, London, 1931.

CAMBRIDGE ANCIENT HISTORY, THE. Cambridge, 1923–39.

CAMBRIDGE HISTORY OF INDIA, THE. Ed. by E. J. Rapson, Cambridge, 1935.

CASO, ALFONSO. 'Middle America', in *Anthropology Today*, ed. by A. L. Kroeber, Chicago, 1953, pp. 226–37.

CHILDE, V. GORDON. *What Happened in History*, Harmondsworth, Middlesex, 1942.
     The Dawn of European Civilization, London, 1947.

CHRISTENSEN, ARTHUR. *L'Iran sous les Sassanides*, Copenhagen, 1944.

CICERO, MARCUS TULLIUS. *Tusculan Disputations*, tr. by J. E. King, London, 1927.

COLLINGWOOD, R. G. *The Idea of History*, Oxford, 1946.

COLLINGWOOD, R. G. and MYRES, J. N. L. *Roman Britain and the English Settlements*, Oxford, 1936.

COLLINS, HENRY B., Jr. 'The Origin and Antiquity of the Eskimo', in *Annual Report of the Smithsonian Institution for 1950*, Washington, 1951.

COMTE, AUGUSTE. *Système de politique positive*, Paris, 1851–4; tr. by F. Harrison and others, London, 1875–9.

CONDORCET, MARIE-JEAN-ANTOINE-NICOLAS CARITAT, MARQUIS DE. *Esquisse d'un tableau historique des progrès de l'esprit humain*, Paris, 1795; tr. by June Barraclough, London, 1955.

CROCE, BENEDETTO. *Teoria e storia della storiografia*, Bari, 1916; tr. by Douglas Ainslie, London, 1921.

   La filosofia di Giambattista Vico, Bari, 1922.

   La storia, Bari, 1938; tr. by Sylvia Sprigge as *History as the Story of Liberty*, London, 1941.

DANILEVSKY, NIKOLAI YAKOVLEVICH. *Rossia i Evropa*, St. Petersburg, 1871; tr. into German by Karl Nötzel, Berlin, 1920.

DESCARTES, RENÉ. 'Discours de la méthode', in *Oeuvres*, Paris, 1897–1910; tr. by E. S. Haldane and G. R. T. Ross in *Philosophical Works*, Cambridge, 1911–12.

DEVEREUX, GEORGE. 'The Social Structure of the Hospital as a Factor in Total Therapy', in *American Journal of Orthopsychiatry*, Vol. XIX, 1949, pp. 492–500.

DILTHEY, WILHELM. *Einleitung in die Geisteswissenschaften*, Leipzig, 1883; tr. into French by Louis Sauzin, Paris, 1942.

DRAY, W. H. *Laws and Explanation in History*, Oxford, 1957.

DROYSEN, JOHANN GUSTAV. *Geschichte Alexanders des Grossen*, Hamburg, 1833.

DU BOIS, CORA. *The People of Alor*, Minneapolis, 1944.

DURKHEIM, ÉMILE. *Les règles de la méthode sociologique*, Paris, 1901; tr. by Sarah A. Solovay and John H. Mueller, Glencoe, Illinois, 1938.

   Les formes élémentaires de la vie religieuse, Paris, 1912; tr. by J. W. Swain, London, 1915.

EDDINGTON, A. S. *The Nature of the Physical World*, Cambridge, 1930.

EVANS-PRITCHARD, E. E. *Social Anthropology*, London, 1951.

FISHER, H. A. L. *A History of Europe*, London, 1938.

FLINT, ROBERT. *Historical Philosophy in France, French Belgium and Switzerland*, Edinburgh, 1893.

FORDE, C. DARYLL. *Habitat, Economy and Society*, London, 1948.

FOSTER, C. M. 'What is Folk Culture?', in *American Anthropologist*, Vol. 55, 1953, pp. 159–73.

FRANKFORT, HENRI. *The Birth of Civilization in the Near East*, London, 1951.

  The Art and Architecture of the Ancient Orient, Harmondsworth, Middlesex, 1954.

FÜTER, EDUARD. *Geschichte der neueren Historiographie*, Munich, 1911; tr. into French by E. Jeanmaire, Paris, 1914.

GALTON, FRANCIS. *Hereditary Genius*, London, 1883.

GARDINER, PATRICK. *The Nature of Historical Explanation*, London, 1952.

GARN, STANLEY M., and CARLETON S. COON. 'On the Number of Races of Mankind', in *American Anthropologist*, Vol. 57, 1955, pp. 996–1001.

GAXOTTE, PIERRE. *L'Age de Louis XIV*, Paris, 1946.

GIBBON, EDWARD. *History of the Decline and Fall of the Roman Empire*, London, 1920.

GOBINEAU, JOSEPH ARTHUR, COMTE DE. *Sur l'inégalité des races humaines*, Paris, 1853–5; tr. by A. Collins, London, 1915.

GOLDENWEISER, ALEXANDER A. *Early Civilization*, London, 1923.

GRUNEBAUM, G. E. VON. *Islam*, Chicago, 1955 (also as Memoir of the American Anthropological Association, Vol. 57, No. 2, Part 2, 1955).

HAIMENDORF, CHRISTOPH VON FÜRER-. *Himalayan Barbary*, London, 1955.

HALL, EDWARD T., JR. and GEORGE L. TRAGER. *The Analysis of Culture*, Washington, 1953.

HALL, EDWARD T., JR., GEORGE L. TRAGER and DONALD H. HUNT. *Technical Aspects of the Theory of the Analysis of Culture*, Washington, 1954.

HEGEL, GEORG WILHELM FRIEDRICH. *Vorlesungen über die Philosophie der Geschichte*, Berlin, 1848; tr. by J. Sibree, New York, 1900.

HERDER, JOHANN GOTTFRIED VON. 'Fragmente über die neuere Deutsche Literatur, in *Sämmtliche Werke*, Berlin, 1877–1909.

  'Ideen zur Geschichte der Menschheit', in *Sämmtliche Werke*, Berlin, 1877–1909; tr. by T. Churchill, London, 1803.

HERODOTUS. *Histories*, tr. by A. D. Godley, London, 1921–4.

HERSKOVITS, M. J. *Man and his Works*, New York, 1948.

HITTI, PHILIP K. *History of Syria*, London, 1951.

HOIJER, HARRY, Ed. *Language in Culture*, American Anthropological Association Memoir No. 79, Vol. 56, No. 6, Part 2, 1954.

IBN KHALDUN. *Muqaddima*, tr. into French as *Prolegomènes* by W. M. de Slane, Paris, 1934–8.

JESPERSEN, OTTO. *Language*, London, 1922.
    Analytic Syntax, Copenhagen, 1937.

JOSEPHUS, FLAVIUS. 'Contra Apionem', in *Works*, tr. by H. St. J. Thackeray, London, 1926–8.

KANT, IMMANUEL. 'Idee zu einer allgemeinen Geschichte in welt-bürgerliche Absicht', in *Sämmtliche Werke*, Berlin, 1912–22.

KARDINER, ABRAM. *The Psychological Frontiers of Society*, New York, 1945.

KLEMM, GUSTAV. *Allgemeine Cultur-Geschichte der Menschheit*, Leipzig, 1843–52.

KLOPFER, BRUNO and DOUGLAS M. KELLEY. *The Rorschach Technique*, Yonkers-on-Hudson, N.Y., 1946.

KLUCKHOHN, FLORENCE. 'Dominant and Substitute Profiles of Cultural Orientations' in *Social Forces*, Vol. 28, 1950, pp. 276–93.

KROEBER, A. L. *Cultural and Natural Areas of North America*, University of California Publications in American Archaeology and Ethnology, Vol. 38, Berkeley, Calif., 1939.
    Configurations of Culture Growth, Berkeley, Calif., 1944.
    Anthropology, New York, 1948.
    The Nature of Culture, Chicago, 1952.

KROEBER, A. L., Ed. *Anthropology Today*, Chicago, 1953.

KROEBER, A. L. and CLYDE KLUCKHOHN. *Culture, A Critical Review of Concepts and Definitions*, Cambridge, Mass., 1952.

LAFITAU, JOSEPH. *Moeurs des sauvages amériquains comparées aux moeurs des premiers temps*, Paris, 1724.

LATOURETTE, KENNETH S. *The Chinese, Their History and Culture*, New York, 1934.

LE BON, GUSTAVE. *Les lois psychologiques de l'évolution des peuples*, Paris, 1894.
    La psychologie des foules, Paris, 1895.

LÉVI-STRAUSS, CLAUDE. 'L'analyse structurale en linguistique et en anthropologie', in *Word*, Vol. 1, No. 2, 1945, pp. 14–19.

'Social Structure', in *Anthropology Today*, ed. A. L. Kroeber, Chicago, 1953.

LINTON, RALPH. *The Cultural Background of Personality*, New York, 1945.

LORIMER, FRANK. *Culture and Fertility*, Paris, 1954.

LOWIE, ROBERT H. *The History of Ethnological Theory*, London, 1937.

MACAULAY, THOMAS BABINGTON. *History of England*, London, 1913.

MACIVER, R. M. *Society, Its Structure and Changes*, New York, 1931.

MACPHERSON, JAMES. *The Poems of Ossian*, Edinburgh, 1830.

MALINOWSKI, BRONISLAW. *Argonauts of the Western Pacific*, London, 1922.

A Scientific Theory of Culture, Chapel Hill, North Carolina, 1944.

MARX, KARL. *Das Kapital*, Hamburg, 1872–94; tr. by S. Moore and E. Aveling, London, 1918.

MEAD, MARGARET. *From the South Seas*, New York, 1939.

'National Character', in *Anthropology Today*, ed. A. L. Kroeber, Chicago, 1953, pp. 662–7.

MERTON, ROBERT K. *Social Theory and Social Structure*, Glencoe, Illinois, 1949.

MINTZ, SIDNEY W. 'On Redfield and Foster', in *American Anthropologist*, Vol. 56, 1954, pp. 87–92.

MOMMSEN, THEODOR. *Römische Geschichte*, Berlin, 1868; tr. by W. P. Dickson, London, 1911.

MONTAIGNE, MICHEL EYQUEM, SEIGNEUR DE. *Essais*, Bordeaux, 1920; tr. by E. J. Trechmann, London, 1927.

MONTESQUIEU, CHARLES LOUIS DE SECONDAT, BARON DE. 'L'esprit des lois', in *Oeuvres complètes*, Paris, 1875–9; tr. by T. Nugent, London, 1896–7.

MORGAN, LEWIS HENRY. *Ancient Society*, London, 1877.

MURDOCK, C. P. *Social Structure*, New York, 1949.

MURRAY, HENRY A. *Explorations in Personality*, New York, 1938.

MURRAY, HENRY A. *et al. The Assessment of Men*, New York, 1948.

MURPHY, GARDNER. *Personality, A Biosocial Approach*, New York, 1947.

NEWMAN, JOHN HENRY, CARDINAL. *The Idea of a University*, Cambridge, 1931.

NORTHROP, F. S. C. *The Meeting of East and West*, New York, 1946.

OGBURN, WILLIAM F. and WILLIAM I. THOMAS. 'Are Inventions Inevitable?', in *Political Science Quarterly*, Vol. 37, 1922, pp. 83–98.

PARSONS, TALCOTT. *The Social System*, Glencoe, Illinois, 1951.

PARSONS, TALCOTT and EDWARD A. SHILS. *Toward a General Theory of Action*, Cambridge, Mass., 1951.

PARSONS, TALCOTT, EDWARD A. SHILS and ROBERT F. BALES. *Working Papers in the Theory of Action*, Glencoe, Illinois, 1953.

PERCY, THOMAS, Bishop of Dromore. *Reliques of Ancient English Poetry*, London, 1906.

POLANYI, MICHAEL. 'From Copernicus to Einstein', in *Encounter*, Vol. 5, No. 3, Sept. 1955, pp. 54–63.

POLYBIUS. *Histories*, tr. by E. S. Shuckburgh, London, 1889.

RADCLIFFE-BROWN, A. R. 'On the Concept of Function in Social Science', in *American Anthropologist*, Vol. 37, 1935, pp. 394–402.
  'White's View of a Science of Culture', in *American Anthropologist*, Vol. 51, 1949, pp. 503–12.
  Structure and Function in Primitive Society, London, 1952.

RANKE, LEOPOLD VON. *Sämmtliche Werke*, Leipzig, 1877.

REDFIELD, ROBERT. *The Folk Culture of Yucatan*, Chicago, 1941.
  The Primitive World and its Transformations, Ithaca, New York, 1953.

RENIER, G. J. *History, Its Purpose and Method*, London, 1950.

ROMAN, KLARA G. *Handwriting*, New York, 1954.

RORSCHACH, H. *Psychodiagnostics*, tr. by P. Lemkau and B. Kronenberg, New York, 1942.

ROUSE, IRVING. 'The Strategy of Culture History', in *Anthropology Today*, ed. A. L. Kroeber, Chicago, 1953, pp. 57–76.

ROUSSEAU, JEAN JACQUES. 'Si le rétablissement des sciences et des arts a contribué à épurer les moeurs', in *Oeuvres complètes*, Paris, 1856–7.

'Letter to Malesherbes', Jan. 12, 1762, in *Correspondance générale*, ed. T. Dufour and P. P. Plan, Paris, 1924–31.

ROWSE, A. L. *The Uses of History*, London, 1946.

RÜCKERT, HEINRICH. *Lehrbuch der Weltgeschichte in organischer Darstellung*, Leipzig, 1857.

RUSKIN, JOHN. *Modern Painters*, Orpington, 1888.
   The Seven Lamps of Architecture, Orpington, 1890.
   The Poetry of Architecture, Orpington, 1893.

RYLE, GILBERT. *The Concept of Mind*, London, 1949.

SANSOM, C. B. *Japan, A Short Cultural History*, New York, 1943.

SAPIR, EDWARD. *Language*, New York, 1939.

SHAPIRO, MEYER. 'Style', in *Anthropology Today*, ed. A. L. Kroeber, Chicago, 1953.

SHOTWELL, JAMES T. *An Introduction to the History of History*, New York, 1922.

SMALL, A. W. *General Sociology*, Chicago, 1905.

SMITH, M. A. 'The Limitations of Inference in Archaeology', in *Archaeological News Letter*, Vol. 6, No. 1, 1955, pp. 3–7.

SOROKIN, PITIRIM A. *Social and Cultural Dynamics*, New York, 1937–1941.

SPENCER, HERBERT. *The Principles of Sociology*, London, 1876–96.

SPENGLER, OSWALD. *Der Untergang des Abendlandes*, Munich, 1918–1922; tr. by C. F. Atkinson, New York, 1932.

STEWARD, JULIAN H. 'Cultural Causality and Law', in *American Anthropologist*, Vol. 51, 1949, pp. 1–27.

TAWNEY, RICHARD HENRY. *Religion and the Rise of Capitalism*, London, 1926.

TAYLOR, ISAAC. *The Alphabet*, London, 1883.

TEGGART, FREDERICK JOHN. *Prolegomena to History*, Berkeley, 1916.
   Theory of History, New Haven, 1925.

THIERRY, J. N. AUGUSTIN. *Lettres sur l'histoire de France*, Paris, 1938.

THUCYDIDES. *Histories*, tr. by C. F. Smith, London, 1920–3.

TÖNNIES, FERDINAND. *Gemeinschaft und Gesellschaft*, Berlin, 1922.

TOYNBEE, ARNOLD. *A Study of History*, London, 1934–54.

TREVELYAN, GEORGE MACAULAY. *England under Queen Anne*, London, 1930–4.

    English Social History, London, 1944.

TYLOR, EDWARD BURNETT. *Primitive Culture*, London, 1871.

VAUVENARGUES, LUC DE CLAPIERS, MARQUIS DE. 'Introduction à la connaissance de l'esprit humain', in *Oeuvres morales*, Paris, 1874.

VICO, GIAMBATTISTA. *La Scienza Nuova*, Milan, 1946; tr. by T. G. Bergin and M. H. Fisch, Ithaca, New. York, 1948

VOLTAIRE (pseudonym for FRANÇOIS MARIE AROUET). 'Brutus', in *Oeuvres*, Paris, 1877–85.

    Lettres philosophiques ou Lettres sur les Anglais, Paris, 1924; tr. by C. Whibley, London, 1926.

    'Essai sur les moeurs et l'esprit des nations', in *Oeuvres*, Paris, 1877–85; tr. by Nugent, Edinburgh, 1777.

    'Lettre à l'Académie française', Aug. 25, 1776, in *Oeuvres*, Paris, 1877–85.

WALSH, W. H. *An Introduction to the Philosophy of History*, London, 1951.

    'The Logic of Historical Explanation' (unpublished paper).

WARD, LESTER F. *Pure Sociology*, New York, 1903.

WEBER, ALFRED. *Kulturgeschichte als Kultursoziologie*, Leiden, 1935.

WEBER, MAX. 'Wirtschaft und Gesellschaft', in *Grundriss der Sozialökonomik*, Tübingen, 1922–7; Part One tr. by A. M. Henderson and T. Parsons, as *The Theory of Social and Economic Organization*, New York, 1947.

    Gesammelte Aufsätze zur Religionssoziologie, Tübingen, 1922–3; a selection tr. by T. Parsons as *The Protestant Ethic and the Spirit of Capitalism*, London, 1948.

    Gesammelte Aufsätze zur Soziologie und Sozialpolitik, Tübingen, 1924; a selection tr. by H. H. Gerth and C. W. Mills as *Essays in Sociology*, London, 1947.

WELLS, HERBERT GEORGE. *The Outline of History*, London, 1923.

WHEELER, MORTIMER. Review of *Roman Britain*, in *The Journal of Roman Studies*, Vol. 29, Pt. 1, 1939, pp. 87–93.

WHITE, LESLIE A. 'Ikhnaton: The Great Man vs. the Culture Process', in *The Journal of the American Oriental Society*, Vol. 68, Pt. 2, 1948.

    The Science of Culture, New York, 1949.

WHITEHEAD, ALFRED NORTH. *Process and Reality*, New York, 1941.

WHORF, BENJAMIN LEE. *Four Articles on Metalinguistics*, Washington, 1950.

WHYTE, WILLIAM FOOTE. *Street Corner Society*, Chicago, 1943.

WILLEY, GORDON R. 'The Prehistoric Civilizations of Nuclear America', in *American Anthropologist*, Vol. 57, 1955, pp. 571–93.

WILSON, DANIEL. *The Archaeology and Prehistoric Annals of Scotland*, Edinburgh, 1851.

WILSON, JOHN A. *The Burden of Egypt*, Chicago, 1951.

WINDELBAND, WILHELM. *Einleitung in der Philosophie*, Tübingen, 1920; tr. J. McCabe, London, 1921.

INDEX

A

Acculturation, 138; studies of, by anthropologists, 172

Achaemenian Empire, 179

Acton, Lord, 47

Aegean civilization, 169, 178

Annamite civilization, 169

Anthropologists: contemporary approach of, 89–90; and culture-traits, 108–9; establishment of universally valid laws by, 135; inferences of, 199

Anthropology: relevance of, 7; cultural, 8–9; social, 8–9; modern, source of, in Romantic movement, 11; origins of, 12; development of, 18–20; scientific approach to, 19–20; general character of, 22; use of concept of culture in, 72; modern technical use of word, 74; relativistic trend in, 90

Appearance, bodily, effect of differences in, 143–4

Arabian civilization, 171

Archaeologists: use of concept of culture by, 128; and secondary civilizations, 172; inferences of, 198–9

Archaeology, 9; comparison of, with history, 28–9

Aristotle: theory of the four causes, 65–6

Armenians, as part of Near-Eastern civilization, 65–6

Arnold, Matthew, 74

Arsacid Empire, 215

Art, in Classical and West-European civilizations, 206–7

Art-historians, and styles of works of art, 108

Assyriologists, 166

Astronomy, as historical science, 33

Augustine, St., 2, 56

Avars, culture of, 180

Aztec culture, 162, 166, 219

B

Babylonian civilization, 165–6, 169, 171: ideographic form of writing in, 184; development of, 216; rationalization process in, 216–17; Early Dynastic Period, 217; Akkadian and post-Akkadian Period, 217; Babylonian Period, 217; period of Kassite rule, 217; political development, 219

Balkan peoples, and Western-European civilization, 168

Barth, Paul., 159

Behaviour: purpose behind, 61–2; patterns of, 63–4; cultural modes of, 81; in particular societies, analysis of, 90

Benedict, Ruth, 19, 192

Berlin, Sir Isaiah, 64

Biography, meaning of, 25

Biologists, inferences of, 200

Biology: ambiguities in, 114; classifications of, 164; differences between species and genera in, 184–5

Bion, W. R., 119

Bishop, Jim, 32–3

Bloch, Marc, 21

Boas, Franz, 18, 20